In the Footsteps of Lewis and Clark

IN THE FOOTSTEPS OF
LEWIS AND CLARK

Early Commemorations and the Origins of the National Historic Trail

Wallace G. Lewis

UNIVERSITY PRESS OF COLORADO

Published by the University Press of Colorado
1580 North Logan Street, Suite 660
PMB 39883
Denver, Colorado 80203-1942

 The University Press of Colorado is a proud member of
the Association of University Presses.

ASSOCIATION
of UNIVERSITY
PRESSES

The University Press of Colorado is a cooperative publishing enterprise supported, in part, by Adams State University, Colorado State University, Fort Lewis College, Metropolitan State University of Denver, University of Alaska Fairbanks, University of Colorado, University of Denver, University of Northern Colorado, University of Wyoming, Utah State University, and Western Colorado University.

Library of Congress Cataloging-in-Publication Data

Lewis, Wallace G., 1943–
  In the footsteps of Lewis and Clark : early commemorations and the origins of the national historic trail / Wallace G. Lewis.
      p. cm.
  Includes bibliographical references and index.
  ISBN 978-1-60732-026-5 (hardcover : alk. paper) — ISBN 978-1-64642-623-2 (paperback: alk. paper) — ISBN 978-1-60732-027-2 (e-book) 1. Lewis and Clark National Historic Trail. 2. Lewis and Clark Expedition (1804–1806) I. Title.
  F592.7.L7157 2010
  917.804'2—dc22
2010017171

Dust jacket design by Caroline Denney
Text design by Daniel Pratt

Portions of the introduction and Chapters 1 and 4 originally appeared as "On the Trail: Commemorating the Lewis & Clark Expedition in the Twentieth Century," in *Lewis & Clark: Legacies, Memories, and New Perspectives*, ed. Kris Fresonke and Mark Spence (Berkeley: University of California Press, 2004).

Portions of Chapter 5 originally appeared as "Following in Their Footsteps: The Birth and Infancy of the Lewis and Clark National Historic Trail," in *Columbia: The Magazine of Northwest History* 16, no. 2 (Summer 2002): 37–42.

In memory of my father, Glenn C. Lewis
1920–2009

Contents

Illustrations

PHOTOGRAPHS

MAP

Preface

THIS BOOK GREW OUT OF MY FASCINATION with both Lewis and Clark and the history of automobile tourism in the West. The now famous Lewis and Clark trail markers that began to appear along two-lane highways in the late 1960s seem to me emblematic of the way highway motoring and public historical awareness became intertwined in the twentieth century. The account that follows seeks primarily to explore and examine ways the Corps of Discovery was commemorated in the period between its centennial and the creation of the Lewis and Clark National Historic Trail by the U.S. Congress in 1978. As highway travel and tourism developed during that time, the public view of the expedition also shifted from a focus on the explorers and Sacagawea to an emphasis on the routes the Corps of Discovery took between 1803 and 1806. The climax of this narrative is not the Lewis and Clark Bicentennial in the twenty-first century but rather the birth of the Lewis and Clark National Historic Trail in the twentieth century. In tracing various aspects of the process that led to that birth, I examined local newspaper stories that describe commemorative activities and express attitudes toward the history of the expedition. Many of them refer to locally installed monuments, markers, pageants, and similar commemorations, although I have not attempted to discuss or list all such instances.

This should not be regarded as a guidebook to historical sites and monuments. Those described are presented as examples, in no sense exhaustive. Further, the book is not intended to be an administrative or institutional history of the agencies and organizations that have cooperated to make the Lewis and Clark National Historic Trail what it is today, as much as such an account deserves to be told.

Starting with the Lewis and Clark Centennial celebration in Portland, Oregon, Chapter 1 examines the use of statuary and other monuments to memorialize the explorers and Sacagawea, particularly during the Progressive Era when overseas imperialism gave the sentiment of Manifest Destiny a new lease. Chapter 2 temporarily diverts the reader from the subject of commemoration to a chronological overview of the expedition's journey, relating land forms and routes taken in 1804–1806 to present-day towns and highways and sketching the background of Native American groups the expedition encountered. Since numerous references to specific locations are made throughout the book, it is important for readers to become familiar with the geography of the expedition's routes—especially because what follows is a discussion of how interest began to shift toward the trail itself and toward later "explorers" who sought to retrace the trail, often by automobile. Chapter 4 examines the 1955 sesquicentennial and its commemorative activities, while Chapter 5 focuses on the five-year existence of the National Lewis and Clark Commission that prepared the way for institutionalizing the Lewis and Clark National Historic Trail. Chapter 6 concludes the book with a discussion of historical authenticity and conflicting viewpoints on interpretations of the trail and the purposes of commemoration.

I am especially grateful to my wife, Marilyn, for her constant encouragement and support and also for helping me research this book. For close readings of earlier drafts of the manuscript, I am indebted to Darrin Pratt, director of the University Press of Colorado, and to Professor Christine Jespersen at Western State College. For their gracious assistance, I thank Patrick Muckleroy at Western State's Savage Library (a master at obtaining interlibrary loans); Keith Petersen, the Idaho Lewis and Clark Bicentennial director; Jennifer Rusk and Chris Mullin at the University of Montana's Mansfield Library Archives; Deborah Knudsen and Donnie Sexton at Montana Travel (Montana Department of Commerce); Peg Owens at the Idaho Department of Commerce; Robben Johnston, archaeologist for the Clearwater National Forest in Idaho; David Nicandri, director of the Washington State Historical Society; Vinola Squires and Bette Hull at the Beaverhead County Museum in Dillon, Montana; Terry Abrams, University of Idaho Library Special Collections; and the staffs of many other libraries and archives, including especially the Montana Historical Society (Helena), Clatsop County Heritage Museum (Astoria, Oregon), Overholser Historical Research Center of the Schwinden Library and Archives (Fort Benton, Montana), University of Wyoming American Heritage Center (Laramie), Idaho Historical Society (Boise), Lewis and Clark Heritage Trail Foundation (Great Falls, Montana), Washington State University Library (Pullman), Three Forks Public Library and Three Forks Headwaters Museum (Montana), and the Nez Perce County Museum (Luna House, Lewiston, Idaho). I am thankful as well for the help and support of Monika Lewis, Jeff Curry, Richard Weholt, and Charlie Knowles.

In the Footsteps of Lewis and Clark

Introduction

THE OFFICIAL OPENING of the national Lewis and Clark Bicentennial in January 2003 ushered in nearly four years of commemorative events and activities that dwarfed all earlier attempts to recognize the expedition's historical significance. The bicentennial celebration represented a variety of purposes with regard to public historical consciousness, including expressing patriotism, maintaining myths of national identity, educating family members through hands-on history, boosting tourism in communities along the expedition's routes, and so forth. For many, it provided an opportunity to enlighten Americans by making their understanding of the past broader and more inclusive.

What should the history of Meriwether Lewis and William Clark's Corps of Discovery mean to us? The answers are varied, but it seems clear that we can no longer accept the white American view of "progress" through conquest that characterized earlier writings and commemorations up until at least around 1975. Regarding Lewis and Clark as simply heroic icons not only glorifies conquest and dispossession but also distorts the nature of the expedition and obscures much else that is interesting in the history of the West. With the exception of Sacagawea, who provided numerous essential services but has been often miscast as the expedition's guide, Native Americans have traditionally been given short shrift in this story. Lewis and Clark's dependence for survival on the help of tribes such as the Mandan, Hidatsa, Lemhi Shoshone, Salish, Nez Perce, and Clatsop was integral to the entire journey, yet it did not fit into a Eurocentric heroic narrative. Since the 1970s, a more enlightened and realistic view has predominated among scholars and students of western expansion. That view was largely reflected in bicentennial efforts to publicize and interpret the history of the Corps of Discovery.

However, what for convenience I call the "standard model" of public attitudes toward the Lewis and Clark Expedition prevailed throughout much of the twentieth century and in some ways continues today. That model, epitomized in the phrase "our national epic of exploration," extolled the frontier past as a glorious march toward "progress" and "civilization." In 1966 Helen B. West, secretary of the Montana Lewis and Clark Trail Advisory Committee, reapplied the label "our national epic" to the expedition. Further, she used the terms "unique saga" and "allegory" and compared "this odyssey" to *Pilgrim's Progress*. Nationalistic rhetoric of this type has more often than not shaped the means by which Lewis and Clark have been memorialized. As a putative American "epic," the collective account of the journey was celebrated as a master narrative of Manifest Destiny and a great adventure tale.[1]

In a commercial sense, these were the expedition's strongest selling points. Pride in the national myth could be easily converted into economic gain. Much of the groundswell for a designated trail during the 1960s and 1970s came from boosters in towns along the routes, who sensed the potential for tourism. It is, in fact, almost impossible to separate such boosterism from the desire to honor national heroes in either the 1905 centennial or the 1955 sesquicentennial, although the same is true of nearly all public representations of the American past. When it comes to tourism, history sells.

The fact that historical commemorations express public memory may seem obvious, but the term "memory" in this sense is open to numerous interpretations. French historian Pierre Nora, for example, distinguishes public memory from written history. History, according to Nora, is studied analysis and representation of the past based on an examination of factual evidence. Memory, on the other hand, entails imaginative and symbolic conceptions of the past and is subject to change according to present interests and circumstances. Public memory, according to Nora, is also tied more to places or "sites" that foster collective identity than it is to historical events. In other words, *where* something occurred is more mythically important than is an accurate account of what actually took place there.[2]

The distinction between scholarly history and public memory is not clear-cut, however. Few historians today would accept Nora's stringent ideal of written history as simply objective analysis based on evidence. Present interests and circumstances appear to affect scholarly work as well. The French theorist's connection between public memory and place, however, does apply particularly to popular attitudes toward the Lewis and Clark trail. Certainly, far more people have established a connection between themselves and the Lewis and Clark Expedition by visiting sites along the trail than by reading journals or interpretive narratives about the expedition. The physical environment and the expedition's narrative are very closely related; visiting a Lewis and Clark site induces a common sense of historical meaning.

In Nora's view, memory consists of more than simply a popular view of history; it encompasses "remembrances, traditions, customs, habits, practices," and similar phenomena—all aspects of what is known as cultural history. In speaking about his native France, Nora assumes a considerable degree of cultural homogeneity, but in the United States there are as many versions of memory as there are groups seeking to define themselves in terms of the past. When it comes to public rituals of commemoration, the question of "whose memory," which often turns on ideological differences, becomes an issue that leads to a variety of representations.[3]

While Nora sees memory as a conception of the past that is free from nationalistic or official history, American public commemoration often transforms popular myths into national institutions. Historian John Bodnar, for example, argues that "public memory emerges from the intersection of official and vernacular cultural expressions." Here, "vernacular" means local and grassroots, while "official" refers to acts by government or "cultural leaders."[4] Applying this concept to commemorations of Lewis and Clark, one might say that communities along the expedition's route have developed their own, often mythical or stylized, versions of related events that occurred in their locales. Once an occasion—such as a centennial—calls for state or national recognition, governments step in to alter local expressions of the event and to establish a sanctioned version.

According to Bodnar, the official expression often co-opts and institutionalizes the vernacular to enlist it for symbols or functions that uphold loyalty to the nation-state. Like Nora, he emphasizes the practical flexibility of public memory, defining it as a "body of beliefs and ideas about the past that help a public or society understand both its past, present, and by implication, its future." Public memory's main "focus," according to Bodnar, "is not the past . . . but serious matters in the present such as the nature of power and the question of loyalty to both official and vernacular cultures."[5] I believe Bodnar is only partially correct. The "matters" he mentions undoubtedly condition the ways we explain the past to ourselves, but they do not completely account for the desire to make authentic, personally intimate contact with that past. Nonetheless, the shifting nature of public memory ensures changes in the ways that past is expressed, a case in point being the Lewis and Clark Expedition. Both the historical meaning of that event and the means for publicly acknowledging it have changed over time at local, state, and national levels.

Differences in the way the Lewis and Clark Expedition is commemorated today compared with its commemoration in the first half of the twentieth century spring from changes not only in attitudes toward history but also in the means of commemoration itself. Monuments and statues have largely given way to historical parks and interpretive centers. The biggest change, however, has been the shift in attention from Lewis, Clark, and Sacagawea as historical icons to the network of routes the Corps of Discovery took from St. Louis to the Pacific Ocean and back (plus, more recently, Meriwether Lewis's route down the Ohio River in 1803).

The growing veneration of the trail, in my view, merges with the development of a federally funded highway system that, in turn, spurred massive automobile tourism. Both scenic and historical landscapes across the country became more easily accessible and popular as destinations for vacation travel. By the late 1920s, community business leaders in the Pacific Northwest and Northern Plains states were hoping to cash in on the relationship between the new long-distance highways and the routes Lewis and Clark took. For tourists aware of the Lewis and Clark trail and the historical associations of the countryside they were passing through, the highway served as a surrogate for the trail. Auto tourists became a new type of explorer in a very broad sense, imaginatively—and now physically as well—reproducing the experience of the historic journey.

An emerging system of highways and the car culture it fostered were preconditions for a significant shift in the way Americans commemorated Lewis and Clark. Until the young states of Washington, Idaho, Montana, and the Dakotas had been sufficiently "settled" by Euro-Americans, consciousness of the Corps of Discovery's route as a significant aspect of the local and national historical heritage probably languished, at least until those states participated in Portland's 1905 Lewis and Clark Exposition. Even then, a lack of transportation routes limited access to most of the sites; and rail tourism, by its nature, was confined to crossing the open spaces as quickly as possible to reach or return from national parks and other resort destinations. It was only when the 1955 sesquicentennial celebrations emphasized statues, monuments, pageants, and other traditional styles of commemoration that the Lewis and Clark story began to give way to an emphasis on the expedition's physical route, although the ingredients for this change had been simmering for half a century.

Highway and tourism history was interwoven with other historical developments in the twentieth century, including movements to preserve both the natural environment and historical heritage sites. Those preservation movements did not become the focus of wide public attention until the 1960s, however, by which time interest in

Lewis and Clark had been regenerated by the expedition's sesquicentennial. Its 150th anniversary—although commemorated mostly in Oregon, Washington, Idaho, and Montana—did much to overcome inertia regarding designation of a national historic route. Compared to preparations for the bicentennial, excitement about a designated route was rather mild and somewhat ad hoc, but interest generated by the 1955 celebration never subsided. Anxiety in the 1960s over degradation of the environment, destruction of wildlife, and loss of historical sites helped spur attempts to preserve Lewis and Clark's route and make it available for the public to appreciate and enjoy. In 1964 the U.S. Congress created the national Lewis and Clark Trail Commission to consider ways of carrying the plan forward.

High on the list of the tasks addressed were designating and marking highway routes and access and developing historical interpretations of important sites. However, these tasks were complicated because many of the expedition campsites along the Missouri River had been inundated by Pick-Sloan Project dams and reservoirs. The loss of much of what could be regarded as the authentic trail—individual sites and long segments of free-flowing rivers—created a gulf that would have to be bridged by interpretation and imagination. Following termination of the Lewis and Clark Trail Commission in 1969, state committees, private organizations, and several federal agencies cooperated to carry on the task. The Bureau of Outdoor Recreation (Department of the Interior) completed a final report for including the Lewis and Clark trail in the National Trails network. The National Trails System Act of 1968 helped finance the Appalachian and Pacific Crest trails and designated other hiking trails across the country. Eventually, the legislation was amended to include partially motorized "recreation" and "historic" routes. In 1978 Congress authorized the Lewis and Clark National Historic Trail.

The subsequent institutionalizing of the various paths the Corps of Discovery took to the Pacific Coast and back in 1804–1806, though beyond the scope of this book, raises issues regarding authenticity and national memory. The route (or skein of routes) exists as a sort of historical replica and a heritage site that extends for thousands of miles. The trail had to be artificially reproduced because virtually no physical trace of it remains, and much of the original trail is covered by water today. Expedition structures, such as forts Mandan and Clatsop, have been reproduced and signs and interpretive centers provided to enhance understanding of the expedition for modern-day travelers, who, by tracing the trail in their automobiles, assume the role of explorers and participate in the trail's historic replication. Yet the interpretation of heritage sites in general has proven problematic because of public attitudes toward history and the authenticity of its artifacts and explanations. Tourists bring expectations of what must be true and respond to a variety of stereotypes. To appeal to those expectations—if not to the stereotypes as well—heritage site developers may sometimes feel compelled to artfully design the appearance of authenticity.

Although the Lewis and Clark National Historic Trail is not free of such issues, its spatial extension and interrelationship with the landscape have a mitigating effect. The trail is largely an imaginative construct anyway, for much of the route represents little more than interpretation applied to landscape, largely in the form of official signage. This makes manifest certain aspects of the journals. The National Historic Trail also differs from most other heritage sites because of its long relationship to highways and personal exploration by automobile. Designated highways merge with the trail and often become equivalent to it, at least in the mind of the traveler.

In fact, highway tourism and the Lewis and Clark National Historic Trail developed virtually in tandem. The first significant stirrings of public interest in Lewis and Clark, stimulated by the 1905 centennial celebration, nearly coincided with the start of a nationwide fascination with transcontinental automobile travel. Up to that time, Lewis and Clark had all but faded from public memory. The Lewis and Clark Expedition garnered relatively little public attention in the nineteenth century. The U.S. government allowed its fiftieth anniversary to pass unrecognized. Local communities, which might later have been expected to celebrate the Corps of Discovery's passage through their vicinities, were few and far between, even after construction of the Northern Pacific and Great Northern transcontinental railway lines. Cultural geographer Wilbur Zelinsky maintains that periodic historical commemorations did not become common in the United States until the late nineteenth century, although it appears that events associated with the Revolutionary War and the nation's founding are major exceptions.[6] In any case, Americans eventually began to commemorate important historical events and figures in quarter-century anniversaries or even more frequently. Thus, it may be significant that Lewis and Clark remained uncelebrated for 100 years following their expedition.

True, there was little or no scholarly interest in the West in general until Frederick Jackson Turner expounded his "frontier thesis" in the 1890s, claiming that westward movement explained American history. Still, Lewis and Clark's relatively low status compared with other individuals regarded as frontier heroes by white Americans in the nineteenth century is curious. During the aggressively expansionist 1840s and 1850s, when the phrase "Manifest Destiny" ruled the rhetoric of nationalism, frontiersmen and exploratory groups of every stripe achieved celebrity. During Andrew Jackson's presidency, for example, Davy Crockett, following the example of Daniel Boone, became a living legend and an even greater heroic icon following his death at the Alamo. Washington Irving's popular 1836 narrative *Astoria,* about the founding of Astor's trading post on the Columbia River, as well as his *Adventures of Captain Bonneville,* indicate that the public was eager for accounts of the western and Rocky Mountain fur trade. Both Benjamin Bonneville and government explorer-surveyor John Charles Fremont, whose 1840s expedition journals fascinated the American reading public, left legacies of place names scattered across the West.

Not even the rising issues of slavery and sectional conflict in the 1850s completely diverted public attention away from western conquest. Hotly debated questions about the spread of slavery into newly acquired territories were at the core of these issues. Captain John Mullan, who built the Mullan Trail across the Bitterroot and Rocky mountains, clearly regarded Lewis and Clark as forerunners of what Anglo-Americans at the time regarded as "civilization." For Mullan, their fame had been memorialized primarily by white settlement. "Here with you," he told the Historical Society of the Rocky Mountains in 1861, "[Lewis and Clark's] monument is to be found, industrious people, who have built towns & cities where there was the wilderness, & their epitaphs are found engraved upon the hearts

& affections of an appreciating people, who are ever willing to pay homage & respect to the very mention of the names of Lewis & Clark." But Mullan castigated the U.S. government for its failure to "maintain the claim . . . established by the explorations" and to publish the complete journals produced by the expedition.[7]

The unavailability of the original journals kept by Clark, Lewis, and four other members of the expedition may help explain why the Corps of Discovery faded in the public imagination during the nineteenth century. After the 1814 Nicholas Biddle/Paul Allen edition, which sold relatively few copies, no legitimate narrative of the journey appeared until Elliott Coues's account in 1893.[8] Coues was a retired U.S. Army surgeon who had developed an interest in the Lewis and Clark Expedition while serving in Dakota Territory in the 1870s. His later reputation as an expert ornithologist and lexicographer earned Coues a commission to produce an expanded reissue of the Biddle-Allen text, *The History of the Expedition under the Commands of Captains Lewis and Clark*. Coues examined as many original sources as he could locate, including the original manuscripts of the journals held at the American Philosophical Society in Philadelphia. The result of Coues's labors was a vastly expanded version rather than simply a "reissue" of the Biddle-Allen book, which in addition to new sources and material contained a great deal of commentary and annotation.[9]

Still, Coues's version was not entirely an original edition of the journals themselves. Such a work did not appear until Reuben Gold Thwaites of the Wisconsin State Historical Society edited a set of the journals that was published in 1904.[10] According to historian Paul Russell Cutright, the first "book of consequence *written about* the Expedition" was Olin D. Wheeler's two-volume *Trail of Lewis and Clark*, also published in 1904.[11] Historian Donald Jackson observed that since the two explorers do not share the frontier mythical space occupied by such figures as Davy Crockett and Daniel Boone, books constitute "the real source of public knowledge about the expedition."[12]

The mythical fame to which Jackson refers would seem to stem more from oral folk tales than from journals and other published writings. Moreover, a number of conditions may help account for the mythical status of Boone and Crockett. For example, Daniel Boone epitomized what Americans in the late eighteenth and early nineteenth centuries regarded as a frontier "hero," and he apparently served as the model for James Fenimore Cooper's main character in the Leatherstocking novels. Davy Crockett died (by legend, heroically) in defense of the Alamo, an almost mythical event in itself. But even earlier he had achieved fame as expert rifleman, Indian fighter, and congressman. Both Crockett and Boone fit the national ethos of individualism associated with the frontier better than did Lewis and Clark, whose exploits were based on cooperation and teamwork. And, as indicated, journals and books constituted the basis for their revival in the public memory during the twentieth century.

Twentieth-century publications of original portions of the journals by editors such as Thwaites, Milo M. Quaife, Ernest Staples Osgood, and Donald Jackson, as well as Bernard DeVoto's popular condensation, largely account for expanding interest in the expedition.[13] During the nineteenth century, however, disillusionment and lack of interest obscured history. The Corps of Discovery's accomplishments had begun to be overshadowed by other events when Biddle's history of them finally appeared. The expedition's scientific observations remained virtually unknown for eighty years, and the path Lewis and Clark blazed fell quickly out of favor. Soon after the explorers' views of the Pacific Northwest had been distorted to promote settlement in Oregon country, Lewis and Clark, as geographer and historian John L. Allen puts it, "receded into the American memory" until the Thwaites edition of the journals and the centennial celebration brought them to the fore. According to Allen, Oregon settlement booster Hall Jackson Kelley ignored the generally negative comments the explorers had made about their surroundings at Fort Clatsop in the winter of 1805–1806 and used Biddle's book "to paint a glowing, rosy picture of the Oregon Country."[14]

A merging of what Allen calls "literate elite" and "folk" images of Lewis and Clark in the twentieth century may help explain the subsequent rediscovery and commemoration of the expedition. The "folk image," according to Allen, has tended to focus on "the explicit purpose of exploring and evaluating the newly acquired lands," essentially the viewpoint expressed by Captain Mullan.[15] Once the

Lewis and Clark Centennial had generated popular writings, this image was over-layered by romanticism and the ingredients of legend, particularly in the case of Sacagawea. But knowledge of the expedition often stops there. In general, according to Zelinsky, American explorers "may have been duly honored by historians, but only casually noted by the general public."[16] Only recently have Lewis and Clark achieved a "heroic apotheosis." Yet a series of questions posed to college freshman in survey courses over several decades in the second half of the twentieth century, designed to determine the extent of their "historical memory," revealed only slight recognition of why Lewis and Clark are historically significant. In the students' responses, Lewis and Clark were usually fused as a single unit or even as one individual. Sometimes they were referred to as "Lewis N. Clark."[17] What Allen calls the "literate elite" image, on the other hand, focuses on the expedition's scientific purposes and, as Donald Jackson stated, the "personalities involved," including those of the enlisted men.[18]

The journals became central to developing the elite image, and they made the specific path of the expedition central as well. Allen notes that the "merging and melding" of the "literal elite" with the "folk" image has resulted in the publication and popularity of "an unprecedented number of popular works which, by and large, have presented the expedition in a light more similar to that of the elite image than did earlier popular histories." Regardless of whether one accepts Allen's categories, it seems clear that a more scholarly or serious approach to the history of the expedition in the late twentieth century tempered the traditional romantic views based on a myth of the West and centered commemorative attention on the trail itself.[19]

The emerging emphasis on designating the Lewis and Clark trail contrasts sharply with earlier attitudes toward the expedition. When the National Historic Trail was created in 1978, eleven states claimed portions of it. But most of those geographic regions were not settled by Euro-Americans until the last three decades of the nineteenth century, which helps explain the previous lack of local interest in the history of the expedition. Accounts in popular magazines occasionally transported the reader to regions through which the explorers had traveled at the beginning of the century, but few attempts seem to have been made to memorialize the route or events associated with it. Early examples included journalist E. W. Carpenter, writing for *Overland Monthly and Out West Magazine* in the late 1860s, who was greatly impressed by the "Citadel Rocks" downstream from Fort Benton on the Missouri River. These are actually the White Rocks Meriwether Lewis lavishly described in May 1805. Carpenter called them "the most beautiful scenery in Montana," although his description appears to have been based on Lewis's description rather than on personal observation, since low water had forced him and his party to cover the last 250 miles to Fort Benton by land through a "desert of dry mud hills" and "badlands" with no redeeming qualities. He agreed with Lewis's assessment of the beauty of the Great Falls but again quoted nearly all of the explorer's passage from the journals. Regarding the rest of the Corps of Discovery's route up the Missouri River from St. Louis, Carpenter admitted a total lack of interest and referred the reader to the daily journal accounts.[20]

In another article from 1869, C. M. Scammon discussed a trip to Astoria, Oregon. He managed to describe Cape Disappointment, Chinook Point, Baker's Bay, and other landmarks now associated strongly with the expedition's arrival and sojourn at the mouth of the Columbia River during the winter of 1805–1806 with barely a mention of Lewis and Clark, and then only as a reference to the river bearing their names.[21] In the context of the times, however, that is not surprising. Scammon's readers were probably more interested in the nature of the small community that had developed around the old Astoria trading post and in commercial and transportation possibilities there. Virtually no one set out to follow and describe any of these places with the purpose of commemorating the expedition, at least not before the 1890s.

In a sampling of mid–nineteenth-century magazines available on-line that contain the names Lewis and Clark, none does more than refer to the expedition in passing. One reference in *Debow's Review* in 1843 mentions Lewis and Clark's "celebrated but ill-conducted expedition across the continent" in a discussion of the Rocky Mountains. Lewis and Clark are briefly alluded to in two other articles in *Debow's Review,* in 1856 and 1857, respectively. One article is about the Mississippi River, and one is about climate in the western regions. Otherwise, nineteenth-century periodical literature tends to mention

Lewis and Clark only in reviews of the Biddle and Coues editions of the journals.[22]

Elliott Coues's expanded and annotated account, although it drew heavily on the original journals, was insufficient to ignite general interest in the Corps of Discovery. As might be expected, however, the 100th anniversary of the expedition did so—but to a degree that may seem rather tepid today. The centennial celebration was mainly confined to Portland's 1905 Lewis and Clark Exposition, and even there the expedition received relatively scant attention.

CHAPTER ONE

Monuments

ON JUNE 1, 1905, PRESIDENT THEODORE ROOSEVELT tapped a telegraph key in Washington, D.C., to officially signal the opening of Portland, Oregon's, Lewis and Clark Centennial and American Pacific Exposition and Oriental Fair. Dignitaries on hand in Portland included Vice President Charles Fairbanks and Speaker of the House Joe Cannon. The fair's motto was "Westward the course of Empire Takes Its Way," and its official emblem included a woman, said to represent "Progress." She had an American flag draped over her shoulder and her arms around two men, presumably William Clark and Meriwether Lewis. The three are standing on the Pacific shore and facing the setting sun, stylized in a way to suggest Japan's Rising Sun. At the time of the centennial, the Pacific Northwest was being touted as the logical jumping-off point for trade with the Pacific Rim and East Asia. The national enthusiasm for imperialistic expansion—whetted by the recent acquisition of Spanish colonial possessions—had brought the United States to the threshold of dominance in the Pacific and an insistence on an "open door" to immensely profitable trade with China. American business leaders and politicians anticipated that the twentieth century would be "America's Pacific century."[1]

The exposition, which Roosevelt had pressured a reluctant U.S. Congress to help fund, thrust Portland into the "mainstream of American boosterism."[2] A national mania for large-scale international fairs had begun in 1876 with the Philadelphia centennial celebration of U.S. independence and was heightened by Chicago's 1893 Columbian Exposition. This had led to such extravaganzas as Nashville's Centennial Exposition in 1897, Omaha's Trans-Mississippi celebration in 1898, and Buffalo's Pan-American Exposition in 1901. Closely preceding the Lewis and Clark Exposition was the 1904 centennial commemoration of the Louisiana Purchase in St. Louis.

As its name indicates, the 100th anniversary of the expedition to the Pacific led by Lewis and Clark was the ostensible occasion for Portland's exposition. Yet like many of the popular international expositions in the United States during the late nineteenth century, the Lewis and Clark Centennial Exposition was much more about the present and the future than about the past. American expositions used historical commemoration as an excuse to display commercial wares, to educate the public on the benefits of economic progress, and to mark the end of one era and the beginning of another. Exposition scholar Burton Benedict and his colleagues called them "mammoth rituals" that utilized clusters of symbols in an attempt to "manufacture tradition" and "impose legitimacy." In the late nineteenth century, international fairs reiterated and justified middle-class morality and goals, linking patriotism with economic growth. They focused national aspirations and provided tangible proof that such aspirations were desirable and just. In short, they symbolized what was thought to be good about America.[3]

For Portland, Oregon, as for many western cities, the extravagant exposition also served as a rite of passage from childhood or adolescence as a booming frontier town to maturity and respectability on par with eastern cities. Further, the Lewis and Clark Exposition represented a chance for Portland to overcome economic stagnation. When planning for the exposition began in earnest in 1900, the city had not fully recovered from the depression of the early 1890s. Portland's collective ego also required a boost in view of the speed with which rival port city Seattle was expanding. A total of sixteen states had exhibits at the exposition. Oregon, Washington, and California, as might be expected, put up the largest structures, but considerable efforts were also made by Massachusetts, New York, and Missouri. Idaho, Colorado, Utah, Illinois, and Maine contributed "modest exhibit buildings." Twenty-one foreign countries were represented. Japan, regarded as key to American Pacific trade dominance in the new century, had the most impressive exhibit—a $1 million display featuring fine silks and porcelains. Paid attendance at the Lewis and Clark Exposition totaled 1,588,000 (although attendance figures range as high as 2.5 million), of which 540,000 were from Portland, 640,000 from elsewhere in Oregon and Washington, and 408,000 (16 percent) from the rest of the United States and Canada. The celebration spurred half a dozen years of rapid economic growth, an impressive increase in real estate values, and a jump in Portland's population.[4]

The city's annual Rose Festival began as a commemoration of the spirit of the Lewis and Clark Exposition and continues to this day. Yet to what extent did the exposition commemorate the Corps of Discovery and its two leaders? The answer, it appears, is "very little." True, the effort considerably exceeded what had been done over the previous century, but little suggests that the expedition was seen as more than a symbol of the "glory" of westward expansion. The world fairs held in St. Louis and Portland in 1904 and 1905, respectively, although stimulating public interest in Lewis and Clark, presented the expedition's story primarily as an emblem of progress and national expansion, in keeping with the true themes of those events.

Public images of both the Lewis and Clark Expedition and the celebration of the Louisiana Purchase flourished as the nation geared up for the centennial anniversaries of the two events. The two celebrations came at a time when America's imperialistic ambitions beyond its shores, particularly in the western Pacific, were in full flood and provided an anodyne to anxiety about the recent closing of the frontier. The image of Lewis and Clark carrying an American flag to the Pacific edge of the continent fit the image of the nation expanding its trade and influence to the very edge of the Pacific Rim. On the other hand, anxiety over the loss of the frontier helps account for a steady increase in popular writings about the West and possibly for increasing interest in Lewis, Clark, and Sacagawea. In celebrating the frontier past, Americans sought what Warren I. Susman has called a "native epic, an epic that extolled the virtues of extreme individualism, courage, recklessness, aloofness from social ties and obligations." An official publication for the Lewis and Clark Exposition, in fact, referred to the story told in the journals as "our national epic" on the basis of the qualities and virtues with which it was seen to represent the nation's ideals at the time.[5]

At the Louisiana Purchase Exposition in St. Louis, the Oregon exhibit included a rather grandiose and non-historical representation of Fort Clatsop, surrounded by a log stockade and "gardens of rose-flushed Clarkia," as well as other plants the explorers discovered. Organizers claimed that "the flag carried by" Lewis and Clark would fly over the structure.[6] Both captains were commemorated at the fair with monuments: Meriwether Lewis, buckskin and moccasin clad, in a heroic- (larger-than-life) sized statue by Charles Lopez and William Clark in a separate statue by sculptor F. W. Ruckstuhl. (Both statues were later shipped to Portland for the Lewis and Clark Exposition, where they mysteriously disappeared.) In addition, a granite obelisk and a bronze bust of Clark were dedicated on October 2, 1904, to mark his grave at Bellefontaine Cemetery in St. Louis.[7] Still, history was overshadowed at the St. Louis fair, even as it had been at the great centennial celebration in Philadelphia and the Columbian Exposition in Chicago, by boosterism and commercialism. Thus the fair became, in Karal Ann Marling's words, "a vast entertainment to which a dollop of history lent some semblance of high-minded dignity."[8]

At Portland's Lewis and Clark Exposition in 1905, ceremonies honored Lewis and Clark, and speakers expounded upon the magnitude of their achievement. An article by H. W. Scott in the fair's official publication states that "the expedition of Lewis and Clark, though as humble an undertaking as the settlement at Plymouth or Jamestown, was the prologue to the theme of our later national expansion."[9] Yet despite the fair's ostensible signs of commemorating that undertaking, it remained overshadowed by the promotion of municipal and regional economic potential. Carl Abbott points out that this made it easier to obtain national funding for the exposition: "No one in Congress had much interest in the historical heroes and their . . . trek." What the members of Congress *were* interested in was the "vision of Pacific trade that had motivated the exploration and settlement of the Oregon Country." To garner support, Oregonians learned quickly in the winter of 1903–1904 to cut the number of references to Lewis and Clark and to hammer home the idea that a Portland fair was "an undertaking of national interest and importance."[10]

The rhetoric commemorating the Corps of Discovery's feat had a distinctly imperialistic ring. In his 1904 article, Scott called the expedition "that Anabasis of the Western World" and explained the "Historical Significance of the Lewis and Clark Expedition" as a "prologue to the theme of our later national expansion [that] pushed our National boundary line to the shores of the Pacific." Scott proclaimed that the expedition "epitomized" the movement of and conquest by the "races of the North" in "one of the great dramas of history." Scott was not shy about using Lewis and Clark to support American expansionism, such as the recent annexation of the Philippines.[11]

Perhaps the fact that they were known at the time primarily as agents of American Manifest Destiny worked against the explorers and their party being idolized as romantic heroes. Abetting national expansion and stimulating economic development, no matter how significant to politicians and boosters in 1905, was decidedly less exciting or dramatic in the public mind than conquering enemies by force of arms or heroically and tragically failing (all but one of the Corps of Discovery's crew, after all, survived the adventure). The figure of Sacagawea, on the other hand, invited celebration of a more human and personal type of heroism in Portland and with increasing frequency throughout the twentieth century. Around two dozen statues, monuments, and markers have been erected to honor Sacagawea; and she is widely celebrated in writings, place names, music, paintings, pageants, motion pictures, and other forms of representation. Public perceptions of Sacagawea, her popularity as a historical icon,

Fig 1.1 *Although dated 1908, this photograph depicts a parade in Helena, Montana, celebrating the Lewis and Clark Centennial. Photo by Edward Reinig. Courtesy, Montana Historical Society Research Center, Helena.*

and the legends that have grown up around her life and death constitute topics unto themselves. As far as commemoration is concerned, Sacagawea often seems to occupy a place apart from the rest of the expedition, perhaps because of the various purposes to which her story—historical or legendary—has been put.[12]

The young Shoshone woman, who had been captured and separated from her people years before she encountered Lewis and Clark at Fort Mandan, accompanied the expedition all the way to the Pacific Coast and back in 1805–1806. She has become perhaps the leading popular icon related to that journey. Some authors have even claimed that the expedition would have failed without her. Donna Kessler has pointed out that different editions of the expedition journals and accounts of the expedition indicate different "versions of Sacagawea's function." One is that she had "no specified role," as Sergeant Patrick Gass's journal and the Biddle edition suggest. Sacagawea was just along for the trip. Accounts by both William Clark and Meriwether

Lewis, however, document several ways the Shoshone woman contributed.[13] Esther Burnett Horne and Sally McBeth categorize them as "interpreter," "guide," "emissary," and "unconventional counselor." The first two categories are probably the most recognized, although there has been some controversy over the question of the extent to which Sacagawea acted as a guide for the expedition. Her husband, Charbonneau, was brought along primarily as an interpreter and possibly also because his wife offered the additional skill of being able to interpret from the Shoshone language.[14]

Horne and McBeth acknowledge that the journals offer scant evidence that Sacagawea was "the guide and pilot" for the expedition and note that her "geographical knowledge was limited to the region near her homeland" in the vicinity of the Three Forks. Yet the fact that she recognized landmarks, such as Beaverhead Rock, was important because it indicated to the captains that they were on the right path. Also, in July 1806 she recommended that Clark's party, seeking a way to the Yellowstone River on the return trip, cross the mountains by way of Bozeman Pass. As "emissary," Sacagawea's dramatic reunion with her brother Cameahwait at Camp Fortunate paved the way for the expedition to obtain Shoshone horses to cross the Bitterroot Mountains. "Unconventional counselor" refers to a number of instances in which Sacagawea contributed to expedition members' morale and provided practical aid. As the mother of an infant born just before the group left Fort Mandan, she signaled to newly encountered Indians the group's peaceful intent and offered the men of the expedition a soothing domestic and maternal touch. She also gathered wild foods, and on one occasion her coolness in an emergency saved important supplies from being washed away when a canoe was nearly capsized on the Missouri River.[15] Historian Laura McCall states unequivocally that "without Sacagawea, the men of the Lewis and Clark Expedition would have either perished or been forced to turn back."[16]

But McCall also refers to Sacagawea as an "enigma." Except for the circumstances of her having been kidnapped by a raiding party near the Three Forks of the Missouri River when she was young and taken to the Hidatsa village in North Dakota, where Clark and Lewis encountered her while in winter encampment in 1804–1805, little is known about Sacagawea's life before she joined the expedition.[17] In addition, unless one accepts the oral tradition that she lived to be rather old and was buried on the Wind River Reservation in Wyoming, little is known about her life after she left the expedition.[18] What Horne and McBeth refer to as the "South Dakota version" of Sacagawea's subsequent life and death is the one most commonly accepted by scholars. Although several records or accounts between 1806 and 1812 apparently refer to her as the Shoshone (or Snake) wife of Toussaint Charbonneau, her actual name rarely appears. Evidence indicates that Sacagawea, her infant son, Jean Baptiste, and her husband, Charbonneau, traveled to St. Louis four years after the expedition returned and accepted a gift of land from William Clark and funds to help educate the boy. They soon left to go back up the Missouri, however, leaving Baptiste in Clark's care, and Charbonneau went to work at one of Manuel Lisa's fur trading posts.[19]

According to this version, Sacagawea became ill and died at Fort Manuel Lisa on December 20, 1812. The supporting evidence is entirely textual, based largely on handwritten notations made by the chief trader at Fort Manuel Lisa (in present-day Nebraska) and by William Clark. Despite questions about the interpretation of this evidence, most scholars accept the South Dakota version. The so-called Wyoming version of Sacagawea's life and death following the conclusion of the expedition is based on oral tradition of several Indian tribes compiled in a 1925 report by Charles Eastman. This version—popularized by Grace Raymond Hebard, then a historian at the University of Wyoming—claims that Sacagawea moved from tribe to tribe after parting from Charbonneau, married a man named Jerk Meat, and settled with Comanches in Oklahoma. After Jerk Meat's death, she "traveled up the Missouri River in search of her own people" and, under another name, eventually settled among the Eastern Shoshone on the Wind River Reservation in Wyoming. According to this version, she lived to be almost 100, dying on April 9, 1884. She was buried on the reservation near Lander, Wyoming.[20] A third version, one that has earned much less support among scholars, is that Sacagawea did live later than 1812 and was killed in northeastern Montana in 1869.[21]

The beginnings of Sacagawea's transformation in the popular imagination can be traced back to Elliott Coues, who emphasized her heroic contribution to the expedition, and to Eva Emery Dye's book *The Conquest: The True Story of Lewis and Clark*, which described Sacagawea as an Indian princess who was as significant to the exploration as were Clark and Lewis. Dye was a suffragette, and her image of Sacagawea provided the movement with what Kessler calls "a prototype for the emancipated woman" and a historically great American woman.[22] Sacagawea assumed the leading historical role at the Lewis and Clark Exposition when the National American Woman Suffrage Association (NAWSA) accepted an invitation to hold its 1905 national convention in Portland. In the convention's presidential address, Anna Howard Shaw called voting rights for women "the logical conclusion of Sacagawea's heroic efforts." Dye "dwelt on the claims of Sacajawea to the patriotism of all true Americans—far greater claims than those of Pocahontas."[23]

The Woman's Club of Portland had already established a Sacajawea Statue Association, with Dye as president, and raised $7,000 for a statue by selling souvenir "Sacajawea spoons" and "Sacajawea buttons." Dr. Washington Matthews of the U.S. Bureau of Ethnology produced what the *Exposition Journal* called "The First Model of a Statue of Sacajawea." One statue had been prepared for St. Louis. The one for Portland was being sculpted in Chicago by Denver sculptor Alice Cooper, who used photographs of Minataree women as studies for the work. Cooper's finished bronze statue for the fair portrayed Sacagawea in a buffalo robe, her baby strapped to her back, pointing the way for the explorers. It was unveiled on July 6, 1905, at a ceremony in which both Susan B. Anthony and Portland suffragist Abigail Scott Duniway praised Sacagawea in speeches. A year later the statue, a potent symbol of the view that Sacagawea had guided Lewis and Clark (because it showed her pointing), was placed in Portland's Washington Park. But Sacagawea symbolized more than progress toward women's rights in the early twentieth century.[24] Kessler points out that she became closely identified with Manifest Destiny and that of the "thirty-three texts [and monuments] highlighting Sacagawea within fifteen years of the publication of Dye's *The Conquest*," fewer than half were by suffragists.[25] For example, a poem about the Portland statue, written by Bert Huffman of Pendleton, Oregon, for the official exposition publication, describes her "glorious fate"

Fig 1.2 *Distant view of* Sacajawea *statue in Washington Park, Portland, Oregon. The statue was central to commemorations of the "Bird Woman" organized by women's suffrage advocates during the Lewis and Clark Exposition in 1906. Photo by Jeffrey Phillip Curry. Courtesy, Jeffrey Phillip Curry.*

to stand upon "fame's pedestal. . . . Bronzed, barefoot, yet a patron saint, / The keys of Empire in her hand."[26]

Veneration of Sacagawea at the Lewis and Clark Exposition was just the beginning of her transformation into a popular histori-

Fig 1.3 *Close-up of Washington Park* Sacajawea *statue. Photo by Jeffrey Phillip Curry. Courtesy, Jeffrey Phillip Curry.*

cal icon. While interest in the two explorers waned, the expedition's female star rose in esteem. Speaking at a meeting of the Montana Federation of Women's Clubs in 1914, Laura Tolman Scott of Armstead called Sacajawea the "unsung heroine of Montana."[27] That same year, the Montana Daughters of the American Revolution (DAR) dedicated a monument to Sacajawea (the spelling of the name preferred at the time and still favored by the Shoshone) at the Three Forks of the Missouri. It was a stone marker with a tablet that cited Sacajawea's "courage, loyalty, and intelligence," which "had done so much towards blazing the pathway to the great northwest."[28] Interest in Sacagawea's role was further stimulated by the republication of Eva Emery Dye's book ten years after Portland's Lewis and Clark Exposition.[29] In 1915 the DAR placed a bronze plaque on granite at the site of Camp Fortunate near Armstead, Montana, to honor Sacagawea. The Oregon Short Line Railroad graded and prepared a concrete site for the memorial. Scott also noted that "the Butte Tombstone Company presented a huge boulder, that was also transported free of charge, and excursions ran from Butte, Dillon and other neighboring cities."[30] Montana senator William A. Clark's speech at the dedication of the memorial called attention to Sacagawea's "services" to the expedition and also to her overall qualities "and her exemplary womanhood."[31] This remark appears to have been underscored by Mrs. Clarence Holt's costumed depiction of Sacagawea and singing of the "Sacajawea Lullaby," composed by Zillah Harris of Portland, to a baby doll as part of the Armstead ceremony (which included personifications of expedition members in a pageant).[32]

Numerous DAR memorials and plaques to Sacagawea followed in Montana and elsewhere. One can still be seen just east of State Highway 28 between Tendoy and Salmon, Idaho, which confidently marks the spot where Sacagawea was born. Based on the alternative theory of Sacagawea's life after the expedition, in 1915 the DAR erected a concrete monument at her purported grave on the Wind River Reservation in Wyoming.[33] The monument contains "a brass plate bearing the inscription 'Sacajawea, died April 9, 1884. A guide with the Lewis and Clark Expedition, 1804–1806. Identified by Rev. J. Roberts, who officiated at her burial.' "[34] In 1929 the Original Hickory Stick Club erected an obelisk commemorating "Sakakawea" near U.S. 12 west of the Missouri River bridge at Mobridge, South Dakota.[35] Five years after Cooper's exposition statue of Sacagawea was moved to Washington Park in Portland, *Bird Woman*, by sculptor Leonard Crunelle, was dedicated on the North Dakota state capitol grounds in Bismarck. Although a 1922 suggestion that a statue of Sacagawea mark "the Trail's End" turnaround in Seaside, Oregon, did not come to fruition,[36] several heroic-sized (life-size or larger) statues of her have been produced since then, including the 1980 painted sculpture at the Buffalo Bill Historical Center in Cody, Wyoming.

It is not surprising that the increase in public enthusiasm for Sacagawea around the turn of the twentieth century would find expression in monuments and statues. Intellectual and cultural historian Michael Kammen reports that the "greatest vogue" for erecting statues to commemorate heroic figures in the United States was during "the 1880s to the 1920s." Kammen suggests that this was a carry-over from the fervor to erect monuments following the Civil War, although it seems likely that both the war with Spain and World War I did much to stimulate the trend.[37] However, early–twentieth-century

Fig 1.4 *Dedication at Traveler's Rest, in 1925, of one of several plaques commemorating the expedition placed by the Daughters of the American Revolution in Montana and Idaho. Laura Tolman Scott, who was also involved in planning and implementing the monument and pageant dedicated to Sacagawea at Armstead, Montana, in 1915, is at the far left. Photo by F. Ward. Courtesy, Montana Historical Society Research Center, Helena.*

public monuments to Meriwether Lewis and William Clark—more substantial than roadside plaques—appeared less frequently than those to Sacagawea and sometimes met with considerable difficulty. In fact, no likenesses of the two explorers appeared in stone during much of the heyday of public sculpture described by Kammen and for fourteen years after the expedition's centennial celebration. The only significant monuments to the two captains erected prior to the Lewis and Clark Centennial were their grave markers. Regardless of whether the existence of statuary reliably indicates esteem for public figures in the early twentieth century, the complete absence of such surely suggests a remarkable lack of such esteem. For Lewis and Clark, however, the situation had begun to change by the 1920s. In fact, enthusiasm for creating and placing sculptures representing the

Fig 1.5 *Although no heroic-sized statue of Clark and Lewis appeared before 1919, the explorers were memorialized with this column monument in Washington Park, Portland, Oregon, as part of the centennial. Photo by Jeffrey Phillip Curry. Courtesy, Jeffrey Phillip Curry.*

central characters of the expedition increased in the decades following the golden age of heroic statuary.[38]

Perhaps the earliest heroic-scale (life-size or larger) statue that includes both Meriwether Lewis and William Clark was created by New York sculptor Charles Keck for the city of Charlottesville, Virginia, and was dedicated in that city's Midway Park in 1919. For the first time, Sacagawea was associated with the two explorers in a major public sculpture rather than presented as a solitary figure (although sometimes with her child). This might suggest that by this time she had come to be regarded more as a member of the expedition than as the singular heroine earlier exalted by the women's suffrage movement, although statues of Sacagawea alone continued to be produced on occasion. The Keck statue in Charlottesville consists of bronze figures of the two men standing and Sacagawea sitting. The work is eight feet, four inches high at its highest point. The sides of the impressive pedestal, which stands more than fourteen feet high, contain bas-reliefs depicting, among other things, Clark and Lewis taking part in an Indian council, York being admired by Indians, a buffalo hunt in which the explorers participated, and Sacagawea returning to her people.[39]

While the Keck sculpture in Charlottesville elevates the stature of the expedition's three "heroes" as larger than life, the bas-reliefs on its base establish a context of particular incidents from the journals. Although this is only a minimal beginning, such contextualizing became even more common in future historical markers and monuments to the expedition. As was the case with Sacagawea, Lewis and Clark emerged from a historical vacuum of sorts, in which they served mainly as iconic figures, and became more widely associated in public memory with the entire journey of discovery and with other historical events and figures associated with the opening of the West.

Along similar lines, the 1926 Astoria Column in Oregon incorporated a frieze depicting events of the Lewis and Clark Expedition and commemorating the explorers as major players in the conquest of the Pacific Northwest. Although not devoted entirely to Lewis and Clark (and not an example of heroic statuary), the Astoria Column stands out as the most grandiose monument to westward expansion in the Northwest and surely the most expensive historical site in the region prior to the nearby construction of a Fort Clatsop replica in the 1950s. This 123-foot-high cylinder, modeled to some extent on the second-century Trajan victory column in Rome, was erected on the crest of Coxcomb Hill, 640 feet above the Columbia River and the Astoria docks. The Great Northern Railway Company and descendants of John Jacob Astor, whose Pacific Fur Company had built the Astoria trading post in 1811, financed the structure to commemorate significant events in the history of Astoria and American expansion into Oregon country. Italian sculptor Attilio Pusterla was commissioned to create a frieze commemorating those events in a sequence of scenes spiraling from the bottom to the top of the column. Over the concrete surface, Pusterla put down layers of colored plaster depicting aspects of Chinook Indian life, Captain Robert Gray's discovery of the Columbia River, the arrival of Lewis and Clark in 1805, Wilson Price Hunt's overland expedition to help establish Fort Astoria, and other historic scenes. Visitors to the Astoria Column could ascend an interior spiral staircase to the viewing platform at the top. The monument's dedication ceremony and the subsequent activities of dignitaries attending as participants in the Great Northern "expedition" indicate that Lewis and Clark were its principal—and heretofore largely forgotten—honorees.[40]

The dedication of the finished monument on July 22, 1926, presided over by Oregon governor Walter M. Pierce, featured speeches by historian Samuel Elliot Morrison of Harvard; Howard Elliot, chairman of the board of the Northern Pacific Railway; and Major General Hugh L. Scott of the U.S. War Department—"a great authority on the American Indian." A descendant of John Jacob Astor, Mrs. Richard Aldrich, replied. In his address, Morrison referred to Astoria as the "Plymouth Rock of the West," having an older pedigree of European discovery even than New England.[41]

General Scott spoke specifically about the exploits of the Corps of Discovery. The reputation of this "great American epic," he said, "grows higher with time as it becomes better known and appreciated." Scott noted that Sacagawea had been commemorated by two bronze statues but that Clark and Lewis had "been forgotten by the government they served so nobly." Scott was unaware of any previous monuments to the two captains along the route except for a 1925 marker indicating the northernmost point Lewis reached during a probe up the Marias River in Montana. Now, through the "patriotic efforts of the Management of the Great northern Railway, which parallels their course for long distances," that neglect was being corrected. Yet, he said, the "great Northwest . . . is itself their grandest monument—may it endure forever."[42]

The Columbia River Historical Expedition, headed by Ralph Budd, president of the Northern Pacific Railway, was the second of two company-sponsored "pilgrimages" to sites related to early exploration—the Missouri Historical Expedition in the summer of 1925 and the foray the following year that climaxed with the dedication of the Astoria Column. According to Kammen, both expeditions did much to arouse public awareness of the West's historical heritage—albeit in a triumphal vein that glorified conquest—and gave numerous historical societies along the routes "a shot in the arm." Budd felt that far too much emphasis had been given to historical locations in the

Fig 1.6 *This 123-foot-high column on a hill overlooking Astoria, Oregon, and the Columbia River estuary was dedicated in 1926, with elaborate ceremony. It commemorates the arrival of Lewis and Clark and other important events in Astoria's history. Photo by Jeffrey Phillip Curry. Courtesy, Jeffrey Phillip Curry.*

Fig 1.7 *A close-up of the Astoria Column shows details of sculptor Attilio Pusterla's historic frieze, including the building of Fort Clatsop just a few miles west of Astoria, where the Corps of Discovery spent the winter of 1805–1806. Photo by Jeffrey Phillip Curry. Courtesy, Jeffrey Phillip Curry.*

eastern United States and too little to those on the Trans-Mississippi Frontier, particularly in the northern portion and on the Lewis and Clark trail. Budd's special train carried a select group of observers, whose purpose was to study the historic areas through which the Great Northern and Northern Pacific lines ran and to dedicate various monuments and works. The 1925 expedition had visited sites in the Dakotas related to fur trade on the Missouri River, including Fort Union, near Williston, North Dakota, and the Bear Paw battleground in northern Montana where Chief Joseph's Nez Perce band surrendered to the U.S. Army in 1877. The 1926 Columbia River excursion went further, traveling west of Glacier Park through northern Idaho to Wishram, Washington, and thence along the Columbia to The Dalles, Portland, and Astoria, Oregon. There, the more than 150 "notables," including Great Northern executives, took part in the dedication ceremony for the Astoria Column.[43]

From Astoria, the group moved on to attend a ceremony dedicating a flagpole at what was believed to be the site of Fort Clatsop. An Astoria newspaper reported that "[t]hey are paricularly [sic] interested in [that] event and in the site of Old Fort Clatsop, wishing to tread the ground where the intrepid explorers passed their winter in the west." From there it was on to Seaside, Oregon, "down to the end of the long, long trail of Lewis and Clark," to dedicate improvements made around the Salt Cairn site.[44] There, during the winter of 1805–1806, a small detail had been assigned to boil seawater to obtain salt for preserving meat. The Salt Cairn site was originally marked by the Oregon Historical Society in 1900 "through the testimony of Jenny Mishel of Seaside, who was born in that vicinity in 1816 and died in 1905. Her Clatsop Indian father remembered seeing the white men boiling water at the site, and pointed out the place to her when she was a young girl." The Great Northern paid to establish a "stonewall base, surrounded by an iron railing," to replace the original "rustic" marker. A recreation of the actual cairn with its row of kettles was produced by the Seaside Lions Club in 1953.[45] North of the Cairn site, a sign and eventually a statue marked the end of the trail at the street turnaround in Seaside next to the Pacific Ocean beach. The designation was apparently made by the Oregon State Highway Commission.[46]

Fig 1.8 *In 1900 the Oregon Historical Society designated the Salt Cairn site at Seaside, Oregon, where a detachment of men from the Fort Clatsop winter quarters (1805–1806) boiled ocean water to make salt. Later, the Great Northern Railway Company provided a wall and an iron railing enclosure for the spot, now located just two blocks from the beach. In 1955 the Seaside Lions Club supplied the replica of a stone cairn and kettles. Photo by Jeffrey Phillip Curry. Courtesy, Jeffrey Phillip Curry.*

Meanwhile, for decades the state of Montana unsuccessfully attempted to establish heroic statue monuments to the explorers, apparently beginning with a proposal around the time of the Portland exposition to place a statue at the site of Camp Fortunate, where the explorers met the Shoshone and bargained for horses, but nothing came of the original proposal.[47] In 1917 a bill introduced in the Montana Legislature called for heroic-sized bronze statues of Meriwether Lewis and William Clark to be erected at Great Falls and at the Three Forks of the Missouri River. The measure, passed by both houses of the legislature, appropriated $5,000 but carried a stipulation that the Society of Montana Pioneers raise an additional $15,000 to help pay for the two statues.[48] The funds were not raised, and the proposal to create bronze figures lapsed.

Fig 1.9 End of the Trail: *Seaside, Oregon's, heroic-sized statue of the explorers, locate inside the street turnaround at the Pacific Ocean beach. Photo by Jeffrey Phillip Curry. Courtesy, Jeffrey Phillip Curry.*

Fig 1.10 *Plaque at the base of the* End of the Trail *statue. Photo by Jeffrey Phillip Curry. Courtesy, Jeffrey Phillip Curry.*

A Montana Governor's Commission, appointed in 1926 to propose means of honoring the explorers, also called for a substantial monument and considered several cities for the site—including Great Falls, Three Forks, Helena, Butte, Bozeman, and Livingston. "During the next two years a series of public meetings were held at which seven communities presented proposals for the new memorial: Armstead, Bozeman, Butte, Great Falls, Helena, Livingston, and Three Forks." The proposals included "monuments with sculptured figures" or "buildings." Bozeman proposed "a building and museum," which the commission liked but did not feel the state could afford at the time. Further, they did not think Bozeman was the appropriate site. Nothing was done, possibly because of the intense municipal rivalry and the commission's apparent inability to decide whether to have several monuments in different places or just one in one location. The commission ultimately recommended monuments in both Great Falls and Three Forks; if only one were approved, however, it should be located in Great Falls.[49]

The competition among the towns continued. In addition to the commercial advantages of luring tourism, community pride and perhaps a sense of local historical identity were at stake. A heroic-sized sculpture, which Montana residents agreed would be *the* symbol of the Corps of Discovery's sojourn in the state, would significantly recognize the historical primacy of the town in which it was located. The winning community would become the official site for both state and national shrines. In 1928 a committee from the Three Forks Chamber of Commerce published an elaborate pamphlet arguing in favor of that town's claim because it was practically on the site of the expedition's "first and most important goal" (the headwaters of the Missouri River) as well as the point where the "great Yellowstone Trail, the National Parks Highway and the Geysers to Glacier Trail" all came together, among other reasons. Montana senator Burton K. Wheeler introduced—fruitlessly, as it turned out—a bill in the U.S. Congress that would have appropriated $50,000 to erect a memorial at Three Forks.[50]

In 1929, the same year the regional Lewis and Clark Memorial Association was formed to address the public neglect of the explorers, the Montana Legislature passed a resolution designating Fort Benton as the sole site for a Lewis and Clark monument, using an earlier design created for Great Falls by artist Charles M. Russell.[51] According to a special 1976 Lewis and Clark edition of Fort Benton's *The River Press*, sculptor Henry Lion of Los Angeles was enlisted to develop Russell's design into a heroic-sized bronze statue. The city of Fort Benton donated the proposed site, a circular turnaround at the north end of Front Street next to the river embankment. However, as the Great Depression deepened in 1930, Montana's state government shied away from appropriating the anticipated cost of nearly $18,000. Nothing came of the design or the resolution, although the legislative act apparently was not rescinded. These attempts by the state of Montana to establish a Lewis and Clark monument during the 1920s—and the attendant squabbling over where it should be located—temporarily raised public consciousness of the expedition's history; however, it is difficult to tell whether this reflected changing public views of Lewis and Clark themselves. The emphasis on the creation and placement of a statuary monument suggests that the "folk" image still dominated public attention paid to the explorers.[52]

Neglect of Lewis and Clark, at least in terms of traditional statuary, proved something of an embarrassment in Montana. While numerous activities were planned for the expedition's sesquicentennial in the 1950s, Fort Benton did not receive its larger-than-life-size sculpture commemorating the explorers until 1976—the year of the nation's bicentennial—when the community unveiled a composite statue of Clark, Lewis, and Sacagawea created by Bob Scriver of Browning, Montana. In 1973 the Fort Benton Community Improvement Association received state approval to revive the 1929 project and raise funds, whereupon a Lewis and Clark Memorial Committee was named to oversee the project. But it is fair to say that Scriver's participation was essential to reviving the Lewis and Clark statue project and that the community supported it with little outside help. Financing came from the sale of small replicas of Scriver's design. The state of Montana contributed no funds. The empty turnaround circle, reserved for the statue since the early 1930s, remains empty to this day. For some reason, the committee ignored it and selected a spot near the embankment, a few feet to the north.[53] The statue is fairly traditional. It depicts the two captains standing, with Lewis looking through a telescope, while Sacagawea is seated with the baby Baptiste beside her. The pattern is similar to that of the 1919 Keck sculpture in Virginia, but without the elaborate frieze.

Scriver's subsequent endeavors to monumentalize the expedition are more original, even audacious. His ambitious project to carve a limestone monolith on Clark's Lookout, the point near Dillon where Clark climbed to view the valley, did not come to fruition. He did complete the fourteen-foot-high bronze group in Great Falls, entitled Lewis and Clark at the Portage, however, which was unveiled at ceremonies for Montana's State Centennial in 1989. The monument portrays Lewis, Clark, York (Clark's African American slave), and the dog Seaman.[54]

The figure of York—who traveled with the Corps of Discovery all the way to the Pacific Ocean and who, along with Sacagawea, took part in a vote held near the mouth of the Columbia River in the fall of 1805 to decide on a location for the winter camp—is central

Fig 1.11 *In the 1970s Montana finally got a heroic-sized statue commemorating Lewis and Clark and Sacagawea, thanks to the community of Fort Benton and sculptor Bob Scriver of Browning, Montana. The statue is located near the turnaround on Front Street in Fort Benton. Photo by Donnie Sexton. Courtesy, Travel Montana.*

to one of Charles M. Russell's paintings depicting scenes from the Lewis and Clark Expedition. In the painting, a somewhat romanticized York is shown impressing his audience in a Mandan lodge. Recently, more attention has been paid to York as a member of the expedition. Writer and historian Steven Ambrose has discussed York's request that Clark free him after the return in 1806 and speculated about York's subsequent life.[55] Historian Robert Betts has devoted a book to York, the most recent edition of which offers newly discovered evidence about post-expedition York in an epilogue by James J. Holmberg. The figure of York in the Great Falls sculptural group reflects the growth of sensitivity in the 1970s toward African American history, as well as a more generally inclusive interpretation of the nation's past.[56]

It is difficult to measure the significance of larger-than-life statues to the public view of Lewis and Clark. There are too few examples to solidly indicate changes over time, although the inclusion of York demonstrates a change in sensibility by the 1970s. However, the history of Lewis and Clark statuary does reveal a curious lack of public regard for the explorers—especially when contrasted with the near idolatry of Sacagawea—at a time when heroic-sized statues were most in vogue. That neglect is remarkable because statues became conventional means for commemorating the exploits of revered individuals in the past. Yet the neglect was fairly general at the national level, even in states through which the expedition's trail runs. Pageants, another means of commemoration, were also popular between 1900 and 1930, although they dramatized group tableaux and actions. While featuring historical figures in the principal roles, pageants tend to mythologize events rather than individuals. As we shall see in Chapter 5, pageants became the preferred method of commemorating the Corps of Discovery during the 150th anniversary of its expedition, which suggests that by the 1950s events described in the journals had become more significant as subjects of commemoration than were the individual personages of Clark, Lewis, or Sacagawea. Those events are closely tied to the route of the Corps of Discovery and, in turn, to the landscape and the modern highways that provide access to the Lewis and Clark trail.

Tracing the Route

A s DESCRIBED IN CHAPTER 1, monuments and statues—once the traditional means of commemorating individuals idolized by the public—were eventually erected to honor William Clark and Meriwether Lewis. But the fascination that cast its spell over an increasing number of history buffs was inspired at least as much by the land and the routes taken through that land as it was by the people who made up the Corps of Discovery, in part because of the written records of the expedition. Without those records there would be no Lewis and Clark National Historic Trail today, since virtually no material trace remains of the group's journey. The journals provide a unique glimpse of the western regions through which the expedition passed—a description of the appearance of the land in the early years of the nineteenth century. The landscape has often changed dramatically since then. The Lewis and Clark trail—the combination

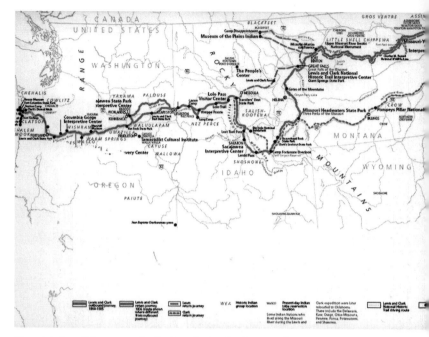

Map 2.1 *Expedition routes, St. Louis to the Pacific Ocean and return, 1804–1806. Large dots indicate locations of natural and historic sites and of Lewis and Clark interpretive centers.*

of routes from Wood River to the Pacific Ocean and back to St. Louis, as described in the journals—became for Americans in the second half of the twentieth century the most genuine memorial to the explorers' names.

Since much of this book discusses events and commemorations held at various times and in various locations along Lewis and Clark's route, it seems helpful to offer a linear and chronological description of the country and the Native American groups encountered, as well as the route's relation to present-day communities and other locations. Furthermore, the summary here relates the path of Lewis and Clark to present-day highways, which provide access to the expedition's historical sites and play a major role in the development of the National Historic Trail—the book's central theme.[1]

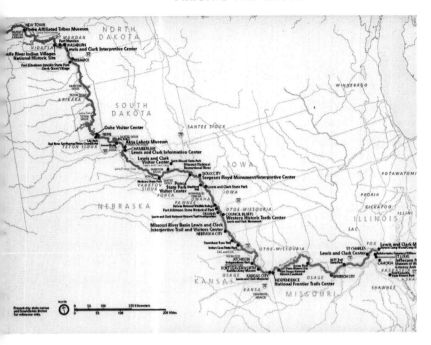

During the summer of 1803, Meriwether Lewis took a specially constructed keelboat loaded with supplies down the Ohio River and picked up William Clark at his home in Clarksville, Indiana Territory. At Camp Wood on the Illinois side of the Mississippi River and near the mouth of the Missouri, the men of the expedition prepared for their journey and spent the winter. President Thomas Jefferson had informed Lewis that his main objective was "to explore the Missouri river, & such principal stream of it, as, by its course & communication with the waters of the Pacific Ocean, may offer the most direct & practicable water communication across this continent, for the purposes of commerce." In addition to finding portage between the headwaters of the Missouri and Columbia rivers, the explorers were to observe and note topographical, botanical, mineralogical, meteorological, and zoological characteristics of the country they passed through.[2]

Lewis and Clark were particularly assiduous in this respect, filling their records of the journey with hundreds of descriptions of new plants and animals and landforms they encountered. Jefferson's instructions also called for conferences and peacemaking among the tribes of the upper Missouri and included a list of social and cultural topics on which he wanted the explorers to collect information. Nearly fifty men comprised the initial party, although there would be some changes as a result of military discipline. A third of those who set out—some soldiers and river boatmen—returned from the Mandan Villages in North Dakota following the winter of 1804–1805 and did not continue to the Pacific Coast. For the first segment of the journey, the Corps of Discovery traveled in a fifty-five-foot keelboat equipped with oars and a sail and two pirogues or dugout canoes, one painted white and one red.[3]

On May 14, 1804, the Corps of Discovery left its winter quarters to join Captain Lewis—who had ridden overland from St. Louis—at the small village of St. Charles, where Interstate 70 now crosses the Missouri River just west of St. Louis. A few days later the expedition continued in a westerly direction. At La Charette, located near Marthasville, Missouri, at a site since washed away by the river, the men left behind the last Euro-American settlement they would see for nearly thirty months. [II, 253n5] For almost 400 miles (by river) they moved westward across the present state of Missouri, past the future sites of Jefferson City, Boonville, Lexington, and Independence and the mouths of the Osage, Moreau, and Chariton rivers and other tributaries. It was, and still is, lush country, described in the journals as fertile prairie interspersed with woodlands. At a point about halfway between Columbia and Boonville, where I-70 crosses the Missouri, William Clark first reported seeing a "buffalo Sign," although another eleven weeks would pass before the group dined on a bison. [II, 282]

West of Boonville and the Lamine River, the Missouri curves north and then southwest before continuing its generally westward course to Kansas City. In this bend the expedition passed a narrow elbow in the river at which a prominent bluff jutted out, now the site of Arrow Rock State Park, downstream from Saline City. Journal entries are replete with descriptions of the natural bounty found in the heavy vegetation along the banks of the Missouri River, which included wild grapes, black raspberries, plums, and crabapples. The bottomlands through which the river shifted and meandered were dominated by large, often even huge cottonwood trees throughout the prairie and high plains regions of Missouri, Kansas, Iowa, the Dakotas, and Montana. Sharing this floodplain were shrubs, willows, and other vegetation characteristic of wetlands created when the river had abandoned and cut off oxbow bends as it changed channels. Away from the floodplain, the terraces and bluffs were thick with upland forests of walnut, ash, hackberry, oak, and sycamore trees.[4]

The currents of the river, "a moody beast," constantly changed speed. The men often had to jump into the shallows near the bank and pull on cordelles (long ropes) attached to the keelboat or push the pirogues when the current was too strong to make headway by poling or rowing. If the wind was favorable, sails could be hoisted to take advantage of it. When the wind blew against them, however, even pulling was ineffective, and the expedition had to put in to shore to wait it out. As if shifting currents and wind were not enough, the Missouri ate away at its banks, causing large chunks to break away without warning and threaten to swamp any nearby craft. Floating obstacles were also a common menace. Enormous cottonwoods that had fallen into the river often became "sawyers," dead tree trunks that floated vertically with their tops just below the surface of the water. With little warning, the bobbing sawyers could rip open the hull of a keelboat or pirogue with tremendous power.[5]

At the mouth of the Kansas River in present-day Kansas City, which it reached on June 26, the expedition paused for several days. On the 28th the men saw their first buffalo but did not kill one. The respite was used to discipline John Collins and Hugh Hall, charged in a court-martial proceeding with drunkenness while on guard duty and with pilfering the whiskey supply. The punishment was harsh: Collins received 100 lashes and Hall 50. This was one of several courts-martial and disciplinary inflictions carried out on the lower Missouri segment of the outward journey. The men celebrated their first Fourth of July near Atchison, Kansas, firing the keelboat bow gun and examining a long-deserted site of a "Kanzas" Indian town in

Donophan County. [II, 349n4] Moving past St. Joseph, they worked their way between present-day Missouri and Nebraska to the mouth of the Platte River, about ten miles south of Omaha.

Today, Interstate 29 follows the river closely on the Missouri and Iowa side. The wild grapes, berries, and wild roses of midsummer could still be seen in profusion along the river's banks, but the prairie land back from the eastern (or northern) bluffs was becoming more open, with fewer signs of timber or vegetation other than grasses. Although the grass became shorter as they moved further west into the interior of South Dakota, the riverine zone of Kansas, Nebraska, and Iowa was dominated by "big bluestem," which could grow as high as twelve feet. Moving out of the prairie region into the Great Plains, the land became progressively drier and higher in elevation. The Platte River, pouring into the Missouri near Bellevue, Nebraska, was known to be a major tributary flowing almost directly from the western mountains. Although not practically navigable, within forty years the Platte would guide and sustain emigrants passing over the great river roads to Oregon, California, and Utah.[6] Clark commented on the Platte: "This Great river being much more rapid than the Missouri forces its current against the opposite Shore . . . with great Velocity roleing its Sands into the Missouri, filling up its Bend & Compelling it to incroach on the . . . shore—we found great dificuelty in passing around the Sand at the mouth of [t]his River." [II, 402]

Concerned about not having encountered any of the Ponca, Oto, Omaha, or Missouri Indians they had expected to see, the captains dispatched hunters George Drouillard and Pierre Cruzatte to look for them and invite them to parley. The Corps of Discovery's first council with Indians was held at a place on the west side of the Missouri River near Blair, Nebraska. Clark referred to this site, south of a large oxbow lake where the DeSoto National Wildlife Refuge is now located, as the "Council Bluffs," but it should not be confused with the Iowa town of the same name across the river from Omaha. There, on August 2, the men addressed a group of Otos and Missouris and handed out Jefferson "friendship" medals to the chiefs. Remnants of the Missouri band, depleted by a smallpox pandemic in 1801, lived among the Otos. Lewis and Clark hoped to negotiate peace between the Otos and their bitter enemies, the Omahas. The once powerful

Omahas, who had not yet been located, had also suffered severe losses from the disease.

In a procedure that would be repeated with other tribes as the Corps of Discovery moved upriver toward the Mandan Villages, Clark spoke to the Missouris and Otos about forging an agreement that would end the raiding and enmity among the river tribes, and he promised trade for all under the sovereignty of the United States. Neither Clark nor Lewis appeared to appreciate the nature of intertribal warfare on the Missouri frontier—what historian James P. Ronda calls "the river realities of raid and truce"—the social role of warfare in the region, or the dynamics of power as related to trade. Hostilities, often rooted in the desire for revenge for insults or for someone having killed a member of the revenger's tribe, would suddenly give way to temporary truces between bands so they could trade horses or food. Once the need for peace had lapsed, warfare could erupt just as suddenly.[7] Still, the Otos accepted the speeches and the gifts and seemed to agree to the plan. The Omahas failed to appear, however. Several days after the council (August 11), Clark, Lewis, and ten other men climbed a high bluff above the river near Macey, Nebraska, to get a good view of the river northward and to visit the grave of the renowned Omaha chief Blackbird. Not far upstream, near present-day Sioux City, Iowa, Sergeant Charles Floyd became the expedition's only fatality, likely a victim of appendicitis. He was buried on a hill above the river bluffs.

From here the river turned to the northwest, between Sioux City, Iowa, and Yankton, South Dakota. On August 23, one of the Field brothers shot the first of many buffalo on which the expedition members would largely subsist as they moved through the high plains. This occurred at the mouth of the Vermillion River near Vermillion in the southeast corner of South Dakota. Another meeting, this time with Yankton Sioux, took place at Calumet Bluff, a whitish outcropping of the chalky Niobrara Formation. [III, 21] The Yanktons listened politely to what would become the standard harangue but indicated that they were interested mostly in assurances of trade in firearms and ammunition. In early September the men passed the mouth of the Niobrara River, which heads far to the west in Wyoming. The captains spent considerable time examining what they took to be an "antient [sic] fortification" similar to the mounds left by an Indian civilization in the Ohio Valley [III, 40, 43n3]. These earth formations have since been determined to have been naturally formed, however. On September 7 they encountered their first prairie dogs near the "tower," a conical landform in northern Boyd County, Nebraska. An effort to catch one alive resulted in most of the crew spending the better part of a day hauling water to force the animal out of its hole. A week later came the first sighting of pronghorns (often erroneously referred to today as antelope) and, near Chamberlain, South Dakota, the coyote and magpie.

Today, Interstate 90 crosses the Missouri River at Chamberlain. A few miles upstream lay Sioux Pass, a major crossing of the Missouri where three creeks enter on the east bank and at the Big Bend, all now within the Lower Brulé and Crow Creek Indian reservations. [III, 91n2] An American Fur Company post, Fort Lookout, was later built near Sioux Pass. The Big Bend, or "Grand Detour," is a nearly closed loop in the river. Clark walked across the neck of the hilly peninsula formed by the loop and pronounced the distance to be no more than a mile and a quarter. The keelboat and pirogues following the river, however, were forced to cover a dozen miles to get to the same place. At this point the river flowed more from the west than the north and would continue to do so up to Farmer's Island and the mouth of the Teton (Bad) River opposite Pierre, South Dakota. Today, the difference between the generally flat agricultural lands east of the Missouri and the hilly grass country west of the river is very noticeable. Here, just downstream from the present-day Oahe Dam and Lake, a nearly fatal series of encounters with a band of Teton Sioux occurred.[8]

Clark and Lewis were leery of the Teton Sioux (Lakota). Missouri traders operating out of St. Louis had warned them about the risks of encountering Teton bands, which did not want upriver tribes to gain direct access to weapons and other trade goods. By 1804 the western Sioux had begun to use their military power both to expand the region within which they could control access to buffalo herds by other tribes and to maintain a role as middlemen in trade among tribes as well as with whites. By the mid-eighteenth century the Sioux dominated an area that comprised most of North and South Dakota, portions of eastern Montana and Wyoming, and western Nebraska.[9] Regarding Sioux expansion, President Jefferson had asked Lewis and Clark to take special pains to "make a friendly impression" on the powerful Sioux.[10] So despite their uneasiness, the two captains agreed to hold council with the Brulé Teton band near the mouth of the Bad River.

The first and third days of the expedition's stay with the Brulé were the most dangerous. The officers and men of the Corps of Discovery began by distributing gifts to the Sioux leaders and putting on their now practiced demonstrations of power in full uniform. They seemed not to have been aware of political rivalries within the Brulé band. According to Ronda, two other chiefs shared authority with Black Buffalo, whom the explorers treated as the headman.[11]

The initial council was followed by a tense situation involving the boats, exacerbated by the surly behavior of one of the slighted chiefs, called "the Partisan." His men grabbed hold of the pirogue cable and mast, and the Partisan told Clark that the expedition would not be permitted to advance up the river. For a few moments it looked as if a fight would break out. Clark drew his sword, and Lewis threatened to fire the swivel guns onboard the keelboat. The danger passed, however, and the following day it was Lewis and Clark's turn to be feasted and regaled with demonstrations. But the Partisan was not finished trying to impress the band with his defiance of the expedition. By the third day, the captains had begun to believe the Brulé would do whatever was necessary to turn them back, while many of the Sioux were expressing disappointment at how miserly the gifts had been from an obviously rich store of trade goods and voicing their suspicion that Lewis and Clark intended to trade upriver with tribes that had come to depend on the Sioux for access to European goods. As the crew prepared to leave, the Partisan demanded more gifts, and his followers again seized a boat cable to prevent the expedition's departure. Although Black Buffalo managed to soothe the situation, bitter words were exchanged. The Corps of Discovery left the Brulé band on bad terms, having largely failed to make the requested friendly impression.[12]

On October 8, around 150 miles upstream from Pierre, the expedition came upon the first of several deserted Arikara villages near Mobridge, South Dakota. The Arikaras, who lived in earth lodges in towns protected by ditches and bristling palisades of sharpened poles, derived much of their food supply and tradable goods from agriculture. They tended to cluster at the mouths of tributaries, such as the Cheyenne, Grand, and Moreau rivers flowing into the Missouri from the west. By the time the Corps of Discovery arrived, the once numerous Arikaras had been reduced by smallpox and Sioux raids and been forced to abandon some of their towns in order to consolidate. The Arikara had a curious symbiotic relationship with the Sioux, trading food for horses, buffalo meat and hides, and European manufactured goods, but sometimes the Tetons simply took what they wanted in raids on Arikara villages. The trader Pierre Antoine Tabeau, who lived among the Arikaras, told Lewis and Clark that the Sioux purposely drove buffalo away from the vicinity of Arikara villages so the tribe would remain dependent on the Sioux. As a result, the explorers came to view the situation as a case of Sioux enslavement of their Arikara victims and resolved to establish alliances with upriver tribes that would help free them. The captains were gratified by the Arikaras' willingness to make peace with the Mandans and Hidatsas. Lewis and Clark spent several days in the Arikara village before continuing upstream.[13]

It was now mid-October, and the captains hoped to spend the winter at the Mandan Villages, a well-known trading center on the upper Missouri. On the 21st they passed the present-day cities of Bismarck and Mandan, North Dakota, and intersected today's Interstate 94. A week later they were camped opposite the mouth of the Knife River and had arranged a counsel with chiefs from the nearby Mandan and Hidatsa villages. Winter quarters were established as Fort Mandan, a triangular-shaped structure built of cottonwood logs and located a few miles downstream near Washburn, North Dakota, across the Missouri from the village of the Mandan chief Sheheke (Big White). The winter spent among the Mandans and Hidatsas in 1804–1805 gave Clark and Lewis an opportunity to study their cultures. As was the case with the Arikaras, these tribes were largely sedentary and tended extensive fields of squash, beans, and corn. They traded agricultural products with other Indians, who often attended trade fairs at this strategic location—central to the Cree, Assiniboin, Crow, and Cheyenne bands, as well as the Sioux.

Fig 2.1 *Replica of Fort Mandan near Washburn, North Dakota. Here, next to the Missouri River, the Corps of Discovery spent the winter of 1804–1805 among the Mandan and Hidatsa Indians. Courtesy, U.S. Army Center of Military History.*

Both the Mandan and the Hidatsa also hunted buffalo, and Hidatsa parties rode as far west as the Great Falls of the Missouri River in northwestern Montana. The captains thus sought information from Hidatsa leaders about the country through which they planned to pass in the spring. They also wanted to conduct diplomacy with both the Native Americans and the Canadian traders in the area around the Mandan Villages. More important, perhaps, they came in contact with Sacagawea, whose husband, Charbonneau, was taken on as an interpreter. Sacagawea was pregnant, and she gave birth to Jean Baptiste, whom Clark would refer to as "Pompy," on February 11, 1805—a little less than two months before he and his parents left to accompany the Lewis and Clark Expedition to the Pacific Coast and back.[14]

On April 7, 1805, a smaller group—consisting of the two captains, thirty men including Charbonneau and York, plus Sacagawea and her child—set out from Fort Mandan to seek the headwaters of the Missouri River and, they hoped, to cross into the Columbia River watershed before winter. The keelboat had departed downstream carrying the members of the original party who were returning to St. Louis. Six dugout canoes and a pair of pirogues would be used for the remainder of the Missouri route. Near the site of Garrison Dam, which today backs up Lake Sakakawea, the Missouri River begins to flow generally from the west. They were still in North Dakota, but further upstream they would move into Montana a few miles west of the confluence of the Yellowstone and Missouri rivers. They were still in the Great Plains, a windswept land of short grass and little rain, and would remain so until midsummer as they followed the Missouri River through western North Dakota and northern Montana.

The Great Plains in this area is a vast extent of glaciated hills, buttes, and shallow coulees, where the only timber is bunched in isolated copses or hugs the bottoms of streams and rivers that cut their way through deep ravines. From the river, Lewis described the North Dakota "upland [as] extremely broken, consisting of high [eroded] nobs as far as the eye can reach on ether side, and entirely destitute of timber" but covered with sagebrush and juniper. Walking along the shore on April 20, Lewis noted within the underbrush of the ubiquitous cottonwood, ash, and box elder trees a variety of rosebushes and currant, gooseberry, and serviceberry shrubs. On the northern fringe of the Dakota badlands the explorers noted sulfurous smoke from fires burning lignite coal seams under the ground. These fires in the Sentinel Butte Formation begin spontaneously and can burn unchecked for years. [IV, 18n5; 21n3].

They soon passed the mouth of the Little Missouri River, which flows out of the Black Hills to the southwest, and proceeded through today's Fort Berthold Indian Reservation. Two weeks out from Fort Mandan the expedition passed the mouth of Little Muddy Creek—where Williston, North Dakota, is located today—and reached the confluence with the Yellowstone, just inside the North Dakota border, on April 25. This river junction became highly important to the upper Missouri fur trade over the next half century. Four trading posts would be built in its vicinity, including the most famous, Fort Union, constructed in 1829. The Yellowstone River, which rises in Yellowstone National Park and flows north to Livingston, Montana, before crossing the southern part of the state and angling up to the Missouri, provided a return path for part of the expedition in 1806.[15]

For the next forty-five days the expedition moved up the Missouri River, westerly through northern Montana. Eventually, the men hoped to make contact with mountain Shoshone—Sacagawea's people—so they could obtain horses to cross over to the Columbia River watershed, but here, between the mouths of the White Earth River in the east and the Milk River in the west, they were skirting the southern edge of Assiniboin hunting territory. They did not particularly wish to encounter these Northern Plains Indians. Since the Assiniboin did little to raise horses, they often raided the Hidatsas and Mandans or traded guns for mounts. Like the Sioux, they were jealous of their middleman trading status. Clark and Lewis regarded them as victimizing the Mandans, just as they saw the Tetons as victimizing the Arikara. Although Clark came across signs of recent Indian encampments while walking along the river's bank in eastern Montana, no actual encounter with the Assiniboins took place.

Almost at the site of Fort Peck Dam, the river runs close to U.S. Highway 2, once known as Roosevelt International Highway. At Big Muddy Creek the expedition moved along the southern boundary of the Fort Peck Indian Reservation and passed the towns of Poplar and Wolf Point. On May 2, near Poplar, an inch of snow fell, coating flowers and leafed-out trees. Clark remarked that it was "a verry extroadernaley Climate." [IV, 101] On May 8, south of Glasgow, they encountered the Milk, the "River Which Scolds All Others." It flows out of Glacier National Park and into southern Alberta before sweeping back into Montana. Beyond the Milk River, which U.S. 2 turns northwest to follow, lay a 180-mile portion of the river now covered by Fort Peck Lake. In the vicinity of Sticklodge Creek on May 14, the group had one of its most disconcerting encounters with a grizzly bear. That evening some of the men spotted a large brown bear lying in the open ground about 300 paces from the river, and six of them set out to shoot it. They were able to sneak up fairly close to the bear, but despite a volley from four muskets, they could not bring it down and were forced to scatter for their lives. Eventually, after being hit by eight musket balls, the bear succumbed, but not before he had driven the hunting party into the river and attempted to pursue one of the men in the water. [IV, 151]

About thirty miles south of Sticklodge Creek (now called Hell Creek) is the town of Jordan, centered and virtually isolated within the immense Garfield County, Montana. Jordan is one of very few communities along the eastern reaches of State Highway 200. That highway, which runs across central Montana between the Missouri and Yellowstone rivers, has a more direct relationship to the Lewis and Clark trail west of the Continental Divide, where it follows the Blackfoot River to Missoula. In late May, still on the portion of the Missouri now inundated by Fort Peck Lake, the explorers killed their first bighorn sheep and spied what Clark assumed was evidence of the Rocky Mountain cordillera but which turned out to be relatively isolated ranges of the Little Rocky, Bear Paw, Judith, and Highwood mountains. Beyond what is now slack water at the foot of Fort Peck Reservoir, the Corps of Discovery passed the future sites of James Kipp State Park and Fred Robinson Bridge. No roads or highways follow the river in this portion of the upper Missouri. They approach from the north and the south and cross at McClellan Ferry and Judith Landing, where the Judith River empties in from the south.

Beyond Judith Landing, the river tends to the northwest before making a great bend southward. As it moved upstream through north-central Montana, the expedition encountered a diminishing supply of firewood and an increasing number of troublesome plants, including prickly pear cactus and thorny greasewood. All journal entries agreed that this was barren desert. This is the region of the Missouri Breaks and the White Cliffs, which must be viewed from watercraft on the river. The area now lies within the Upper Missouri Wild and Scenic River segment. As the expedition passed the "nearly perpendicular" White Cliffs on May 31, Lewis marveled at the intricate formations within the 200- to 300-foot-high bluffs. From a distance, he wrote in his journal, they exhibited "a most romantic appearance." Over time, water trickling down the white sandstone had carved columns, niches, statuettes, and "a thousand grotesque figures" that could appear—with some use of the imagination—to be the work of human hands. [IV, 225][16]

Fig 2.2 *The White Cliffs, at which Meriwether Lewis marveled as the expedition passed en route up the Missouri River on May 31, 1805, are now part of the Upper Missouri Wild and Scenic River segment. Photo by Donnie Sexton. Courtesy, Travel Montana.*

Highway access to the expedition's route picks up again at Loma, Montana, where U.S. 87 crosses the Marias River near its mouth. Here the two captains made camp on June 2 and paused to consider whether to follow the Marias fork northwest or to continue on the southward-tending fork. For several days small groups carried out a reconnaissance of the two forks of the river. Lewis led one group perhaps sixty miles up the Marias, which flows in from the northwest, while Clark took another group up the southerly fork. The Marias was narrower but seemed to carry a greater volume of water. After weighing the evidence, the two captains determined that the main stem of the Missouri River must be the south fork, although their followers disagreed. Once the decision had been made, the men dug a cache to deposit equipment, supplies, and specimens they would not need for the final dash to the Pacific Coast and also hid one of the pirogues.

As preparations for departure continued at the Marias camp, Meriwether Lewis and four other men set out to look for the Great Falls of the Missouri, which the Hidatsas had told them would require a

Fig 2.3 *Big Falls on the Missouri River, twelve miles east of Great Falls, Montana, photographed in 1910, long before it partially disappeared underwater behind a hydroelectric dam. Photo by G. V. Barker. Courtesy, Montana Historical Society Research Center, Helena.*

short portage to circumvent. Moving upstream above the river bluffs, they could see two massive flat-topped buttes to the west and beyond them the Rocky Mountains and the crest of the Great Divide. On June 13, 1805, Lewis, who was alone while his companions searched for game on the plains south of the river, came upon the Great Falls. This confirmed that he and Clark had taken the right course. What Lewis call a "sublimely grand specticle" was located approximately thirty miles upstream from the future Fort Benton. He described "a sheet of the whitest beaten froth for 200 yards in length and about 80 feet" in height. The outcrop where Lewis stood seemed "to reverberate" as the water pounded against it. As the torrent fell, it swelled "into half formed billows of great hight which rise and again disappear in an instant." Below the falls Lewis noticed the skeletons and

PHOTO BY G. V. BARKER
LEWISTON IDAHO,

No 7.

remains of many buffalo that had fallen into the river while drinking and been precipitated over the cascade. In his description of the
lower and largest of the waterfalls, Lewis is the most eloquent in
his observations of nature. [IV, 283–285] But there were four more
beautiful waterfalls upstream: Crooked Falls, Rainbow Falls (current
name), Colter Falls (no longer visible), and Black Eagle Falls, which
lies within the present-day city of Great Falls, Montana. [IV, 296n2, 3]
Between Rainbow and Black Eagle falls was the eight-foot-high Giant
Spring, described by Clark as the "largest fountain or Spring I ever
Saw," boiling up from under the rocks near the edge of the river and
emptying into the Missouri. [IV, 307]

It was necessary to portage around all of the cascades, a task
that consumed three weeks and involved building axles and solid

wheels cut from cottonwood trunks on which to pull the dugout canoes. This portage route swung south of the river, passing through Malmstrom Air Force Base and the southwestern edge of Great Falls before returning to the river at the White Bear Islands. These islands, three miles upstream from the mouth of the Sun River (which Lewis and Clark called the Medicine River), provided a base for refitting before the expedition continued southward up the Missouri toward the Three Forks.

At the White Bear Islands, Lewis put together the iron skeleton for a shallow draft boat. The portage, which began on June 22, was often excruciatingly difficult and painful. The men pulling the dugout canoes and their cargo suffered especially from mosquitoes, hailstorms, and the spines of prickly pear cactus that often had to be removed from the soles of their feet at the end of each day. During one cloudburst, Clark, Charbonneau, Sacagawea, and the baby Baptiste almost perished from a flash flood in the ravine where they had sought shelter. Clark described the countryside as having a "romantick appearance [with the] river inclosed between high and Steep hills Cut to pieces by revines but little timber and that Confined to the Rivers & Creek." There were so few trees that his men had to gather driftwood to light their campfires. Along the river below the red bluffs was a profusion of chokecherries, currants, and gooseberries. [IV, 332] Thousands of bison roamed the area, and the grizzly bears ("white" bears) attracted by the animals' drowned corpses constituted a frequent nuisance, if not a menace, to the men working in the vicinity of the island camp.

Meriwether Lewis's "iron boat" was launched on July 9. However, lacking the proper pitch to caulk the seams, the elk and buffalo hides that covered the frame were unable to keep out water. Without the boat, it was necessary to fashion new dugout canoes from cottonwood trunks before proceeding. Finally, on July 15, the Corps of Discovery resumed its journey to the headwaters of the Missouri River, leaving the open country around the falls and entering a canyon in which the Missouri River cut its way through the western end of the Big Belt Mountains. Today, Interstate 15 follows the canyon as far as Wolf Creek and then parallels the river a few miles to the west. Through the Gates of the Mountains north of Helena, Montana's

Fig 2.4 *Gates of the Mountains on the Missouri River, north of Helena, Montana. Meriwether Lewis noted "a dark and gloomy aspect" to the narrow six-mile stretch of canyon as he passed through it on July 19, 1805. Much of the effect today has been eliminated by water backing up from Holter Dam. Photo by Donnie Sexton. Courtesy, Travel Montana.*

capital, the main group continued by water under Lewis's guidance. On July 19 Lewis noted that the river was now between 100 and 150 yards wide and deepening, and the current was increasing in velocity. That evening the eight dugouts entered a stretch pressed on both sides by cliffs, which Lewis estimated to be about 1,200 feet high: "[E]very object here," he wrote, "wears a dark and gloomy aspect. The tow[er]ing and projecting rocks in many places seem ready to tumble on us." Lewis dubbed the nearly six-mile passage beneath these forbidding cliffs, which today lie between Holter and Hauser dams, the "Gates of the Rocky Mountains." [IV, 402–403, 405n4]

It was William Clark's turn to scout ahead with an overland party. South of Townsend and Canyon Ferry Reservoir, which now inundates this portion of the river, Clark and his party reached the area where the Gallatin River, coming from the east, helps form the main stem of the Missouri and the very sinuous Madison and Jefferson rivers join together a few miles north of Interstate 90 and the town of Three Forks. Clark's men also checked out part of the canyon

Fig 2.5 *A view of the Three Forks (headwaters) of the Missouri River, looking south. DeCamp was the photographer who accompanied Olin D. Wheeler on his search for Lewis and Clark campsites through the Lolo country. Photo by R. E. DeCamp, Courtesy, Montana Historical Society Research Center, Helena.*

through which the Jefferson River entered the valley and passed close to the site of Lewis and Clark Caverns State Park before returning to join the main party, whose river journey had proceeded along U.S. Highway 287 to Toston, Montana, and then through another canyon to the Three Forks of the Missouri.

Today, Interstate 90 climbs out of the valley about fifteen miles west of the town of Three Forks before dropping down to the Jefferson River Valley, at the foot of which is the town of Whitehall. U.S. 87 and Montana Highway 2, however, remain on the water grade of the Jefferson River canyon and on the expedition's original route. From near Whitehall, the group continued in a southwesterly direction to Twin Bridges, Montana, close to where the Beaverhead, Ruby, and Big Hole rivers come together to form the Jefferson. (Lewis and Clark named the latter two the "Philanthropy" and "Wisdom" rivers, respectively.) A dozen miles south of Twin Bridges they came upon

Beaverhead Rock, which—as noted earlier—Sacagawea recognized, thereby assuring them that they were on the right track. They were moving up one of several valleys in southwestern Montana that run generally north from the Continental Divide. Yet the Divide was also directly west because the crest of the Bitterroot Mountain range, along which the Divide runs for some distance, turns dramatically to the northwest. From the Great Falls, the elevation had risen 2,000 feet by the time the explorers reached Beaverhead Rock. The streams were becoming narrower and shallower, and the two captains were convinced that they would soon arrive at the point where the Missouri River's main tributary rose on the Divide itself. Still, there had been no sign of the Shoshone Indians, Sacagawea's people, from whom they desperately hoped to obtain horses on which to cross the last range of the Rockies.

On August 9 Lewis, accompanied by four men—including the hunter Drouillard—walked on ahead of the main party, which was toiling up the Beaverhead River south of Dillon, Montana, to locate a band of the Shoshone. Lewis named the two imposing rocks that marked the entrance to the Beaverhead River canyon just south of Dillon "Rattlesnake Cliffs." The route through the canyon is now followed by I-15. At the juncture where the Red Rock River joined with Horse Prairie Creek to form the Beaverhead, the men turned west through the broad Horse Prairie Valley, where they spotted Indians who quickly retreated into the mountains. Lewis and his men followed, climbing to the summit of Gibbons Pass on the Continental Divide. It was not actually the "most distant" tributary of the Missouri River but tiny Trail Creek, which leads almost to the summit, that gave the men an opportunity to finally "straddle" the mighty Missouri. From the largely bare crest of the Divide, they gazed westward into Idaho.

The Missouri segment of the outward journey had ended, but any expectations that the expedition would be able to easily slip down the Pacific slope to the Columbia River on tributaries were quickly dashed. In his entry for August 12, 1805, Lewis reported that he had "discovered immence ranges of high mountains still to the West of us with their tops partially covered with snow." [V, 74] There would be no easy portage to the Columbia. It became even more urgent to obtain an adequate supply of mounts. Lewis and his men soon

Fig 2.6 *Gibbons Pass, where Clark's party crossed the Continental Divide into the Big Hole Valley of Montana en route to Camp Fortunate and the Yellowstone River in late summer 1806. The (undated) photograph was taken not far from Lost Trail Pass, which the expedition had taken on the outward journey, just before meeting with Flathead (Salish) Indians. Photographer unidentified. Courtesy, Montana Historical Society Research Center, Helena.*

encountered a Shoshone band and returned with them to the forks of the Beaverhead, where Clark and the main party arrived to set up Camp Fortunate. After the captains had parleyed with the Shoshone and their chief, Cameahwait (Sacagawea's brother), the entire group crossed over Lemhi Pass.

The Shoshone had been among the first Indians in the region that is now Idaho, Montana, and Wyoming to obtain horses from the Spanish Southwest in the mid-eighteenth century. This gave them a major advantage in hunting buffalo and in warfare, and for decades Shoshone bands dominated the plains region north and south of the upper Missouri River. But their power was eventually countered by tribes that possessed firearms. In particular, the Piegan, Blood, and Gros Ventres bands of the Blackfoot Confederacy, which possessed both guns and horses, were effective in pushing back the Shoshone. By the time Lewis and Clark arrived on the Northern Plains, the Lemhi Shoshone band had been forced into the Bitterroot and Beaverhead mountains of eastern Idaho and western Montana. Without guns, they faced great risk in venturing onto the plains to hunt buffalo. Like the Flathead (Salish) Indians to the north, they had to avoid Blackfoot war and hunting parties and return to the protection of the mountains as quickly as possible. Cameahwait's band, languishing from hunger when the Corps of Discovery arrived, had been about to leave on a hit-and-run attempt to obtain buffalo meat for their village. It is not surprising, then, that Lewis and Clark represented a great opportunity to them. If the Americans would supply the Shoshone with guns and ammunition, Cameahwait's people would have a chance to equalize power in buffalo country.

Now on the Pacific side of the Continental Divide, the expedition had to linger for more than two weeks at the Lemhi Shoshone camp near present-day Salmon, Idaho, to bargain for horses. Clark took a small party to see if the westward-flowing Salmon River would provide a water path to the Columbia, but the canyon walls proved to be steep and treacherous and the rapids far too dangerous to attempt to navigate.

At the beginning of September, members of the Corps of Discovery were forced to move north and re-cross the Bitterroot crest, although they remained on the west side of the Divide. Working their way through heavy timber, they descended from Lost Trail Pass to Ross's Hole in Montana, where they picked up additional horses from a band of Flathead Indians and struck the Bitterroot River (which they dubbed "Clark's River"). With them was a Shoshone called Old Toby, who would guide them westward over the mountains further north by way of the Lolo Trail, a pathway used by Nez Perce and other tribes to cross from the plateau country of Oregon and Washington into the buffalo-hunting regions east of the Rockies. The jumping-off point for the Lolo Trail was at a place Lewis and Clark named Traveler's Rest, down the Bitterroot River past Darby, Hamilton, and Stevensville, Montana. At Traveler's Rest, near the confluence of the Bitterroot River and Lolo Creek (present-day Lolo, Montana), they stopped on September 9, 1805, to prepare to cross a mountain range whose peaks already showed signs of heavy snowfall.

After leaving Traveler's Rest, the explorers began to move west through the narrow valley of Lolo Creek. On September 12, William Clark, with an advance party, encountered hot springs in the vicinity of very large boulders and stony outcroppings. From there to the head of Lolo Creek the trail was often steep or choked with beaver dams or deadfall, but near the summit the terrain opened up as they followed Glade Creek to Packer Meadows, near the point where U.S. Highway 12 crosses Lolo Pass. From this point they could see the higher mountains "Covered with snow." [V, 203] Their Shoshone guide failed to pick up the Lolo Trail right away, and the expedition followed a path down to Colt-killed Creek (so named because they dined there on a colt after reaching the fork of the Lochsa River). On September 15 the narrowness of the river passage forced them to climb out of the canyon on a steep switchback trail. After several mishaps with horses losing their footing, including one that rolled forty yards down the slope and smashed Clark's writing desk against a tree, the party reached the top of Wendover Ridge and followed it to the main Lolo Trail. From there Clark wrote, "I could observe high ruged mountains in every direction as far as I could See." [V, 207] They melted snow for drinking water. Game was virtually nonexistent. This set the stage for the Lolo crossing of the mountains in what is now Idaho and the group's descent to the Weippe Prairie, which took another ten days and nearly resulted in starvation.

From the summit of Lolo Pass, the trail proceeds along high mountain ridges—occasionally above the timberline—and past numerous peaks. The men ate horsemeat and powdered soup to survive, nearing starvation before emerging from the mountains onto a broad, rolling plain and practically falling into the laps of Nez Perce Indians camped near the present-day towns of Weippe and Pierce, Idaho. This is rolling prairie, bordered by timbered mountains and cut by chasms formed by the Clearwater River and its forks. Covered at that time by grass meadow broken by patches of pine trees, the Weippe Prairie and the similar Camas Prairie south and west of the Clearwater canyons are now largely planted to grain.

The Nez Perce, called "Chopunnish" by Lewis and Clark, inhabited villages along the Clearwater, Salmon, and other tributaries of the Snake River and in the Wallawa Valley of northeastern Oregon. Their food-gathering and hunting area included the Blue Mountains to the west, the Bitterroot Range to the east, and the rolling prairie plateaus in between. They seasonally harvested a variety of berries, roots, and the bulbs of the camas flower to process and preserve, and they also fished for salmon. Similar to the Shoshone, the Nez Perce occasionally ventured eastward to the plains to hunt buffalo, although they also lacked the armaments necessary to protect them from the Blackfeet, Crows, and Hidatsas. Well-worn trails through the Bitterroots, including those taken by the expedition, attested to numerous such journeys. The depleted members of the Corps of Discovery could have done little to prevent the Nez Perce party they encountered on the Weippe Prairie from taking their weapons and ammunition. Tribal tradition maintained that an elderly woman (Watkuweis), who had been well treated by whites after they retrieved her from being a slave of the Blackfeet, begged the warriors to spare the men of the expedition. But Chief Twisted Hair and other Nez Perce leaders also likely hoped for a future steady supply of weapons from U.S. traders.[17]

After recovering from their ordeal, the members of the expedition dropped down into the canyon of the Clearwater River near Orofino, Idaho, and built five canoes, leaving their horses in the care of the Nez Perce and Chief Twisted Hair. On October 7 the expedition set out on water for the first time since leaving Camp Fortunate. From the mouth of the North Fork of the Clearwater, the group proceeded west to the Snake River at the sites of Lewiston, Idaho, and Clarkston, Washington. The Snake River took them through a segment of the route now flooded by slack water from the Lower Granite and Little Goose dams. Although one canoe struck rocks and was lost, the party made it to the confluence of the Snake and Columbia rivers, at a point just east of the Tri-Cities in Washington, without serious incident. In this vicinity the expedition encountered the villages of the Walula (Walla Walla), Yakima, and Umatilla Indians. Bands of these plateau tribes were harvesting sea-run salmon—their main food supply—and drying the fish in large stacks. The meetings were amicable, particularly with the Walulas, whose Chief Yellepit enthusiastically welcomed the explorers.[18]

After hooking southeast in a bend at this point, the Columbia River turns generally westward between the Horse Heaven Hills to

Fig 2.7 *Clearwater River west of Orofino, Idaho, near the spot where the expedition built new dugout canoes for the journey to and down the Columbia River, for which it departed on October 7, 1805. Photo by Peg Owens. Courtesy, Idaho Department of Commerce.*

the north and the Blue Mountains to the south. Black basalt bluffs rise above both banks of the river, and before irrigation the region was dominated by dry grasslands, juniper, and sagebrush. But just west of The Dalles, Oregon, the Columbia narrows and deepens as it cuts a spectacular gorge through the Cascade Mountains. Above the soaring cliffs the mountains are green with fir and other coniferous trees. From the crest of the Cascades to the Pacific Coast the heavy rainfall has produced thick forests replete with the huge Sitka spruce and Douglas fir trees Lewis marked with astonishment in his journal entries. Today, Interstate 84 follows the south bank of the Columbia from near Hermiston, Oregon, to Portland. Washington State Highway 14 parallels the route on the north bank. Working its way down the Columbia River in late October, the Corps of Discovery was forced to negotiate dangerous rapids at several points, particularly in approaching The Dalles. Celilo Falls near Wishram, Washington, and the Short and Long narrows, which comprised The

Fig 2.8 *Columbia River east of the gorge. Photo by Jeffrey Phillip Curry. Courtesy, Jeffrey Phillip Curry.*

Dalles, could only be passed by portaging and guiding the dugout canoes with ropes from the bank.

On October 23, assisted by Indians who fished for salmon from the rock islands, the expedition portaged around Celillo—long called the "Great Falls" of the Columbia—on the north side. Here the group found the great commercial marketplace of the Columbia, presided over by the Wishram Indians on the north bank and the Wasco on the south, where goods from the Pacific coastal region were traded for those from the inland plateau. Not far downstream lay the Short and Long narrows. A day after completing the Celilo portage, the party observed two stretches at which the river was suddenly confined by enormous rocks. The first, a quarter mile long, funneled the entire river through a 45-yard channel. The second, the Long Narrows, William Clark noted as 50 to 100 yards wide, swelling and boiling "with a most Tremendeous manner" over a distance of about three miles. [V, 329] The dugouts and most of the baggage had to be ridden through both of these chutes, as the portage path along the rock faces was narrow. The narrows were not the last river obstacles the group faced. On the first two days of November the party encountered a long series of rapids and chutes, the Cascades, which required similar time-consuming handling of canoes and portaging of supplies.[19]

Past the present site of Hood River, Oregon, into the Columbia Gorge, the dry country gave way to timber and green undergrowth as the Corps of Discovery entered the coastal climatic zone. The explorers gazed with wonder at landmarks that today are among the main attractions of the Columbia River Gorge National Scenic Area: Beacon Rock, Rooster Rock, Phoca (Seal) Rock, and Multnomah Falls. At Vancouver, Washington, north of Portland, Oregon, the Columbia River turns to the north and then, near Longview, Washington, west once more to the Pacific. By November 7, near Pillar Rock, the expedition was close enough to the mouth of the Columbia to hear ocean breakers. In his journal Clark wrote, "Great joy in camp we are in *View* of the *Ocian.*" [VI, 33, 34n9] But what they were actually seeing was the wide Columbia estuary; there was still some distance to travel. At Chinook Point on the Washington side the expedition beached its canoes and sent exploratory parties out along the shore of Baker's Bay ("Haley's Bay") to the hook-like peninsula dubbed "Cape Disappointment" and through the vicinity of Ilwaco and Long Beach.

The company, whose members—including Sacagawea and York—voted on the issue, elected to spend the winter of 1805–1806 not in Baker's Bay but instead across the estuary on the banks of the Netul (now Lewis and Clark) River, south of Astoria, Oregon. There they built Fort Clatsop and made forays to the ocean's coast near Cannon Beach and Seaside to see a beached whale and to set up a salt works to produce salt from seawater. Bad weather, much of which was rain or fog, plagued them and made it difficult to preserve game. To acquire game, in fact, they had to range further and further from Fort Clatsop. Much of their food, including wappato roots and fatty "candle fish," had to be obtained by trading with the local Clatsop Indian tribe. Other Chinookian-speaking peoples in the vicinity included the tribe Lewis and Clark called the Wahlakkums, north of the Columbia estuary, and the Tillamooks down the coast to the south of Fort Clatsop.

Fig 2.9 *Columbia River estuary, seen from a hill above Astoria, Oregon. The expedition followed the Washington shoreline when it arrived in early November 1805. On the left can be seen Chinook Point, on the distant horizon Cape Disappointment, and in the middle ground the Astoria Bridge connecting Oregon and Washington. Photo by Jeffrey Phillip Curry. Courtesy, Jeffrey Phillip Curry.*

But the members of the Corps of Discovery found trading with the Clatsops more congenial.

Because of the nearly constant rainfall, everyone in Fort Clatsop became eager to leave the coastal range, even though they knew the high country of the Bitterroots would be impossible to cross before June because of the snowpack. On March 22, 1806, the expedition departed anyway, retracing its path up the Columbia. Moving past St. Helens, Oregon, and parallel to the route of Interstate 5, the party came upon a large river flowing from the south and entering the Columbia 142 miles upstream from its mouth, by Clark's reckoning. [VII, 66] They had missed the mouth of the Multnomah River on the outward journey because it was screened by a long island. From this point, on April 2 Clark reported that he was able to view the snow-capped volcanic peaks of Mount Rainier, Mount St. Helens, and Mount Adams in Washington and Mount Hood in Oregon. While

Lewis and the main body set up camp near present-day Washougal, Washington, Clark led six men to take a look at the Multnomah River. They encountered several villages of Chinookian-speaking people within the environs of Portland before returning to the main camp on the Columbia. For most of the rest of April the expedition repeated the portages of the previous fall around the Cascades and The Dalles. Tempers grew short as they dealt with the demands of, and thefts by, the Indian bands that controlled them. The captains were determined to cover much of the return route to the Nez Perce by land, but a dwindling supply of trade goods made it difficult to obtain horses.

On April 29, rather than continue up the Snake River, the Corps of Discovery struck out overland at the juncture of the Columbia and Walla Walla rivers, about thirty miles west of Walla Walla, Washington, to the Touchet River and through the sites of Prescott, Waitsburg, and Dayton, Washington. Lewis described the Touchet as "a bold Creek 10 yds. Wide," its fertile bottom thick with cottonwood, birch, wild roses, and various berries, but the "surrounding plains," he wrote, "are poor and sandy. The hills of the creek are generally abrupt and rocky." [VII, 186–187] The nearly bare plain cut by tributaries flowing from the Blue Mountains to the south is now used primarily for dry-land wheat farming. On May 3 they crossed the Tucannon River and proceeded along the valley of Pataha Creek to Pomeroy and down a steep gulch to the Snake River and its tributary, the Clearwater, west of Clarkston, Washington, and Lewiston, Idaho. They marched up the north bank of the stream they had floated down the previous fall, crossed it at the mouth of Potlatch ("Colter's") Creek, then climbed up the south wall of the canyon downstream from the Canoe Camp site, on a rolling plateau called the Camas Prairie. This area south and west of the Clearwater River breaks is much like the Weippe Prairie from which the expedition had emerged the previous fall following the harrowing crossing of the Lolo Trail. Paralleling the main stem of the Clearwater, the party descended into the canyon by way of Lawyer Creek.

Just across the Clearwater from Kamiah, Idaho, they set up Long Camp, where they would stay while they rounded up the horses they had left with the Nez Perce and waited for the snow level to drop in the towering Bitterroot Mountains to the east. In the meantime, Sergeant John Ordway led a small scouting expedition back west across the middle of the Camas Prairie to search for "Lewis's River," the Snake River south of Lewiston, and to bring back salmon for provisions. Ordway's group left Long Camp on May 27 and crossed the route of Highway 95 between Craigmont and Ferdinand through Lawyer Creek Canyon, en route to Wild Goose Rapids on the Snake. On their return they skirted the Salmon River, which joins the Snake just a few miles south of Wild Goose Rapids. This was the river on which Clark had ventured downstream while looking for a way across Idaho from the Shoshone village near Salmon, Idaho. Ordway's men had taken just three days to reach the Snake River, but they needed another week to complete the reconnaissance and return to Kamiah by way of Cottonwood. They generally followed Cottonwood Creek, north of Grangeville, down to the South Fork (Clearwater) Canyon to Stites, then north to Kooskia and Long Camp across the Clearwater River from Kamiah.

In mid-June the Corps of Discovery, outfitted with supplies and horses, moved up out of Clearwater Canyon to the Weippe Prairie and the path the group had taken across the mountains in 1805. But on June 17 they had to turn back from "Hungery Creek" because snow banks still obscured the Lolo Trail. After obtaining the services of Nez Perce scouts, the group set out again. This time they easily made it along the ridges to Lolo Pass and down to the hot springs on Lolo Creek ("Traveler's Rest Creek"), where they bathed and relaxed on June 29. A day later they emerged from the shadows of the Bitterroot Range and rejoined the Bitterroot River at Traveler's Rest, where they split into two groups. Clark led the main body southward over Chief Joseph Pass into the Big Hole Valley and back down to Camp Fortunate, where the dugouts had been cached after the journey up the Missouri. Then the group retraced the outward-bound route down the Beaverhead and Jefferson rivers to the Three Forks.

At the Three Forks Clark divided the men once again. Sergeant Ordway took one party down the Missouri River, northward, with the canoes. Clark and the remainder, including Sacagawea and her infant son, Jean Baptiste, went up the Gallatin River past the site of Bozeman, Montana, and over Bozeman Pass to the Yellowstone River

Fig 2.10 *Vicinity of Long Camp, looking west across the Clearwater River to Kamiah, Idaho. Photo by Peg Owens. Courtesy, Idaho Department of Commerce.*

at Livingston. At that point the Yellowstone River, flowing north from Yellowstone National Park, bends to the northeast. With difficulty, because they had insufficient horses and could find no adequate cot-

72

Fig 2.11 *William Clark's party, returning by way of the Yellowstone River in July 1806, came upon this monolith. Photo by Donnie Sexton. Courtesy, Travel Montana.*

tonwood trunks to make into dugouts, Clark's group worked its way down the Yellowstone past Big Timber and Columbus. On July 20, 1806, near Laurel, Montana, just east of Billings, they finally found trees suitable for canoes. A few days later the group came to an unusual and noticeable sandstone tower, upon which Clark carved his name and the date. He named it Pompey's Pillar, after the nickname he had bestowed on Jean Baptiste—"Little Pomp." They continued on in late July and early August past the future sites of Miles City, Fallon, and Glendive, Montana. On August 3 Clark's party camped at the confluence of the Yellowstone and Missouri rivers, where they planned to reunite with Lewis's group, which would be coming down the Missouri.[20]

Back at Traveler's Rest, Meriwether Lewis—accompanied by Drouillard, the brothers Joseph and Reuben Field, Sergeant Patrick Gass, and Privates William Werner and Robert Frazer—had proceeded north a dozen or so miles along the Bitterroot River to the point where it empties into the Clark Fork River at Missoula, Montana. The men then turned east, passing through "Hellgate" gap from which the Clark Fork emerges. The Nez Perce scouts, who had left them at the confluence of the Blackfoot and Clark Fork rivers, had told the explorers that an easy overland shortcut would take them back to the

Great Falls of the Missouri along a long-used route to buffalo hunting grounds. The route was so widely traveled that they could not miss the path. Following the Blackfoot River Canyon northeast from Bonner, Montana, the party emerged into the broad Blackfoot Valley on June 7. A few miles east of Lincoln, the buffalo road cut north to Alice Creek, which headed on the Continental Divide. North of Rogers Pass, where Highway 200 crosses the Divide, Lewis's party reached a narrow saddle. Today it is known as Lewis and Clark Pass, although no roadway crosses over it. From the 7,452-foot elevation, the men could look out upon the prairies beyond the Great Falls. On the east side of the Divide they proceeded north to the Sun ("Medicine") River near Augusta, which they followed due east to the White Island Camp south of Great Falls, the terminus of their portage route the previous July.

In the first of two strokes of good timing, Sergeant Gass's party, bringing the dugout canoes up the Missouri River, arrived at the same time. The second stroke of good timing occurred following a side trip Lewis, Drouillard, and the Field brothers made to explore the Marias River, which entered the Missouri downstream from Fort Benton. On July 16 the four men set out from the camp at the Great Falls north to the Marias River, which they followed upstream to Cut Bank Creek, passing the site of Cut Bank, Montana. On July 26 they stopped following the tributary at the location Lewis dubbed "Camp Disappointment," since it was clear that the Marias River headwaters were not far to the north but rather in the near rampart of mountains, now part of Glacier National Park. After proceeding southwest to Two Medicine River (the Marias south fork), they encountered a group of Piegan Blackfoot warriors, who spent the night with them. In the morning Lewis and his men scuffled with the Piegans over a rifle and the horses. Two of the Blackfeet were killed. For the rest of the day and through the night, Lewis's party fled toward the Missouri River, knowing the Piegans would return in force. En route, they passed the site of Conrad, Montana. On July 28 the four men were enormously relieved to reach the bank of the Missouri just in time to meet Sergeant Gass's canoe party and be taken onboard.

On August 7, 1806, Lewis, Gass, and their men arrived at the junction of the Yellowstone and Missouri rivers, just inside the present

North Dakota border. A message there told them that William Clark and the rest of the expedition had moved downstream after waiting a week. Lewis followed, hampered by discomfort from an accidental gunshot wound in the buttocks.[21] They caught up with Clark about thirty miles before reaching the mouth of the Little Missouri. The final leg of the journey, from Fort Mandan to St. Louis, went relatively quickly. What had taken the initial expedition party the entire summer of 1804, traveling upstream, passed by at a clip of nearly eighty miles per day when they were going downstream. By September 23 they were back in St. Louis.

CHAPTER THREE

The New Explorers

A s CHAPTER 2 INDICATES, most of Lewis and Clark's path from St. Louis to the Pacific Ocean and back follows, crosses, or closely parallels the highway system that developed during the 1920s and 1930s. Easy automobile access to the trail may help account for its growing popularity; by the mid-twentieth century it began to upstage the expedition personnel in the public's historical consciousness.

Reinvigorating the historical memory of a western trail was not new, nor was associating it with a designated highway route. The Oregon Trail, for example, had become celebrated by the 1920s, largely through the efforts of Ezra Meeker. Meeker, who had come over the Oregon Trail in 1852, devoted his later years to building public recognition of its historical significance. In 1906–1907 he drove a wagon back over the route all the way to Washington, D.C., where he lobbied the government for funds to adequately mark the trail. He failed to get the funding, but his odyssey attracted attention in communities along the way, most of which were inspired to create historical markers.[1]

Lewis and Clark's trail eventually attracted attention for many of the same reasons and, as we shall see, inspired similar attempts to commemorate the route through designated highways in its name. The Corps of Discovery's 1803–1806 route and its many sites became the central "hero" of the exploration narrative. For many enthusiasts, the most inspiring and appropriate way to commemorate Lewis and Clark has been to follow in their footsteps, to personally trace as much of the route as possible while relating journal entries to segments of the countryside. Lewis and Clark aficionados go further than tourists by studying maps and attempting to pin down the locations of expedition campsites. In general, however, the practice of retracing the route is closely related to the development and effects of transportation in the West, particularly long-distance highways and automobile tourism. The Lewis and Clark National Historic Trail, created during the 1970s, came into being in part because tourists in automobiles became, in a sense, the new explorers of the West.

The tradition of following in Lewis and Clark's footsteps dates back to the turn of the twentieth century and Olin D. Wheeler's two-volume book, *The Trail of Lewis and Clark*. In the late 1870s Wheeler served as a topographer for John Wesley Powell's survey of the Colorado Plateau. By 1892 he had become a publicist and was named chief advertising executive for the Northern Pacific Railway, where he apparently began to view history as a way to promote tourism. Wheeler researched and wrote about the economic development the railroad sparked in the West, as well as historical lore accessible to travelers along the Northern Pacific route from Minnesota to the Pacific Coast. For example, as the author of the Northern Pacific's annual travel magazine, *Wonderland*, Wheeler offered colorful narrative and descriptions of the Battle of the Little Bighorn, which occurred not far south of the Northern Pacific line through southern Montana. He was next drawn to the story of the Lewis and Clark Expedition as a saga associated even more with the geography traversed by the company's tracks.[2]

To prepare a separate chapter on Lewis and Clark for the 1900 issue of *Wonderland*, Wheeler set out "to more particularly visit many places that were important and critical points in their exploration." In his preface to *The Trail of Lewis and Clark*, Wheeler stated that one of his purposes was to show that tourists routinely failed to connect the areas through which they traveled with the explorations of Lewis and Clark. Closely relating sites and landmarks tourists visited to passages in the journals, Wheeler attempted to match them with the geographic features he encountered, the names of which had frequently changed from those the explorers assigned—in short, to connect "the exploration with the present time." Armed with a print copy of the journals and accompanied by various photographers he engaged along the way, Wheeler spent at least four years traveling the route by train, steamboat, and horseback. Clearly, more than the promotion of tourism was at stake. Wheeler had turned into a hard-core buff, willing to take great pains to document the Corps of Discovery's trail. Now, however, Meriwether Lewis and William Clark as individual makers of history—in what was long regarded as the "Great Man" view—were superseded by a re-experiencing of the historic journey.[3]

Wheeler collected so much data that he eventually expanded the feature article into a two-volume book, written to increase public understanding of the expedition for its centennial celebration. Locally hired photographers contributed 100 pictures showing locations along the trail a century after Lewis and Clark passed through. Wheeler walked, rode, and sailed the entire length of the trail but did not confine himself to the Corps of Discovery's exploits. His book offers background on the practices of various Indian peoples encountered along the route, as well as later nineteenth-century historical events. Wheeler also describes and extols evidence of changes in the land since the time of Lewis and Clark as a result of settlement and economic development. Later enthusiasts following the same path decried rather than extolled the changes, however, and an environmental ethic was behind the mid–twentieth-century push to establish a national trail. Still, *The Trail of Lewis and Clark* is a clear landmark in public thinking about the expedition, the beginning of a slow shift away from the focus on individual frontier "heroism" toward a focus on the trail and its significant locations. Wheeler provides maps that feature particular segments of the route, as well as foldouts showing the trails in relation to railroad lines. Having originally intended to increase the historical awareness of travelers on the Northern Pacific, Wheeler eventually undertook an examination of portions of the trail far from the view of train tourists.[4]

Between 1898 and 1902, as one example, Wheeler set out to trace the expedition's September 1805 crossing of the Bitterroot Mountains in Idaho and Montana, perhaps the most dangerous passage of the expedition. The Corps of Discovery followed the Lolo Trail, a pathway the Nez Perce Indians used for traveling to buffalo country in Montana. At the east end of the trail was Lolo Pass; to the west, the trail followed high mountain ridges and crossed deep side canyons to emerge onto a rolling prairie. Later, Captain John Mullan, who built a wagon road from Walla Walla in Washington Territory to Fort Benton on the Missouri River in the mid-1850s, rejected Lolo Pass in favor of one further north (Lookout Pass) for crossing the Bitterroot Range. "Of all the sections of the Bitter Root Mountain chain," Mullan stated in an 1861 speech to the Historical Society of the Rocky Mountains, "there is no doubt in my own mind but that Lewis and Clark crossed by the most difficult section. The whole region for miles in every direction is one immense sea of rugged, frowning mts. & once in them your condition is well likened to that of the sea wrecked mariner tossed from one mt. to another."[5] In Mullan's opinion, the explorers had chosen this route at "the instigation" of Indians, who presumably wanted to impede their progress. For Wheeler, tracing Lewis and Clark's route by way of the Lolo Trail proved the most difficult and time-consuming task of those he undertook, in part because in 1898 it remained almost as close to being wilderness as it was nearly a century earlier.

As was the case with the White Cliffs portion of the Lewis and Clark route on the Missouri River upstream from Fort Benton, Montana, the crossing of the Bitterroot Mountains offered Wheeler no access by way of railroad lines. In addition, no roadway paralleled the Lolo passage before the 1930s. Various attempts had been made in the late nineteenth and early twentieth centuries to build track over this portion of the Bitterroot barrier, but nothing came of them. In 1887 engineer C. C. Van Arsdol, who reconnoitered numerous railroad routes in Canada and the western United States, undertook a survey of a path over the Bitterroots between Lewiston and Missoula for a regional line apparently allied with the Oregon Railway and Navigation (OR&N) Company. This was a time, Van Arsdol's son wrote, "when there was considerable publicity about what appeared to be a struggle between the major railroads for control of the Mullan Pass and the Coeur d'Alene mining section" to the north. No construction resulted, but by the end of the century railway companies were once again squaring off over the region between Clearwater Canyon and western Montana. Tracks had been laid into the canyon about ten miles upstream from Lewiston in 1898, thereby tying Lewiston to the Northern Pacific system and to Spokane, Washington. Once again, the OR&N sent a survey group into the Bitterroots. Van Arsdol, now leading a Northern Pacific crew, followed. A Yakima, Washington, newspaper characterized the struggle as "one of the most bitter railroad wars ever waged in this country."[6]

Although Olin Wheeler had closely read Elliott Coues's 1893 presentation of the journals many times so he could set the record straight concerning specific sites, the Lolo Trail presented particular difficulties. The Lolo passage, he wrote, was "a point where, metaphorically, [the expedition's trail] has been washed out. That is to say, hitherto the topography of the region has been so little known, and the maps have been so worthless, that no one has ever been able to do more than vaguely guess at their trail across this wild, craggy range." Determined to change that state of affairs, Wheeler traveled portions of the Lolo Trail over portions of three summers.[7]

Wheeler first approached the Lolo in 1898, making what he called a "flying trip" to Boyle's Hot Springs (now Lolo Hot Springs), described in the journals as a welcome resting stop for the Corps of Discovery after it returned over the Lolo Trail in the spring of 1806. Boyle's Hot Springs was the end of the road, and Wheeler was still seven miles short of the pass. The following year he returned, accompanied by local guide and historian W. H. Wright.[8] The occasionally rough and narrow passage of Lolo Creek on the Montana side was now much easier to negotiate. "The first time I made this trip," Wheeler wrote, "the road crossed the stream something like forty times, but recent improvements have cut out almost all of these crossings." By 1903, Wheeler noted, stagecoaches were running daily from Missoula bringing excursionists to the hot springs. Along the "wild and rugged" canyon, the Indian trail followed by Lewis and Clark was "distinctly visible at several points on the sides of hills and ravines." From Boyle's Hot Springs, the traveler would have to follow one of several trails on foot or horseback to the pass at the crest of the Bitterroot Range and on into Idaho.[9]

Wheeler quoted a U.S. Geological Survey report that described the region as "a vast mass of curving, winding, peak-crowned spurs, constituting the watersheds of the Clearwater basins," and a "perfect maze of bewildering ridges" running out from the main crest of the Bitterroot Range, itself "a succession of sharp, craggy peaks and 'hogbacks.'"[10] To penetrate such country, Wheeler depended heavily on Wright's knowledge of the trail the Nez Perce had used to cross eastward to hunt buffalo. Wright had spent years exploring "nearly every square mile of the Clearwater country," the region encompassing the Lochsa and Clearwater river canyons and what is now the Selway-Bitterroot Wilderness.[11] From Boyle's Hot Springs, Wright and Wheeler packed in to Glade Creek, where they set up camp. Demonstrating his desire to walk as closely as possible in the steps of Lewis and Clark, Wheeler wrote: "Mr. Wright and I camped at the forks of Glade Creek, where Lewis and Clark first came out upon it, in a bed of delicious strawberries."[12]

The two men then hiked the rugged area around Lolo Pass in an effort to identify the route taken in 1805 and to locate the expedition's campsites. Wheeler noted that on the outward-bound journey, the expedition used only portions of the main Indian trail. The profusion of trails over the pass made it extremely difficult to locate the precise route Lewis and Clark had taken. Wheeler compared the Lolo to a trunk railroad line with numerous branches and parallel sidings. Yet all paths led to the wide meadow (now Packer Meadows) from which Lolo Pass was visible. West of Lolo Pass, it was essential to "determine and identify beyond doubt" the location of Colt-killed Creek, where the Corps of Discovery had camped before climbing back out of the non-traversable Lochsa Canyon.[13]

From the campsite Wheeler and Wright followed a nearby trail over the mountain to Colt-killed Creek but soon discovered that it was one of those "parallel railway sidings" converging on the same point, not the trail used by the explorers.[14] This was one example of the difficulties with which Wheeler and other trail locators since his time have struggled in their attempts to match certain sites and routes with the accounts left by members of the expedition. In some ways the new explorers faced problems finding the path similar to those Lewis and Clark experienced (without the same challenges to their survival). Wheeler and Wright had no Shoshone guide, but they did possess a rendering of the expedition journals. Juxtaposing the written record with the physical reality of the landscape posed difficulties of interpretation, however.

Wheeler and Wright did not attempt to trace the route west beyond Colt-killed Creek and the headwaters of the Lochsa River in 1899, but three years later they teamed up again and brought along landscape artist Ralph E. DeCamp to investigate the trail from its western end. DeCamp, later commissioned to paint murals for a law library addition to the Montana capitol, served as the photographer for this exploration of the western portion of the Lolo pathway across the Bitterroots.[15] Wheeler was now seeking to locate the expedition's 1805 route in *reverse* order rather than pushing westward from where his party had halted in 1899. Thus, in his second attempt to study the Bitterroot Wilderness, Wheeler shortened the distance he would have to travel from established settlements and railheads. That, of course, was not an option for Lewis and Clark, who had to struggle over the entire length of the Lolo Trail both on their way out in 1805 and on their return in 1806.

After emerging from the canyon of the Lochsa River (which the journals refer to as the Koos koos kee), Lewis and Clark's party faced the most difficult hardships of their journey. On September 16, Clark reported, it "began to Snow about 3 hours before Day and Continued all day . . . and by night we found it from 6 to 8 inches deep." Snow made locating the trail difficult, and the men had to trace it by looking at rubbings on trees made by Indian travelers over the Lolo Trail. [Moulton V, 209] On September 18 Clark and a small party of hunters went ahead to search for game, while Lewis and the remainder of the drenched company ate portable soup reconstituted with melted snow. Clark's hunters, camped by a creek they appropriately named "Hungery Creek," had nothing to eat. The following day they came upon a horse, which they killed. They ate some of the animal and left the rest for the main party. At last, on September 20, Clark and his men emerged from the mountains onto level country of grass and pine trees, where they encountered a village of Nez Perce. The Indians fed them camas root and dried salmon, and Clark sent Reuben Fields with provisions back to the main group, which by September 22 was eight miles from the village. [Moulton V, 228] The Corps of Discovery was reunited and saved from starvation on what today is called the Weippe Prairie, northeast of Clearwater River Canyon in Idaho.

Fortunately for Olin Wheeler nearly a century later, a rail line up the Clearwater River from Lewiston, Idaho, offered access to the western end of the Lolo Trail. From there, Wheeler and his entourage could reach such locations as Hungry Creek, Weitas Meadows, and Camp Choppunish without having to follow the treacherous (and unmarked) route over nearly 100 miles of mountainous terrain. In addition, their supply line would be considerably shorter. Near the present-day towns of Weippe and Pierce, Idaho, Wheeler, Wright, and DeCamp planned to pick up the Lewis and Clark trail and move eastward along the Lolo, identifying places related to the September 1805 trek and to the expedition's return path in 1806. Locating the Hungry and Collins creeks precisely was an essential goal.[16]

With a pack train, the three men set out northeastward from the town of Kamiah on the Clearwater River, which they had reached by means of Northern Pacific subsidiary branch lines from Lewiston. In their tent each night they studied a copy of Coues's book on Lewis and Clark, "a rough, unpublished reconnaissance map of the United States Geological Survey," and a copy of C. C. Van Arsdol's surveys for the Northern Pacific Railway. In addition to Wright's expertise, the search for campsite locations benefited from the "criticism" of Nez Perce Indian James Stuart, "a graduate of Carlisle [the Indian industrial school in Pennsylvania]," who "is familiar with the old Indian trails in the Clearwater country." Almost immediately, DeCamp was able to photograph what they believed was the site of the spring 1806

"Camp Choppunish" (Long Camp) on the bank of the Clearwater opposite the Kamiah town site, where the Corps of Discovery spent a month waiting for snow to melt on the Lolo Trail before retracing its steps across the mountains.[17]

From Clearwater Canyon they proceeded to the headwaters of Hungry Creek and Collins Creek, apparently along the route the Corps of Discovery took eastward in 1806, where they set up camp in Weitas Meadow. From that vantage point, they calculated the distances Clark and his advance group of hunters had traveled along both streams in September 1805, as well as the subsequent passage by the main party under Lewis during the period when it suffered the most from lack of food. Wheeler pointed out that game was virtually nonexistent, both in Lewis and Clark's time and when he was writing, at the elevations through which the Lolo Trail passed. It is unclear just how far eastward Wheeler and his companions trekked during their 1902 inspection of the Lolo Trail. Wheeler's book suggests that it was not far beyond the Weitas Meadows camp, probably only as far as the explorers had gone by June 17, 1806, before running into eight- to ten-foot snowbanks and losing the trail. Lewis and Clark had been forced to turn back, wait for more snow to melt, and engage the services of Nez Perce guides before continuing their homeward journey.[18]

West of the Bitterroots, the remainder of Wheeler's investigations could be carried out from the comfort of a train, with occasional short side trips by road. He took several trips along the Columbia looking for significant Lewis and Clark sites and having photographs taken for his book. In 1902, for example, Wheeler closely studied the area around The Dalles on the Columbia River. He and his local guide, S. L. Brooks, drove to the Narrows and "struggled across a part of the river bed which, at high water, is a rushing torrent, to the brink of the long narrow channel and chasm through which Lewis and Clark took their canoes, where I overlooked the swirling waters as they boiled and raged."[19] Wheeler was rowed to Memaloose Island and the Indian burial site described in the journals. Later, he visited what was assumed to be the location of Fort Clatsop, as well the Salt Cairn site near Seaside, Oregon, where some of Lewis and Clark's men had boiled seawater to obtain salt during the winter of 1805–1806.[20]

Wheeler's efforts to trace Lewis and Clark's route faintly echo at least one aspect of the original expedition in ways that apply to later, similar attempts. In response to instructions from President Thomas Jefferson, William Clark drew maps of the expedition's route, indicating the rivers, mountains, and as much of the surrounding areas as he could observe. He later used this cartographic record to produce a map of the entire region of the upper Missouri and the Pacific Northwest through which he had traveled. This was perhaps the most immediately practical product of the journey west. Intentionally or otherwise, Wheeler endeavored to carry out—nearly a century later—a mapping project that produced a secondary representation, or imitation, of Clark's original task. While Clark had mapped the topography, Wheeler mapped the expedition's path through that topography.

Publications demonstrating both the changes in the landscape that had occurred since 1806 and the pleasure of locating sites mentioned in the journals have followed Wheeler's lead over the years. In a series of black-and-white photographs—a graphic surrogate for the journals, one could say—Ingvard Eide and Albert and Jane Salisbury effectively depicted the look of the ground Lewis and Clark covered as it appeared in the mid-twentieth century, before a number of the sites had been inundated by reservoirs. Several enthusiasts and local historians—including Walter Sewell, John P. Harlan, Elers Koch, Ralph Space, and John J. Peebles—have attempted to plot routes and pin down the locations of campsites in northern and central Idaho.[21] Sewell, a longtime resident of Orofino, worked to locate portions of the Lewis and Clark trail for the 1905–1906 centennial. He was aided by close friends in the Nez Perce Ahsaka band. In the 1920s local historian John Harlan, also from Orofino, became an authority on Lewis and Clark campsites in the area and participated in the first signing of the expedition's route on or adjacent to the Lolo Trail. In 1935 Harlan placed three historical plaques for the Daughters of the American Revolution on the Lolo Trail, including one at the top of Lolo Pass marking Lewis and Clark's "Squamish Glade Camp" of September 13, 1805.[22]

In 1970 Ralph Space wrote that he had "first crossed the Lolo Trail in 1924" and had "no idea how many times" he had traveled over it since. Little had changed on the Nez Perces' "Road to the Buffalo," he noted, since the gold mining boom of the mid-1860s, when a road-building expedition led by engineer Wellington Bird and surveyor Sewell Truax made alterations to portions of the trail. Congress had appropriated $50,000 in 1865 for a road connecting the gold camp of Pierce, located just east of the Weippe Prairie, with Missoula by way of the Lolo Trail and Lolo Pass. The funding was woefully inadequate for constructing a wagon road across the Bitterroots. By July 1866 the Bird-Truax party had been able to do no more than survey and mark a route and rebuild some of the Indians' trail. The remainder of the summer and fall was spent working on the trail and rerouting portions of it. In the process, the Bird-Truax party made a number of changes to the Lolo Trail as it had appeared to Lewis and Clark. The changes, Space noted, included rerouting a segment east of Sherman Saddle to avoid having to descend into, and climb out of, the Hungry Creek ravine. In general, the surveyors and their crew "graded from saddle to saddle, thus eliminating many steep sections and generally easing the grade." The overall route as marked and altered by Bird and Truax would substantially remain the Lolo Trail thereafter, and Space believed they gave a number of locations along the trail their present names, including Snowy Summit, Sherman Peak, Noseeum Meadows, and Indian Post Office.[23]

In 1907 the recently formed Clearwater and Lolo national forests received funds to clear and open up the Lolo Trail, which had been choked by undergrowth and timber deadfall over the forty years since the Bird and Truax construction party made its improvements. According to Space, work began at both ends and was completed in August when the crews met at Indian Post Office, about thirty miles west of Lolo Pass. The U.S. Forest Service maintained the trail until a forest road, the Lolo Motorway, was constructed in the 1930s that approximated most of the Lolo Trail and much of the route taken by Lewis and Clark (discussed later in this chapter). From that point on, the Forest Service began to provide historical markers at points along the Lewis and Clark trail. Space credits Lolo National Forest supervisor Elers Koch with locating Lewis and Clark's campgrounds and, in 1939, having the first historical signs installed along the route. When Ralph Space became supervisor of the Clearwater National

Forest, he continued Koch's efforts. But many of the sign boards that were put up had to be placed "where turnouts could be installed for the safety of the people who stopped to read them" rather than at the precise location they described.[24]

John Peebles, who has also devoted considerable attention to the location of Lewis and Clark's campsites and routes, published two extensive articles on the subject in the mid-1960s. Peebles expressed gratitude to his predecessors in tracing the expedition's passages along the Lolo Trail, particularly Ralph Space, whom he described as "perhaps the foremost authority on locations of the trails and campsites of the Expedition in this region."[25] The Bitterroot portion of the route, Peebles noted, presents particular difficulties: "There probably is less detailed information available concerning [the route] through northern Idaho than for any other portion of the explorer's [sic] epic journey." This, he pointed out, is a result of the complexity of the topography and the "sketchy descriptions" in the journals made by men who were "half-starved and in a desperate situation." Only recently "have adequate topographic maps and air photographs been available for the use of investigators attempting to trace the route and plot it on maps." As others had before him, Peebles "traversed most of the trail and visited all of the known campsites," armed with the journals of Clark and Lewis and also those of Sergeants John Ordway and Patrick Gass and Private Joseph Whitehouse. He had Clark's maps and "compass traverse notes" from the Reuben Gold Thwaites edition of the journals. Particularly important for comparing the lay of the land in 1805–1806 with the geographic characteristics of the Lolo Trail region in the 1960s, Peebles was able to refer to "air photographs and several types of maps," including township survey maps and various Forest Service and U.S. Geological Survey topographical charts, as well as "Planning Survey maps published by the Idaho Department of Highways."[26]

Before tackling the Lolo crossing, Peebles had gone over the expedition's route through western Montana, from the Three Forks up the Jefferson and Beaverhead rivers to Lemhi Pass, the location of present-day Salmon, Idaho, and over Lost Trail Pass to Traveler's Rest on the Bitterroot River, from which the Lewis and Clark party had approached the Lolo Trail. The first of his articles contains several detailed survey maps that show the expedition's route superimposed on land sections, town sites, and other mid–twentieth-century signs of habitation. According to a map legend, solid lines indicate route locations "accurate to within a few hundred feet," broken lines those portions "in error by as much as a half mile," and dotted lines those "in error by as much as 1 or 2 miles." Locations of campsites are partitioned into the same categories, with appropriate symbols.[27]

The cumulative efforts of Koch, Space, Peebles, and numerous other researchers since have gradually provided a more accurate physical understanding of the Lewis and Clark trail. Some locations, however, will always be difficult to pinpoint, since readings of the various journals provide the only evidence and the journals are often ambiguous, as Wheeler pointed out 100 years ago. While specifically locating material evidence requires more stringent location criteria, tourists following highway maps and searching for Lewis and Clark campsites are generally satisfied with approximations.

The automobile age that began at the turn of the twentieth century opened a new frontier in the American West. Armed with guidebooks offering mile-by-mile advice on how to locate landmarks, cowpaths, and intermittent roadways, an intrepid breed of motorists picked their way across the plains and mountains. Although they rarely encountered dangers greater than mechanical breakdowns, adverse weather, or becoming mired in mud, auto tourists repeated many of the patterns of earlier explorers, at least generally. Despite a lack of continuous highways, they followed well-worn paths into regions largely unknown to them and about which they entertained complex sets of expectations about the landscape and inhabitants that experience would modify, as had happened with Lewis and Clark, Fremont, and others before them. They planned their expeditions, carrying as many necessities as possible and depending on strangers along the way to provide their sustenance for a price. They often kept journals and later narrated their adventures in popular accounts.

Western tourism was not new in 1900. Railway companies had quickly tapped the potential market by promoting scenic wonders and whisking vacationers across the continent in Pullman sleeper cars. The railroads even established their own resorts as destinations, such as the Northern Pacific in Yellowstone National Park and the Union Pacific (in the 1930s) in Sun Valley, Idaho. Railway travel, similar to later interstate travel, provided a regularized and protected experience for the tourist. As historian Anne Farrar Hyde put it, "Encased in a steel train and swaddled in Victorian luxury, wealthy American tourists could now look out at the far western landscape with no thought of danger."[28] The landscape, sometimes seen and sometimes not, slid past relentlessly. There was little sense of interaction with the environment outside the passenger cars. Even a tourist who possessed a copy of Olin D. Wheeler's guide to the Lewis and Clark trail vis-à-vis railroad routes would have barely been able appreciate the historical scenes and landmarks that passed. Since railroad travelers were destination tourists in the early 1900s and the destination was usually a posh resort, lodge, international exposition, or national park, they were generally confined to the vicinity of the rail lines.[29] As mentioned earlier, Wheeler himself had complained about railway tourists as largely "oblivious" to the historical import of nearby segments of the Lewis and Clark trail.[30] Historical legacy did not compete with scenery, luxury, and recreational activities on cross-country rail vacations. Still, train tourism did introduce those who could afford it to the wonders of the western landscape, an experience heavily promoted by the See America First movement during World War I.

Even as railroad passenger service dominated tourism, however, automobiles began to present a new dimension in long-distance travel for pleasure. Automobiles freed tourists from the confines of rail routes and resort destinations and introduced new elements of uncertainty and adventure, especially in the era before federally funded highways spanned the West. As the use of automobiles increased, the economic benefits of tourism spread, bringing business not only to towns and cities situated along rail lines or within national parks but to roadside enterprises as well. By the late 1920s, scenic two-lane blacktop routes, such as U.S. 40 and Highway 66, had become tourist destinations in themselves. Olin Wheeler's desire to relate historical heritage tourism to cross-country travel was eventually realized, but only after the new highway system had increased access to historical sites. Automobile tourism (often referred to as "auto tourism" in the literature) evolved in fairly distinct phases.

In the years before World War I, cross-country touring remained largely the province of well-off adventurers and professional drivers sponsored by automobile manufacturing companies. As inexpensive, mass-manufactured automobiles became available, some democratization occurred, although only a few isolated stretches of improved roadway existed across the West. In the 1920s the western states, aided by the federal government, built a system of paved interstate highways. Auto tourism took off as a result but was heavily dampened during the Great Depression in the 1930s. Perhaps the final phase occurred in the 1950s and 1960s as middle-class prosperity boomed and the National Defense Interstate Highway system was constructed. Each phase of development, beginning in the 1920s at least, influenced public awareness of, and interest in, the concept of a Lewis and Clark trail. As we shall see, businesses and community promoters along the new highways were eager to tout both historical and scenic wonders. The routes of Lewis and Clark seemed perfect for attracting tourism because they traversed so much of the country and so many miles of the highway system ran close to or paralleled those routes.

Auto touring began as a sporting activity for a handful of specialists and wealthy enthusiasts. Between 1897 and 1903 hardy motorists with considerable time on their hands struggled across the countryside over rural roadways dotted with gumbo mud, over rocky and rutted wagon roads, even over two-track paths through sagebrush plains and deserts. In 1903, three automobile touring expeditions crossed the continent. The first to successfully make it from coast to coast was a two-cylinder Winton piloted by Vermont physician H. Nelson Jackson and mechanic Sewall Crocker. They set out from San Francisco on May 23, 1903, and drove nearly 6,000 miles through Oregon, Idaho, Wyoming, Nebraska, and eastward to New York City in sixty-four days.[31] The publicity the Winton Company reaped from Jackson and Crocker's odyssey encouraged other automobile manufacturers to sponsor attempts to duplicate the feat and set new time records. Lester Whitman, who had also crossed the country in 1903, cut the time record in half the following year; he and his co-pilot Clayton Carris halved it again, to just over fifteen days, in 1906, driving an air-cooled Franklin automobile.[32]

As the quality and power of automobiles improved, so did their endurance and the average time of a cross-continental run. By 1916 a professional race driver, Ralph Mulford, with the help of relay drivers, was able to make the journey from San Francisco to New York in just over five days.[33] The improvement in automobiles was not matched by the roadways they traveled, however, and drivers and the companies that supported them soon began to call for construction of a transcontinental touring highway. In 1905 the federal government's Office of Public Road Inquiry and the Olds Motor Company tried to draw attention to that need by "promoting a transcontinental race between two Oldsmobiles . . . from New York City to the Lewis and Clark Centennial Exposition in Portland, Oregon," although apparently no attempt was made to follow the explorers' route west. Thousands of affluent motorists had already taken to the road, or what there was of it, the previous summer in "moderately priced" Packards and curved-dash Oldsmobiles.[34]

Armed with *Blue Book* guides that offered mile-by-mile descriptions of landmarks, hazards, and routes that varied from unmarked double tracks to country roads, this new breed of explorer contended with breakdowns, mud, and other obstacles without the benefits tourist services later provided. The pioneer motor tourists engaged in what John Jakle has called "an athletic relationship with their environment," and drivers enjoyed the experience of "mastering" their machines by being their own repairmen.[35] Many later described their journeys in print, establishing a new journalistic subgenre. Hugo Alois Taussig, for example, wrote a short account privately published in 1910 entitled *Retracing the Pioneers: From West to East in an Automobile*. Others seem to have made the trip for the express purpose of writing about it. The most famous accounts were Emily Post's *By Motor to the Golden Gate* (1916) and Mary Roberts Rinehart's Southwest tour in *The Out Trail* (1923).[36]

While such feats were widely publicized in motorist periodicals and books describing individual adventures, automobile touring did not become widely popular until the advent of Henry Ford's Model T in 1908. At a price of $400 or less, the "Tin Lizzie" or "flivver" was available to almost anyone. By the time the United States entered World War I, Ford was selling about half of the new cars purchased in the country. According to historian James J. Flink, Ford's Model T and other American mass-market vehicles were simple to repair, had the power and clearance to "readily negotiate steep grades and wretched roads, and were easier to drive [than earlier vehicles] because they required less frequent shifting of gears." Long-distance travel by automobile, even transcontinental touring, was no longer confined to the wealthy. While the vehicles were readily available, however, the requisite highways still were not—or at least no coherent system was in place before the 1920s.[37]

The lack of highways did not completely deter automobile tourism in the West, however. Aided by detailed guides and transcontinental automobile route associations, intrepid motorists made their way across the landscape on fragments of improved roadways, interconnecting farm roads, and double tracks worn through sagebrush. The route associations raised money from the public and corporate sponsors to construct cross-country highways piecemeal. The first to be completed, and perhaps the most famous, was the Lincoln Highway. The Lincoln Highway route, much of which later became U.S. 30, began at Times Square in New York City and "ended at the Pacific Ocean in San Francisco's Lincoln Park." In the plains and western states it ran through Nebraska, southern Wyoming, and Utah to Salt Lake City; from there it went across eastern Utah and Nevada to Donner Pass in the Sierras and on to the Bay area. Long portions of the route followed that of the Pony Express, and travelers passed close enough to some of the station sites to be able to eat lunch in the ruins.[38]

The Lincoln Highway, which took more than ten years to develop, was the brainchild of Carl Graham Fisher, promoter and builder of Miami Beach and founder of the Prest-O-Lite automobile headlight manufacturing company. Fisher proposed a coast-to-coast highway in 1912 and the following year helped organize the Lincoln Highway Association. With financial contributions from Prest-O-Lite, the Packard Motor Car Company, Goodyear Tire Company, and other corporations associated with the automobile and tourist industries, the Lincoln Highway Association began to coordinate and plan what was expected to be an all-weather paved route across the country.[39]

In fact, the Lincoln Highway was a piecemeal operation, in the beginning little more than a marked route that often zigzagged along preexisting rural roads or deteriorated into a pair of tire tracks across the prairie. "In the beginning," according to Drake Hokanson, "the highway afforded its patrons more adventure than many of them had bargained for. . . . The association's first mapmakers drew it as a thick, black line across the country's midsection. In reality, however, it was a poorly marked assortment of existing roads, full of doglegs and detours, stretching 3,389 miles and lacking all but the most casual maintenance and conveniences." States, counties, and local community groups contributed to upgrading the highway. An official of the Lincoln Highway Association estimated that, even before paving, between 5,000 and 10,000 automobiles had carried people across the country to visit the 1915 Panama-Pacific Exposition in San Francisco. The Lincoln Highway captured the public imagination and became the model for a spate of transcontinental routes that bore colorful names.[40]

In addition to the Lincoln Highway, by 1924 the National Old Trails Road (later Route 66) from Washington, D.C., to Los Angeles; the Theodore Roosevelt International Highway from Portland, Maine, to Portland, Oregon, across the northern tier of states; the Bankhead Highway from Washington, D.C., through the South and Southwest to Los Angeles; the Old Spanish Trail from Florida to California; the Pikes Peak Ocean to Ocean Highway from New York City and Philadelphia to San Francisco; and the Yellowstone Trail from Plymouth Rock through Illinois and the north-central states to Puget Sound were added to lure traffic east and west. The Evergreen Highway, promoted in 1916 by caravans of motorists who called themselves the "Evergreen Pathfinders," sought an all-season touring route between Galveston, Texas, and the northern Pacific Coast.[41] In Wyoming, the Yellowstone Trail Association was formed to develop and promote a route from Denver to Yellowstone National Park. Later, the route grew in two additional directions, eventually linking Massachusetts with the Pacific Northwest.[42] In Montana, historian Marilyn Wyss points out, association members "were recruited all along the route and special Trail days were designated when entire communities . . . turned out to work on the road." Soon, Montana automobile clubs were promoting the construction of a "good all-weather road" between Glacier and Yellowstone national parks. Dubbed the Park-to-Park Highway, it became part of a system of similar routes connecting national parks in the West (the Great Parks National Automobile Highway).[43] "At one time," Bill Rishel of the *Salt Lake Tribune* reported, "there were no less than fourteen highway and trail associations claiming State Street [in Salt Lake City] from South Temple to Twenty-first South as their own particular route."[44]

People in the Pacific Northwest were likely to find the Columbia River Scenic Highway more impressive than any of the transcontinental trails. Running above and along the walls of the Columbia Gorge east of Portland, the Scenic Highway opened in 1915. S. C. Lancaster, the engineer who designed this new sightseeing route, paid exceptional attention to aesthetic and environmental considerations. Lancaster's highway was undoubtedly the first constructed that closely paralleled a portion of the Lewis and Clark trail. For those who built highways through the mountainous West during the 1920s and 1930s, the Columbia Gorge route was the ultimate model of achievement. But advances in automobile technology and speed, as well as the advent of long-distance freight trucking, quickly doomed this beautiful and imaginative segment of the highway, and it fell into disuse.[45] Today, however, a segment can be traversed between Troutdale and Bonneville Dam, descending from the high bluffs near Multnomah Falls.

In 1916 Congress responded to the demands of motorists and a burgeoning Good Roads lobbying movement by passing the first federal aid to highways act, which established uniform road construction specifications and matching funds for states. Federal funding, increased by subsequent legislation, was essential for building long-distance, paved highways within the states of the high plains and interior West because of the area's low population and small tax base. By the end of the 1920s, improved roadways linked western state capitals and the national parks.

Automobile tourism quickly overshadowed the more expensive and elite destination tourism associated with rail travel. For auto campers, or "tin can" tourists, the process of getting there was at least as important as arriving. In time, however, improved highways and the plethora of new services that sprang up along them removed much of the uncertainty and adventure associated with early auto touring. In addition, the increasing speeds the better highways permitted tended to isolate motorists from their immediate surroundings, putting greater emphasis on getting someplace than on experiencing the journey.[46] Yet for many, the essential aspects of personal exploration remained. While aristocratic wilderness enthusiasts may have bemoaned the mass movement of automobile tourists throughout the West as representing a loss of connection with the pioneering past, the new motorized explorers "craved" the experience, according to Hal K. Rothman, "as a rite of passage, and the sense of power that came from navigating the roads, trails, and paths of the American West."[47] Or, as Robert Athearn pointed out, "the West again was a frontier," and "the new frontiering was a family matter."[48]

Except for the Columbia River Scenic Highway, which Oregon had opened in 1915, any highway that commemorated Lewis and Clark's route would have to be built from scratch. Although federal highway matching funds had been increased since their inception in 1916, few western states had made much progress by the time the federally numbered interstate highway system was designated in the late 1920s.[49] Auto tourists who might have wished to follow the route the Corps of Discovery took faced a daunting challenge, at least north and west of Iowa and Nebraska. Virtually no paved highways existed in the Dakotas or Montana in 1925. Major gravel roads in North and South Dakota ran east and west, with only in a few segments beyond the Missouri River. South Dakota did build three highway bridges across the Missouri in 1924. South to north, they were the U.S. 14 crossing at Pierre, in the vicinity of the nearly violent confrontation between the Lewis and Clark Expedition and a Teton Sioux band on the group's upriver journey; the U.S. 212 crossing; and the U.S. 14 crossing near Mobridge, the site of the Arikara villages Lewis and Clark visited in 1804.[50] Bismarck, the capital of North Dakota, also had a new bridge across the Missouri River by 1925, but it was accessed in both directions by dirt roads. A gravel roadway in North Dakota ended 100 miles east of Bismarck and the Missouri River in 1925 but included a segment north of the Missouri between Minot and Williston and the Montana line. Often proceeding in right-angle jogs, the gravel road afforded occasional approaches to a portion of the river the Corps of Discovery followed when it was outward bound in the spring of 1805. Only county or unmarked prairie roads were available for actually paralleling the river route.[51]

Prospects for following the river in Montana were also meager. At the point where the Yellowstone River joins the Missouri southwest of Williston, North Dakota, segments of gravel road followed both rivers—one to just beyond Glendive, Montana, on the Yellowstone, and one straight west along the Missouri. Otherwise, motorists could be assured of gravel road only as far west as Glasgow or connecting such cities as Great Falls, Butte, Helena, and Missoula. The route that later became U.S. Highway 2 proceeded on to Shelby, Cut Bank, and East Glacier on a path far to the north of the Missouri River that intersects the one Lewis and the Field brothers took up the Marias River in 1806.[52] After their grueling portage around the Great Falls of the Missouri, the explorers had continued south, up the river through the present-day sites of Holter and Canyon Ferry dams near Helena and on to the Three Forks. In rainy weather the unpaved road, which during the mid-1920s covered only the 100 miles from Great Falls to Helena, could take nearly twelve hours to traverse. The often zigzagging road that continued southeast to Three Forks and Bozeman by way of Townsend was also slow going. Motorists contending with swampy areas near the river where the roadway deteriorated into mud might be lucky to average ten miles per hour. Highway construction in all these states developed rapidly thereafter, however. By 1939, for example, about 5,000 miles of Montana's highways in the federal system had been surfaced with oil. Roadway width tended to be somewhat narrower than it is today, and safe speeds ranged from ten to forty miles per hour.[53]

One of the first initiatives for relating these and other new highways that spanned the West to the path of the Lewis and Clark Expedition was launched in 1929. Concerned about the nation's failure to adequately commemorate the explorers' 1804–1806 journey to the Pacific Ocean and back, delegates from more than twenty communities in the Pacific Northwest and Montana gathered at Lewiston, Idaho, to form the Lewis and Clark Memorial Association. "It seems almost incredible," the group's initial report stated, "that through all those years there has been no national monument erected in their [the explorers'] honor. . . . Perpetuated only in a few place names, they claim but scant present attention, except from close students of western history." The 1905 Portland Exposition, the delegates pointed out, "created nothing permanent, was as much commercial as sentimental, and many of those connected with the movement have gone to their reward." They referred to the nearly twenty years that had "intervened" since the centennial as a "vista of silent years."[54]

A committee appointed by the Lewiston Chamber met with Idaho congressman Burton L. French, who offered his "unqualified endorsement" of the association. Directors and officers were elected and articles of association drawn up. In its list of aims, the Lewis and Clark Memorial Association sought to commemorate the two captains. No other member of the expedition is mentioned. Second on the list, the group vowed to "expedite the completion of a highway following the route" that would "through its utility stand as a lasting memorial" to the explorers. Rescuing "important historical points along the route from oblivion" came next, followed by "a campaign of education" and erection along the route of "suitable monuments and markers" indicating the significance of events in various locations. Anyone could join the association, and other chambers of commerce along the Lewis and Clark route were invited to become members, with dues graduated according to the size of the community. Lewiston, Idaho, would remain the organization's seat of business.[55]

Although its inaugural report reflected a growing sense that the expedition's exploits had been largely ignored in the twentieth century—despite the centennial celebrations—the Lewis and Clark Memorial Association failed to stir much enthusiasm for the approaching 125th anniversary of the trek, which occurred during the depths of the Depression. Nevertheless, it gave some thought to promoting local celebrations of the expedition's 125th anniversary in appropriate states that would be "more fitting than" one planned for the spring of 1930 in Mandan, North Dakota, which would merely commemorate the date on which the explorers left Fort Mandan to head west. The report suggested the possibility of forming an automobile "caravan to follow as nearly as possible the route taken by the explorers."[56] The idea of designating a commemorative highway was not completely ignored. In September 1933 a stretch of paved highway connecting Lewiston, Idaho, with Umatilla, Oregon, by way of the Wallula Gap on the Columbia River was dedicated as an "Important link of [the] Lewis-Clark Memorial Route," indicating that sentiment behind the Lewis and Clark Memorial Association's proposals established an important precedent.[57]

The enshrinement of Sacagawea as a heroic figure, publication of the original journals, and celebrations of both the Louisiana Purchase and Lewis and Clark centennials occurred during a surge of U.S. imperialism that had already thrust the expedition and its chief figures into the public consciousness following a long period of neglect. Yet this was not enough recognition for some, as indicated by the 1929 lament that the nation had lost interest in the expedition. It was significant for the future that the promotion of a multistate Lewis and Clark highway route had been central to the association's agenda. The association's prediction that a "better understanding" of the expedition and those who conducted it would "inspire a higher conception of what is suitable to commemorate them" turned out to have been accurate. Highways and automobile tourism eventually became essential components in recreating the trail as a form of commemoration.[58]

Even without an officially designated memorial highway, it would have been possible in the early 1930s to trace most of the Lewis and Clark trail by automobile if one knew which routes to follow. Major exceptions were the Missouri River downstream from Loma, Montana, to Fort Peck Reservoir and the crossing of the Bitterroot Mountains in Idaho. The Bitterroot gap was partially closed during the Great Depression when U.S. Forest Service crews succeeded in constructing a crude road that connected Pierce, Idaho, with Lolo Pass. The Forest Service began building roads up to the ridges above the Lochsa River in 1931. These were only "low standard 'truck trails'," however, in accordance with an agreement made with the Bureau of Public Roads. The roads were needed for fire management and access for other Forest Service practices.[59] Most of the construction of what became known as the Lolo Motorway took place between 1930 and 1935. Work proceeded on a "single track

Fig 3.1 *Lolo Motorway, a forest road completed in 1935, follows portions of the Lolo and Lewis and Clark trails through northern Idaho. This vista is from a site on the motorway called "Smoke Place." Photo by Peg Owens. Courtesy, Idaho Department of Commerce.*

road with turnouts" each summer during those years to approximate portions of both the Lolo Trail and the route taken by Lewis and Clark.[60]

By 1933 the Lolo road had been extended eastward as far as Sherman Saddle, along the 1806 portion of the route, north of the 1805 diversion down into Hungry Creek, and about ten miles from Weitas Meadows where Olin B. Wheeler had established his main camp in 1904.[61] The Lolo Motorway was completed in late summer of 1935. Seventy-five men, working in two groups moving from opposite directions, met up at Indian Grave. On September 24 they celebrated connecting the first roadway across the Bitterroots with a chicken dinner and a day off.[62] With the opening of the Lolo Motorway (Forest Road 500), automobilists who wanted to trace the trail as authentically as possible gained a significant addition to the route, including its most awesome and beautiful segment.[63]

Experiencing the Lewis and Clark trail by highway and roadway has been the goal of many enthusiasts and has engendered a body of related writings. Ralph Gray, for example, who brought his family over most of the trail in 1953—including the Lolo Motorway—wrote an article for *National Geographic Magazine* that seems to have set the stage for the many subsequent accounts of automobile excursions along the Lewis and Clark route. In June 1953, Gray, his wife, and three children set out in a station wagon crammed with camping equipment and topped by their red canoe, *Trout,* to do a motoring tour of the Lewis and Clark route from east to west. As the guide, Gray brought along a set of the journals and other books about the expedition. They picked up the explorers' trail at Wood River, Illinois, site of the first winter camp in 1803–1804. From there, Gray wrote, he and his family "logged 10,000 miles in three months," a journey that included a major side trip to the Wind River Shoshone Reservation to see what some claim is the resting place of Sacagawea.[64]

After Wood River, a first major stop was St. Charles, Missouri, "the only community on the westward Lewis and Clark Trail that existed when the explorers passed." After visiting the Charles Floyd memorial near Sioux City, Iowa, Gray and his family continued to follow the Missouri River through South and North Dakota. They witnessed the work in progress to complete the Oahe and Garrison dam-reservoir projects and the construction of the Fort Randall and Gavins Point dams. Then, "over modern highways that would have astounded our predecessors," Gray wrote, "we steered the Orange Crate [a nickname for the station wagon] toward Bismarck, capital of North Dakota."[65]

The canoe dubbed *Trout* enabled the Grays to follow portions of the route inaccessible to most tourists. They must have been among the last visitors to encounter areas of the Missouri River bank roughly as Lewis and Clark and their party had seen them before the massive Pick-Sloan dams inundated them in the late 1950s. "We entered Montana's Lewis and Clark County and launched *Trout* . . . in the swift-flowing Missouri beside U.S. 91. We paddled about in the vicinity of the expedition's July 17th camp." Shortly thereafter, they took a motorboat through the Gates of the Mountains and, near Helena, observed construction in progress on the 225-foot-high Canyon Ferry Dam being built by the Bureau of Reclamation. At the town of Three Forks, the Grays spent a night in the historic Sacajawea Inn and then drove six miles to the spot where the Madison, Jefferson, and Gallatin rivers join to form the main stem of the Missouri.[66]

After continuing south to the fork of the Jefferson River and seeing Beaverhead Rock, they drove south of Dillon to Armstead and the site of Camp Fortunate, now under the waters of Clark Canyon Reservoir. They might have continued south from there, staying on federal highways and skirting the central Idaho massif—which includes the all but impassable (at that time) Salmon River and Bitterroot mountain ranges—to pick up the Lewis and Clark trail in eastern Washington. But this was not a casual retracing of the route only on available paved highways. For the sake of *National Geographic Magazine*, as well as for the education and delight of his family, Ralph Gray was intent on experiencing as much of the original route as possible. After a lengthy side trip to Wyoming, the Grays returned to Armistead, Montana, and took a "narrowing" dirt road straight west through Horse Prairie Valley and up to the summit of Lemhi Pass on the Continental Divide. From there they dropped into the Lemhi River Valley and thence to Salmon, Idaho.[67]

Once again, they could have struck south on U.S. 93 to southern Idaho's lava plain and then followed a major east-west highway to the lower Snake River and rejoined the Lewis and Clark trail. Or they could have followed the historic route north to Missoula and crossed the mountains on U.S. 10, another east-west highway route, and then gone south to Lewiston, Idaho, at the point where the Clearwater River flows into the Snake. Until the Lewis-Clark Highway was completed along the Lochsa River, most automobile tourists following the trail would have taken one of these detours, perhaps after driving up to Lolo Pass on the Montana side. The Grays, however, were committed to traversing the Lolo Motorway, Forest Road 500. "This wild Idaho upland has seen little change since Lewis and Clark's day," Ralph Gray wrote. "We discovered that forcing passage through the stubbornly resisting forests and crags still was an adventure in the 20th century." For 100 miles after turning onto the road they encountered no gas stations or buildings of any kind. Sometimes skirting "the brink of yawning chasms," they "averaged 10 miles an hour." To make the trip even more of an adventure, one of their tires blew out after only 5 miles. Amazingly, they persevered for the 95 miles to

Pierce, Idaho, and the Weippe Prairie "without a spare." The following day, after they had driven just 13 miles on pavement, a second tire blew. After that, the final phase of the trip to the Pacific Ocean and Ecola Point, Oregon, near Seaside was a snap by comparison.[68]

Another family journey to trace the Lewis and Clark Expedition's route became the subject of a book published in 1970. Gerald S. Snyder combined a narrative about the Corps of Discovery with an account of the trip he and his family made to retrace the route from east to west. By this time the Arikara villages site near Mobridge, South Dakota, had been covered by the reservoir behind Oahe Dam. But the family did its best to emulate portions of the water route, taking a twenty-foot open-deck barge on a five-day trip from Kipps State Park in Montana to Fort Benton on the Missouri River and a motor launch tour of the Gates of the Mountains north of Helena. Snyder hired horses to ride over Old Toby's Trail across Lolo Pass, and the family later drove the lonely Lolo Motorway across the Bitterroots, as Ralph Gray had done before them.[69]

Although the Lolo Motorway would be improved over the years, relatively few tourists accepted its challenges, even if they wanted to follow Lewis and Clark's route. Not until an actual paved highway was constructed to follow the course of the Lochsa River between Lolo Pass on the Montana-Idaho line and Clearwater River Canyon—where the Corps of Discovery had once again taken to dugout canoes on its journey to the Pacific—was the dream of a designated Lewis and Clark Highway through the Bitterroot Wilderness realized. In the relationship between the Lewis and Clark trail and the highway system, the Lochsa segment had long been a missing link.[70]

Designated by the Idaho State Highway Commission in 1916, the Lewis-Clark Highway remained little more than a line on a map for decades, the fate of many mountainous routes in areas where the tax base was too low to finance their construction. During the 1920s and 1930s the states of Idaho and Montana slowly built toward each other—Montana westward from Traveler's Rest on the Bitterroot River and Idaho eastward from Kooskia on the Clearwater River—planning to meet at Lolo Pass. Although construction west of Traveler's Rest was difficult, Montana had a much shorter distance to cover. The Idaho segment was nearly three times as long and even more rugged.

From Kooskia, where on its return in the spring of 1806 the Lewis and Clark Expedition settled into Long Camp to prepare to cross the Bitterroots and to wait for snow to melt on the Lolo Trail, the Lewis-Clark Highway eventually proceeded (west to east) up the Clearwater middle fork to the confluence of the Selway and Lochsa rivers at present-day Lowell, Idaho. From Lowell the roadway followed the Lochsa River upstream to its headwaters, the fork of Colt-killed Creek and Crooked Fork, near the point where the Corps of Discovery had descended from Lolo Pass and—having determined that passage through the river canyon was impossible—elected to climb up to the Lolo Trail. Today, most of this nearly 110-mile stretch of highway passes between two major wilderness areas.

The U.S. Forest Service took on the responsibility for completing the segment along the Lochsa, but construction was extremely slow, in some years consisting of little more than clearing timber from the right-of-way. During World War II, federal prisoners and Japanese internees were brought to the Lochsa to help blast a roadbed through the difficult Black Canyon section, but they made little progress. By 1949, thirty-six miles remained completely untouched. As the project dragged into the 1950s, hope faded that the missing highway link could be completed in time for the sesquicentennial celebration slated to begin in the summer of 1955. It was not. A year after the sesquicentennial ended, there was still a thirteen-mile "gap" halfway between Kooskia, Idaho, and Lolo, Montana.

To some extent, the highway had fallen victim to the National Defense Highway program, created in 1956 to create an interstate superhighway system. Yet, while the Lewis-Clark Highway suddenly seemed much less important to the public at large, a group called the U.S. Highway 12 Association lobbied for a route that would be designated the "Lewis and Clark Highway" all the way from Mobridge, South Dakota, on the Missouri River to Hoquiam, Washington, on the Pacific Coast. The U.S. Highway 12 Association continued to call for the gap in Idaho to be filled, as did communities along Montana State Highway 200 (then 20), which ran eastward from Missoula to Great Falls and on to Lewistown, Jordan, and Sidney near the North Dakota line. With strong support from Senators Frank Church of Idaho and Albert Gore of Tennessee, funds were finally appropriated

Fig 3.2 *Lochsa River, a tributary of the Clearwater River in northern Idaho. The Lewis-Clark Highway (U.S. 12), which follows the bank to the left in the photo, took forty-four years to build. It connects Missoula, Montana, with Lewiston, Idaho, via Lolo Pass and the Lochsa River Canyon, running roughly parallel to the Lewis and Clark trail. Photo by Peg Owens. Courtesy, Idaho Department of Commerce.*

to complete the Idaho portion of the project. The route, later designated as a segment of U.S. Highway 12, officially opened in 1963. An article in the California Automobile Club publication *Westways* referred to it as "A New Northwest Passage."[71]

New interstate superhighways completed during the 1960s directed the flow of tourists away from much of the Lewis and Clark trail and discouraged travelers from stopping or even slowing down to examine individual sites. The two-lane highway system had initiated a new way of commemorating Lewis and Clark through automobile exploration of their path west. But despite making access more remote, the advent of the interstate superhighway era did not generally diminish interest in the Corps of Discovery's exploits. During the very years in which the U.S. Congress debated and authorized the interstate freeway system, observations of the Lewis and Clark sesquicentennial stimulated a wave of enthusiasm that continued to grow throughout the rest of the twentieth century.

CHAPTER FOUR

The 1955 Sesquicentennial

W HAT I HAVE TERMED THE "STANDARD MODEL" of understanding Lewis and Clark—glorifying the explorers as forerunners of civilization—informs the array of celebrations that marked the 150th anniversary of the expedition. Still, the commemorations covered a wide gamut of sophistication, running from "folk" to "literate elite" images.

In the spring of 1955, Hollywood offered its contribution when Paramount Pictures released the film *The Far Horizons*, starring Charlton Heston as William Clark, Fred MacMurray as Meriwether Lewis, and Donna Reed as "Sacajawea." The movie virtually ignored historical fact in favor of rather typical cinematic clichés about the West. Even traditional views of the explorers appear to have been ignored. *Time Magazine* complained that "the very qualities that made Meriwether Lewis and William Clark great explorers—coolheadedness, caution and iron self-discipline—are precisely the ones the moviemakers have thrown out the window." While Clark and Lewis were depicted as "a pair of buffoons who would have trouble finding the mailbox," Donna Reed played Sacajawea as "a high-fashion pulse-thumper turned out in beautifully tailored buckskin." Conveniently for Clark and their romantic relationship, in the movie she was unmarried and had no child.[1] Citing frequent Indian onslaughts and a "monosyllabic script" spiced up by an ongoing feud between Clark and Lewis, a critic for *The New York Times* concluded: "As for Paramount's idea of what Lewis and Clark did, was this trip necessary? Shucks, no."[2] For most of the country, *The Far Horizons* was probably the final word in remembering the famous journey of exploration. But while most of the national audience appeared to accept Paramount's version of the expedition, an increasing number of enthusiasts at the local and regional levels took a more serious view. Even at the folk level, residents of communities on or near the trail knew the Hollywood version failed to accord with commonly understood events in the Lewis and Clark narrative.

By 1955 the heritage of the Corps of Discovery's 1804–1806 journey had achieved more than purely historic or even nationalistic interest in the states through which the route had passed. For cities and communities in the region, the memory of Lewis and Clark represented growing commercial and promotional opportunities. Such opportunities, as indicated earlier, were closely tied to the national highway system, which, in the far West at least, had come into being in the late 1920s and the 1930s. Automobile tourism, especially after World War II, breathed new life into many dying towns. As described earlier, from the very beginning of the automobile age, promoters had touted particular highway routes in an effort to attract tourists, and, when possible, regional boosters attached colorful names and historical themes to these routes. The Lewis and Clark Expedition route seemed to be a natural for this sort of promotion, and highways played a major role in commemorations during the mid-1950s and thereafter.

With the advent of the sesquicentennial in 1955, local and regional activities increased sharply. The governors of Washington, Oregon, Idaho, and Montana proclaimed 1955 "Lewis and Clark Year" and ap-

pointed a joint committee of representatives from the sesquicentennial committees in those states that met in Spokane, Washington, in
December 1954 to plan commemorative celebrations. Events were
scheduled to take place between May and October 1955 and were
spaced so that none would conflict. In some cities a Lewis and Clark
theme was added to regular annual events, while others staged elaborate celebrations dedicated to the sesquicentennial.[3] Ever since the
1905 Lewis and Clark Exposition, the Seaside, Oregon, Chamber of
Commerce had been determined to "hold an annual festival commemorating the first Americans to cross the continent." In Astoria,
Oregon, a full week of activities accompanied the dedication of a
newly completed replica of Fort Clatsop, the small log habitation
where the Corps of Discovery spent the winter of 1805–1806.[4]
Special guests included William Glasgow Clark, said to be a "direct
descendent" of William Clark, and Lydia Large, whose lineage as
"Sacajawea's . . . great-great-grand niece" had been sworn to by the
superintendent of the Wind River Reservation in Wyoming. From
August 20 through August 28, 1955, the Astoria celebration included
dances and athletic contests, a regatta, various teas, and guided historical tours, to name a few of the activities. Days were devoted to
commemorations in both Seaside and Cannon Beach, but commemorative activities in Oregon were spread among the communities of
Gearhart, Warrenton, and Hammond as well.[5]

The public was also invited to inspect the new replica of Fort
Clatsop. This site, considered one of the most important historical
sites in Oregon, had been shabbily marked until recently. For years,
a local newspaper noted, the site's supposed location on the Lewis
and Clark River five miles southwest of Astoria near U.S. Highway
101 had been indicated by a "simple flag pole" and a plain "concrete
marker." By the late 1940s the marker was overgrown with berry
vines. Its plaque, which contained historical background, had been
removed for safekeeping, and the rotted flagpole had been cut down.
No clear directions from the nearest roadway existed to guide visitors
to what remained of the marked site. As the newspaper story put it,
"From there the pilgrim is on his own, much as were Lewis and Clark.
If he turns off by instinct (there is no sign) over a muddy lane, he will
find a pile of beer cans, the trail markers of civilization. There in an

unkempt grove hangs a small wooden sign 'site of Fort Clatsop.' "
Funds were not available to organizations in the area—including the
Oregon Historical Society, the Clatsop County Historical Society, and
the American Pioneer Trails Association—that were interested in improving or maintaining the site. In 1946 historian Bernard DeVoto
followed the Lewis and Clark trail west as part of his research for
what would become a hugely popular abridged edition of the expedition journals. When DeVoto publicly "expressed his horror" at the
condition of the Fort Clatsop site, the general response was that "the
war had prevented financing" its improvement. The writer of the
news story added that it is "high time that something be done about
Fort Clatsop."[6]

An attempt to more accurately pin down the location of the fort
was announced in 1948 by Walter Johnson, president of the Clatsop
County Historical Society. "That summer," the Astoria *Evening Budget*
recalled, Louis Caywood, an archaeologist for the National Park
Service, "began excavations at a location suggested by old surveys
and photographs." Caywood quickly encountered a layer of char-
coal and uncovered several stone-lined firepits, which he concluded
had been made and used by white men. Caywood's findings convinced the Oregon Historical Society and other interested persons
that the location of the actual fort was only about ten feet from the
marker the society had placed in 1901.[7] As part of its preparations
for the Lewis and Clark sesquicentennial celebration, the Oregon
Historical Society—which owned the land on which excavations
had been carried out—sponsored and oversaw the construction of a
replica of the fort in 1955, based on the description in the journals.
The Crown-Zellerbach wood products corporation agreed to provide logs for the replica, and local architect John Wicks designed the
structure based on a drawing by Rolf Klep, formerly of Astoria. The
"second-growth hemlock logs" were pre-fitted and marked so they
could be easily assembled on the site. In May 1955, Astoria Jaycee
and Lions club members began constructing the Fort Clatsop replica and completed it in time for Astoria's sesquicentennial celebration. Members of the American Legion Auxiliary hand-sewed an
American flag with fifteen stars to fly over the replica of the fort.
In July, Oregon senator Richard Neuberger introduced a bill to es-

Fig 4.1 *Doorway at the first Fort Clatsop replica near Astoria, Oregon. Following several years of archaeological work to determine the probable location of the expedition's 1805–1806 winter quarters, the replica was constructed in time for the Lewis and Clark sesquicentennial in 1955 and was designated a national monument. An interpretive center was added in the early 1960s. Photo by Jeffrey Phillip Curry. Courtesy, Jeffrey Phillip Curry.*

tablish what was believed to be the original site of Fort Clatsop as a national monument.[8]

As part of the 1955 commemoration, the Northern Pacific Railway Company agreed to finance a special sesquicentennial book with maps to familiarize readers with events in the journals and the nature of the country the explorers traversed. A section by northwestern author James Stevens extolled the expedition's role in blazing a trail for settlement and development. Included in the rather modest booklet is the text of a speech by Northern Pacific president Robert MacFarlane to the Western Railway Club in Chicago. In his address, entitled "The Lewis and Clark Country a Century and a Half Later," MacFarlane tied Lewis and Clark to the march of "progress" represented by the great transcontinental railroads. There seems to be no conscious irony in his emphasis on the just-completed Missouri River reservoirs, which had yet to be filled and would obliterate much of the Lewis and Clark trail. The booklet's cover lists the members of the Northwest Sesquicentennial Organizing Committee, which included three representatives from the Dakotas. Chapin D. Foster from South Dakota was co-chair.[9] Yet except for the fact that some groups tracing the trail passed through the Dakotas, little evidence exists that the sesquicentennial was widely commemorated east of Montana. South Dakota officials, in fact, admitted that there would be "no exclusively Lewis and Clark celebrations" in the state in 1955 and stated that communities would refuse to support a series of planned pageants.[10]

It is understandable that residents of the Pacific Northwest, Idaho, and Montana would show greater interest in the Lewis and Clark Expedition than people further east. In many communities between Seaside, Oregon, and Great Falls, Montana, the names of the explorers and their exploits appear ingrained in the public consciousness. At the confluence of the Clearwater and Snake rivers in northern Idaho and eastern Washington, for example, the names were ubiquitous long before the creation of the National Trail. The Corps of Discovery passed this way twice, in 1805 and 1806. A bridge across the Snake River connects Clarkston, Washington, with Lewiston, Idaho. Lewiston boasts the Lewis and Clark Hotel, Lewis-Clark State College, and Lewis-Clark Memorial Gardens, to name a few. "Nowhere along the route of the explorers," an Associated Press story claimed, "are the names of Lewis-Clark so commercially evident" as in Lewiston and Clarkston.[11] Yet the names are unavoidable elsewhere throughout the region as well. Both Clark and Lewis counties are found in Washington and Idaho, and Montana's capital is in Lewis and Clark County.

A site that, along with the Fort Clatsop replica in Oregon, played a particularly significant role during the sesquicentennial was Missouri Headwaters State Park near the town of Three Forks, Montana, about thirty miles northwest of Bozeman. In late July 1805 the Corps of Discovery had spent several days at the location where the Madison, Jefferson, and Gallatin rivers come together to form the Missouri. It was near this spot, Sacagawea had told the men, that a Minataree (Hidatsa) raiding party had attacked her Shoshone band

and taken her captive. From the Three Forks of the Missouri, the expedition proceeded up the Jefferson River. The park at the Three Forks was founded in conjunction with the most celebrated enactments of pageantry along the Lewis and Clark trail.

The idea of establishing a state park at the famous Headwaters of the Missouri dates back to the summer of 1928, when Clark Maudlin, a cement plant worker in nearby Trident, Montana, was picnicking with his wife and son at the Three Forks. Maudlin's wife, a former schoolteacher, pointed out that Lewis and Clark had visited that spot and that "this would be [an] ideal place for a park." Both she and their son, Billy, succumbed to influenza the following summer, but years later, as he drove past the forks on his way to work each day, Clark Maudlin often remembered her words and was inspired to create a park to commemorate the expedition. He purchased the only parcel available for sale at the site and donated it to the state of Montana. The state was unable to fund further purchases, but it gave Maudlin the authority to raise the money needed to complete the park. By 1946 he had convinced civic and business leaders throughout the state to join "historical-minded" residents in the community of Three Forks in supporting the project and had recruited John G. Buttelman to head a new fund-raising organization called the Founders Club of Montana, of which Maudlin became vice president. More parcels were purchased, and in July 1951 the Missouri Headwaters State Park was officially opened.[12]

Although responsibility for the park passed to a state commission in 1957, Maudlin stayed on as caretaker. That same year he traveled to St. Charles, Missouri, to visit one of the jumping-off points for the expedition and publicly expressed disappointment at the lack of any marker commemorating the event in that historic location. In 1961 the Three Forks of the Missouri in Montana was designated a National Historic Landmark. Clark Maudlin died in 1972, just a few years before the creation of the Lewis and Clark National Historic Trail.[13]

Although cultural historian David Glassberg never refers to Lewis and Clark or Sacagawea in his study of historical pageantry in the United States, the outdoor productions of the sesquicentennial seem

113

to echo what he saw as an earlier golden age of local historical pageants. These commemorative local history pageants, Glassberg notes, combined boosterism and community patriotism with an "idealized" representation of the "behavior of past generations." The pageants usually reflected "cultural conservatism" in their imagery, and their texts often contained a great deal of "saccharine moralism."[14]

According to another scholar, Naima Prevots, American pageants flourished particularly between 1905 and 1925, during which time the aesthetic and social values of the American Pageant Association (APA) encouraged proliferation of the form and influenced the quality of productions. The desire "to develop popular art of quality in every community . . . and [to] develop American thematic material" engaged the talents of such writers, directors, and educators as Percy MacKaye, George Pierce Baker, and Frederick H. Koch. To be sure, during the Progressive Era in the early twentieth century, pageants that involved the widespread participation of community members were also seen as means for reform and for reviving democracy through art. MacKaye especially believed that theater should be treated as "an important civic institution [with the] power to reach the masses" and to instill such democratic values as "cooperation, clear thinking, and true moral action." Pageant performances, held in appropriate outdoor settings, drew audiences of between 2,000 and 80,000 people and depended mostly on community members to assume the performance roles.[15]

Between 1908 and 1917 the APA reported performances of several hundred pageants, of which more than eighty were historical in nature. Most of these pageants depicted history east of the Mississippi, particularly in the upper Midwest and New England. The figures of Lewis and Clark and Sacagawea were represented, however, in one of the most spectacular events, *The Pageant and Masque of St. Louis*, performed for four days in May 1914 on the site of the 1904 Louisiana Purchase Centennial Exposition. The pageant portion, written by Thomas Wood, presented significant periods in the region's history, including those of the Plains Indians, early French explorers, and the founding of St. Louis. The departure of the Lewis and Clark Expedition in boats was depicted, as was the later arrival of settlers. The pageant carried through to the end of the Civil War and was followed by Percy MacKaye's symbolic masque about Cahokia, the center of the early Native American mound-building culture, which was tied in somehow to the life of the French king for whom the city was named.[16]

The Lewis and Clark Expedition played a much greater role in *A Pageant of the Northwest*, written by Frederick H. Koch and "eighteen of his students" at the University of North Dakota and produced outdoors in the Bankside Theatre on the Grand Forks campus. Koch, who had taken a leave of absence from the university to study "dramatic literature" at Harvard University with George Pierce Baker, became closely associated with the burgeoning pageant movement and "a leader in the APA." The outdoor theater in which the pageant was performed in 1914 was constructed especially for the production, making use of a stream that "flowed across the university campus." "The Bankside Theatre," Koch later wrote, "was the first to utilize the natural curve of a stream as the foreground of the scene, between the stage and the amphitheatre. It is unique in that entrances and exits can be made by water as well as by land. . . . [O]n this very spot, by this same stream . . . the buffalo herds ranged at will and the Indians met the white man in friendly trade. . . . [*A Pageant of the Northwest*] marked a distinct contribution because it demonstrated that the community, under proper direction, can not only enact its own traditions and outlook, but, more than this, [can] actually create the pageant-form, thus cultivating communal literary as well as histrionic art." This also, according to Prevots, marks the first spelling of the "Bird Woman's" name as "Sakakawea," the spelling preferred in North Dakota today.[17]

The first pageant in Montana to reenact an aspect of the Lewis and Clark Expedition occurred at Armstead, about fifteen miles south of Dillon. On August 30, 1915, at the unveiling of the Daughters of the American Revolution's *Sacajawea* plaque, residents of Armstead depicted the Corps of Discovery's meeting with the Lemhi Shoshone and Sacagawea's return to her band and her brother Cameahwait. Conceived by Laura Tolman Scott, the pageant took place at the confluence of Horse Prairie Creek and the Beaverhead River, the approximate site of the expedition's Camp Fortunate. According to a newspaper account, the cast included around thirty "Shoshone Indians from the Lemhi reservation" who (oddly, considering the peaceful nature of the meeting with Lewis and Clark) "gave their famous war dance following the program."[18] Seven years later a procession and pageant depicting scenes from the city's history "kicked off" the grand opening of the five-story Lewis and Clark Hotel in Lewiston, Idaho. Capping the Lewis and Clark segment, "Sacajawea," represented more as a promotional icon than as a historical figure, was presented with keys to both the city of Lewiston and its newest hotel—which she ceremoniously tossed into the Snake River. A "scalp dance" (again, rather inappropriate) was performed with the help of Nez Perce Indians.[19]

The enlistment of Native Americans, usually as supernumeraries to the main action, was characteristic of pageants held at various places along the Lewis and Clark trail. Referring to urban historical pageants and festivals around the turn of the twentieth century, tourism scholar Catherine Cocks argues that something more than historical authenticity was at work in the battles and dances commonly staged by Indians. "Without the proper accoutrements and stylized activities," she writes, "onlookers might have to encounter the Indians as fellow citizens rather than living souvenirs of a dying, primitive, and alien race. The requirement that the Indians perform their culture as a series of entertainments reduced irreconcilable conflicts to sideshows."[20]

The popularity of historical pageants in general declined rapidly in the 1920s, in part as a result of increasing competition from motion pictures and radio. Today, Lewis and Clark pageants have largely given way to a variant: the historical reenactment, which places a premium on technical and factual accuracy. But in a general sense, the early–twentieth-century history pageant described by Prevots and Glassberg provided a model for commemorating the 150th anniversary of the Lewis and Clark Expedition, although in pageants in the 1950s, noble rhetoric and symbolism seemed tempered by more vernacular speech and realism.[21]

One of the major pageants performed in the summer of 1955, the one at the Missouri Headwaters where Clark Maudlin and others were establishing a memorial park, had some history. In 1949 Albert Erickson, advertising director for the Montana State Highway Commission, informed Maudlin that he had visited Professor Bert

Hansen at the University of Montana in Missoula and discussed putting on a pageant at the Three Forks during the summer of 1950. Hansen responded by co-writing (with Virginia Buttleman), directing, and producing an outdoor program that would be presented during four consecutive summers leading up the sesquicentennial.[22] Professor Hansen was well prepared for the task. He had been writing, producing, and directing historical pageants in Montana for several years. This grew out of his interest in using the pageant form as an educational tool, as Henry Koch had done. Hansen advocated broadening the understanding of students in speech and drama programs by having them participate in creating group psychodramas he called "sociodramas," a term coined by Dr. Jacob Moreno in the 1930s. As a means for "analyzing and treating [the] social problems of a group," sociodramas begin with spontaneous role playing and evolve into productions written and rehearsed for public performance.[23] Beyond the classroom, Hansen believed participation in sociodramas at all levels would foster unity and community cohesion. Years before being asked to create an outdoor spectacle using nonprofessionals to depict the Corps of Discovery and Sacagawea at the Three Forks of the Missouri, Professor Hansen was working on ways to evoke local history by harnessing community creativity.

He put the sociodrama process to work as part of a grant-supported research program called the Montana Study, funded by the Rockefeller Foundation. The purpose of the Montana Study was to find ways to develop community culture in small towns throughout the state and prevent flight to larger cities. Two of the eleven small towns that participated were Darby and Stevensville, both near Hamilton in southwestern Montana.[24] Hansen took a leave of absence from his academic duties to establish a "dramatic vehicle" that would involve as many residents as possible. He took care to distinguish community-based "sociodrama in the form of a pageant" from the commonplace historical pageant. The method was intended, at least in part, to foster community identity and not just be a vehicle for perfunctory celebration of past events.[25]

Beginning with Darby, which in the mid- to late 1940s was facing the loss of much of its lumbering operations (a perception not shared by many of Darby's residents), Hansen initiated basically the same process he had used with speech classes. To make "the whole community conscious of its predicament," a group of residents wrote a sociodrama entitled *Darby Looks at Itself* and performed it in early December 1945. Fifty-three people out of a population of 500 participated in the writing, and 127 residents took part as actors.[26]

After the Darby project, Hansen engaged the citizens of Stevensville. The town was one of the oldest in the region, but Hansen said its residents lacked an "appreciation of its singularly historic past," a "vision for its future," or even "an interest in its present."[27] According to historian Carla Homstad, "Nearly three thousand people—roughly one-fourth of the population of Ravalli County"—saw a production of *A Tale of the Bitterroot* in August 1946.[28] One aspect that seems to have set the Stevensville pageant apart from run-of-the mill dramatized historical celebrations was, Hansen stated, "its solemn adherence to a belatedly recognized truth that had never before been told by Indians and whites together at a public gathering." In four episodes that dealt with the Christianizing of the Flathead Indians and their eventual removal from the Bitterroot Valley, the sociodrama "portrayed the story of a fifty year period of ruthless aggression on the part of the white men, and of their determination to drive the Flathead Indians from their native lands in the fertile Bitter Root Valley where Stevensville is located." Hansen insisted on "realistic treatment" and authenticity, seeking to incorporate, among other things, "real Indians with their tepees." But they were not merely extras. Participants in the Stevensville pageant included descendants of the Flathead Indians who had been removed in 1891. Paul Charlot, chief of the Salish tribe, played the part of his grandfather, Chief Charlot, an important historical figure during the removal period.[29]

A year later, in 1947, Hansen helped study groups in the towns of Arlee and Dixon to dramatize local history related to the Flathead Indian Reservation and the founding of the communities north of Missoula, Montana. Homstad points out that performances of the pageants ceased after the Montana Study concluded in 1948. For Bert Hansen, however, they proved to be a warm-up for the Lewis and Clark pageants for which he would be best known.[30]

Hansen's 1950 Lewis and Clark pageant, performed at the Three Forks of the Missouri, depicted four episodes related to the expedition. Although most of the dialogue is fictional, the pageant is a far cry from Hollywood's conception of the Lewis and Clark Expedition. Its title, *Corridor of an Empire*, reflects a traditional and popular view of western expansion and of the expedition's significance to white America. The "corridor" referred to is virtually the trail of the Lewis and Clark Expedition. Yet, as in the case of the first Stevensville pageant Hansen supervised in 1947, the Three Forks script demonstrates sensitivity to Native American viewpoints well ahead of its time. As a historical pageant, it also presented a refreshingly realistic approach that paid close attention to the historical record, particularly the Lewis and Clark journals.[31]

The pageant does contain a certain amount of celebration of conquest and destiny, but *Corridor of an Empire* avoids much of the chauvinism and mawkishness that characterized occasional pageants at the time. It also avoids the typical high-flown rhetoric and stiff attempts to imitate language of the period, and symbolic poses are kept to a minimum. Many of the speeches Bert Hansen and Virginia Buttleman devised are intended to realistically represent normal conversation, and the usage tends to have a rather modern ring. The content of the dialogue among expedition members is closely based on actual comments in entries from the journals, yet the completely fictionalized scenes about Sacagawea and her people tend to have a poetic and prophetic character. For example, Episode I of *Corridor of an Empire* presents an imagined scene from Sacagawea's childhood in which her mother vaguely glimpses the destiny of her "little Bird Child," and the chief of the Lemhi Shoshone band suggests that the river formed by the Three Forks seems aware of having a "mission."[32] This betrays an underlying celebratory theme. Despite its overall attempt to present a more inclusive and realistic view of history, the pageant occasionally turns Indian characters into cheerleaders for western expansion.

In the second episode, at a social event Meriwether Lewis and Thomas Jefferson discuss Jefferson's "dream" of sending an expedition to the headwaters of the Missouri River. This is a highly compressed bit of exposition that contrives to be conversational but also to present Jefferson's views on the possibilities of a Northwest Passage and the purchase of Louisiana Territory from France. Jefferson tells

Lewis, his secretary, that he has been selected to lead a "scientific" expedition up the river. After initial astonishment at the news, Lewis requests that his "longtime friend," William Clark, be allowed to go along to share the experience. Significant aspects of the expedition's initiation and purpose are, fairly deftly, presented to the audience, albeit highly telescoped in time because of the constraints of the dramatic presentation. At the end of the scene, "Lewis stands in wonderment as Jefferson blends into the crowd."[33]

New Year's Day 1805 at Fort Mandan on the Missouri River is the setting for Episode III, which explains why and how Sacagawea was allowed to accompany the expedition westward from the 1804–1805 winter quarters. It also offers conversation between York and Meriwether Lewis and a dancing exhibition by York. Sergeants Ordway and Pryor also have a few lines of dialogue. But central to the episode is Clark and Lewis's discussion of Sacagawea's background, as well as her husband, Charbonneau's, efforts to persuade them to bring along the "Indian princess." The two captains are particularly interested in Sacagawea's knowledge of the Missouri River headwaters and the fact that she was kidnapped from her Shoshone band near there and brought to the Mandan and Hidatsa villages. They are concerned about her advanced state of pregnancy but have come to understand how important she would be to the journey, with or without Charbonneau's florid and blustery arguments. The Frenchman storms offstage, dragging his wife with him, after Clark suggests that they would prefer to take her along rather than Charbonneau. Ultimately, of course, the explorers decide to accept both Sacagawea *and* "the windbag and faker."[34]

The final episode brings the audience back to the site of the first episode, which depicted Sacagawea and her parents. Now, however, it is Saturday, July 27, 1805. Stage directions call for boats to "come out from behind some trees about 400 yards" from the point of land on which the dramatic action will take place. As the boats approach, conversations begin that involve a number of the men, including John Ordway, Silas Goodrich, George Gibson, John Collins, and Joseph Whitehouse. They present more exposition about their experiences coming up the Missouri, as recorded in the journals. They also grumble about having to continue on to the Pacific Ocean, for which they will need horses from Sacagawea's people so they can cross the mountains. Clark and Lewis agree that "this is the place," the headwaters of the Missouri River. But Lewis notes that Jefferson was wrong. This was not "a low-lying watershed, easily portaged." Before them were mountains, the magnitude of which they had "never dreamed." He observes that "the men don't seem exactly thrilled over our discovery" and bows to Private Whitehouse's suggestion that "an extra portion of brandy" be distributed "to celebrate this Three Forks Place." (The journals indicate that the brandy was finished off earlier to celebrate the Fourth of July at the Great Falls.) Lewis drinks to "an even more interesting experience into the unknown" and dubs the path they are blazing "a Corridor of an Empire." The 1950 performances at the Three Forks of the Missouri set the pattern for sesquicentennial pageantry there and for numerous future revivals.[35]

On July 23–26, 1955, Hansen's pageant became a significant event in the celebratory schedule. Episodes depicting the expedition's outward- and homeward-bound journeys were each performed twice, on alternate evenings. Bound scripts of former pageants were offered for sale. In conjunction with the Three Forks celebration, the American Pioneer Trails Association—national sponsor of the sesquicentennial—held its twenty-sixth annual "Rendezvous" at the Sacajawea Hotel in Three Forks. Patrick Gass's grandson, James S. Smith, a retired California teacher, was slated to attend the festivities.[36]

Just five days after the pageant at the Three Forks, an estimated 5,000 spectators crowded a "natural amphitheater" near the site of Camp Fortunate on the Beaverhead River as Dillon offered its commemoration, a two-hour dramatization directed by Professor Joe Ryburn of Western Montana College of Education that featured a cast of "more than 100." The Camp Fortunate pageant opened with a "Shoshone prayer and Indian tribal songs" and depicted, among other things, members of the Lewis and Clark Expedition "hauling their boats up the narrowing Beaverhead River," the recognition scene between Sacagawea and her brother, and "the smoking of the pipe of peace by the Indians and whites."[37] The printed program pointed out that the pageant's "colorful tipis" were not used by the Shoshones at the time they met the expedition and that Drewyer (Drouillard) was incorrectly portrayed as speaking Shoshone but otherwise

Fig 4.2 *Encampment on Horse Prairie Creek near Armstead, Montana, for the 1955 Dillon Lewis and Clark Sesquicentennial Pageant—held before Clark Valley Reservoir inundated the site of Camp Fortunate. Photo by Joe Ryburn. Courtesy, Beaverhead County Museum, Dillon, Montana.*

vouched for the presentation's accuracy as based on passages from the journals.[38]

In the summer of 1955 Bert Hansen, who was a member of the state Lewis and Clark Sesquicentennial Committee, had also been commissioned to write, direct, and produce a "triple" commemoration pageant for the Missoula, Montana, Kiwanis Club and the U.S. Forest Service. Performed on August 12 and 14, the pageant celebrated the sesquicentennial of Lewis and Clark's passage through the Missoula area, the centennial of Isaac Stevens's Council Grove Treaty with the Flathead Nation that would open that nation to white settlement, and the fiftieth anniversary of the founding of the U.S. Forest Service in 1905. The first episode of *Your Land Forever* dramatized Thomas Jefferson's role in launching the Lewis and Clark Expedition and depicted the Corps of Discovery at Traveler's Rest (south of

Fig 4.3 *Men pulling boats up the Beaverhead River as part of the 1955 Dillon Sesquicentennial Pageant. Photo by Joe Ryburn. Courtesy, Beaverhead County Museum, Dillon, Montana.*

Missoula, near present-day Lolo) on September 10, 1805, as the group prepared to cross the Bitterroot Mountains on the outward-bound journey. During the pageant, about 100 members of the Flathead, Salish, Pend Oreille, and Kootenai tribes occupied an encampment on an island in the Clark Fork River in downtown Missoula. Two of the Indians, Aggie Woodcock and Adolph Ninepipe, played the roles of Sacagawea and the Shoshone guide Old Toby, respectively. The day following the performances, a motorcade sponsored by the Missoula Automobile Dealers Association drove to the top of Lolo Pass on the Montana-Idaho state line for a picnic.[39]

Montana did not monopolize dramatizations of the Lewis and Clark story during the sesquicentennial, however. A historical pageant entitled *Salmon River Saga*, written and directed by Vio Mae Powell, director of speech and drama at Idaho State College in Pocatello, was performed in Salmon, Idaho, on August 20 and 21, 1955, following six weeks of rehearsal. Salmon is north of the location where the Lemhi Shoshone band of Cameahwait (Sacagawea's brother) was encamped when visited by the Corps of Discovery in August 1805. The company had lingered there for about two weeks while the explorers bargained for horses to carry them over the Bitterroot Mountains. Under the stars at the Lemhi County fairgrounds, with the silhouetted Salmon River Mountains as a "dramatic backdrop," an impressively large cast combined drama, music, poetry, and narration to tell the story of Lewis and Clark and Sacagawea in the Salmon area. Eight episodes were depicted, beginning with Sacagawea's abduction by the Minatarees (Hidatsas) and concluding with the Shoshone guide Old Toby leading the expedition over the Bitterroots. The pageant was "acted in pantomime, with actors dubbing in the dialogue over a public address system." This was the method used in all the large outdoor presentations, including the pageants at Three Forks. At Salmon, the Horace Johnson group of dancers from the Fort Hall Shoshone-Bannock Reservation in eastern Idaho performed "authentic" Indian dances during intermission. Total paid admissions for the two nights amounted to 2,274, and between 500 and 600 schoolchildren were admitted for free, setting a record for attendance at the fairgrounds.[40] A newspaper story proudly pointed out that "cars from five states" other than Idaho "were noted on the parking lot within the fairgrounds gates."[41]

While historical pageants were the most complex sesquicentennial activities, the schedule included numerous other events spread over the years 1955 and 1956 and planned to correspond to the weeks the expedition was in a particular area. Lewiston, Idaho's, turn came in the fall of 1955 and featured a three-day "water pageant," a buffalo barbecue, breakfast with the governors of Idaho and Washington, and a Nez Perce encampment. The featured speaker at a convocation on Friday night, October 7, was Pulitzer Prize–winning novelist A. B. Guthrie Jr., author of *The Big Sky* and other books about the early West.[42] Similar events took place throughout the Clearwater Valley. A barbecue at Kamiah drew 2,000 people, and the winning parade float depicted—significantly—the uncompleted Lewis-Clark Highway route against a backdrop of snow-covered mountains.[43]

However, not all events were specifically tied to towns or cities in the region. Approximately 1,000 Boy Scouts gathered in Great Falls, Montana, to begin retracing the expedition's route from the great portage to Astoria, using dugout canoes and packhorses. The

Greater Clarkston (Washington) Association sponsored an "automobile caravan" that traveled over the Lewis and Clark route for nine days between Bismarck, North Dakota, and the Oregon coast. The caravan planned to camp along the way and to stop at "all Lewis and Clark museums and roadside markers." More than 100 pilots prepared to fly an air tour over the trail from St. Louis to Astoria, with stops in Missoula, Montana, and Walla Walla, Washington. A pair of Air Force F-84 jet fighters "retraced" the expedition's path between St. Louis and Great Falls, Montana.[44] The Montana State Committee announced that it would help pay expenses for seventeen-year-old Meriwether Lewis of Tacoma, Washington, "a seventh direct descendant of an uncle" of the famous explorer, to travel the length of the trail. The Washington State Committee prepared outlines for talks on Lewis and Clark and lists of available speakers and offered suggestions for program topics and activities, including art displays, pageants, and radio and television programs.[45]

In 1956 the Northwest Sesquicentennial Organizing Committee turned its attention to the exploration party's journey back to St. Louis from the Pacific Coast in the spring and summer of 1806. Even as the summer of sesquicentennial celebrations in the Pacific Northwest came to a close with Lewiston, Idaho's, two-day gala, interest in preserving and interpreting the trail of Lewis and Clark as a national memorial began to gain momentum. Montana's 1945 celebration of the 140th anniversary of the expedition had centered on a rededication of the trail, "planned," according to the *Great Falls Tribune*, "as a special highlight of the American Pioneer Trails Association's 1945 project, Explorers of America."[46] Meetings and programs were scheduled in communities from Missoula to the North Dakota line and on parts of the Missouri and Yellowstone rivers. The principal activity appears to have been another automobile caravan, led by Esther Horne of Wahpeton, North Dakota, who claimed to be a "direct descendent of Sacajawea." This retracing of the route from west to east was also intended to build support for a Lewis and Clark "National Tourway." The tourway was a more ambitious version of a 1948 proposal by the National Park Service, calling for a designated highway route along the Missouri River between St. Louis and Three Forks, Montana. The 1956 National Tourway campaign, headed by Senator Warren

Magnuson of Washington, would extend all the way to the Pacific Coast and include, incidentally, State Highway 14 on the Washington side of the Columbia River.[47]

Enthusiasm for this plan remained lukewarm east of Montana. The secretary of the South Dakota Historical Society expressed the view that, although the idea was "picturesque," numerous pioneers besides Lewis and Clark had "used the Missouri as a path to the Northwest."[48] The remark suggests that Lewis and Clark represented something different in the Pacific Northwest than they did in the Northern Plains states. In fact, the sesquicentennial celebration had been focused primarily in Montana, Idaho, Washington, and Oregon, while the Dakotas and states further downstream had barely participated. That would change, however, once the idea of commemorating the entire route from the mouth of the Missouri River to the Pacific Ocean gained currency. While the issue of appropriately selecting and labeling highways remained, emphasis in the 1960s shifted to the actual path of exploration and the campaign to establish a national historic trail.

There was little initial interest in the Dakotas, Kansas, Missouri, Nebraska, and Iowa for commemorating Lewis and Clark with historic highway markers. Many residents of Idaho and Montana, moreover, would have preferred that the U.S. Congress provide the means for completing the Lewis-Clark Highway between Lewiston, Idaho, and Lolo Pass on the Idaho-Montana state line. The highway (now U.S. 12), which follows the route Lewis and Clark took down the Clearwater River and roughly parallels the Lolo Trail for about 100 miles, still had not been completed forty years after construction began. Less than thirty miles remained to be completed along the Lochsa River in 1955 as the region celebrated the Corps of Discovery's 150th anniversary. Once the missing link was finally spanned and the Lewis-Clark Highway was dedicated in 1963, the regional goal of a continuous highway commemorating the expedition's route resurfaced. State commissions, appointed (as the sesquicentennial committees had been) by western governors, began to surface in the early 1960s. Soon those states along the route that had virtually ignored the sesquicentennial—the Dakotas, Iowa, Nebraska, Kansas, and Illinois—joined in.

Although the National Park Service did establish an interpretive center at the Fort Clatsop replica in Oregon, the federal government's involvement in the sesquicentennial had been minimal. Part of the reason may have been that the National Park Service focused on individual historical locations and was highly selective in choosing which ones to interpret and improve for public visitation. The Jefferson National Expansion Memorial and the Gateway Arch in St. Louis fit the pattern. So did battlefields and famous structures. But the trail of Lewis and Clark consisted of numerous significant sites spread over thousands of miles, and the terrain through which it ran was inextricably tied to the expedition's historical significance. As we shall see in Chapter 5, the momentum for commemorating the Corps of Discovery's journey, which increased in intensity during the sesquicentennial, was maintained at the regional level into the next decade. The federal government weighed in as well, stimulated by the public's demand for reform. By the mid-1960s nationwide fears that traces of the past were rapidly being obliterated combined with concern over the environmental health of rivers and wildlife to stimulate the assumption of new responsibilities by the federal government, and an expanding movement to create a Lewis and Clark National Trail captured the public's imagination.

CHAPTER FIVE

The National Commission

Public opinion had begun to swing in favor of preserving wilderness and cleaning up parklands by the time John F. Kennedy became president. A new vision of "wilderness" as something human beings would define and manage took hold as a basis for national government policy. Secretary of the Interior Stewart Udall's push for legislation to preserve natural places and roadless areas resulted in the 1964 Wilderness Act, which established a new set of rules for wilderness. The act stands as a landmark for preservation, but the struggle over which lands should be set aside for that purpose continued. The Wilderness Act was followed by a stricter Water Quality Act and Lady Bird Johnson's Highway Beautification bill in 1965. The Johnson administration also turned its attention to establishing recreational hiking trails and expanding the number of historical sites to be preserved. "Environmentalism," writes historian Walter Nugent, "frequently appealed to the same people who supported historic preservation, and the aging of those born from the 1920s through the baby boom provided a more affluent and nostalgic demographic base." The focus in western communities in the 1960s began to shift from "slash-and-burn renewal" to preservation of historic sites.[1]

The Missouri River portion of the Lewis and Clark trail, at least, brought together initiatives affecting clean water and wildlife preservation, demands for additional outdoor public recreation, and historical interpretation.[2] In May 1961 conservationist and celebrated political cartoonist J. N. "Ding" Darling proposed that the Missouri River be incorporated into "a national outdoor recreation and natural resources ribbon along the historic trail of Lewis and Clark." Gravely ill, Darling knew he would not live to see such a project carried out. However, he secured banker and fellow conservationist Sherry Fisher's promise to initiate a campaign for the proposal. Darling, who had helped found the National Wildlife Federation, was famous for his syndicated editorial cartoons for the Des Moines Register promoting wildlife sanctuaries and opposing dam construction, particularly on his beloved Missouri River. Following his friend's death in February 1962, Fisher helped form the J. N. "Ding" Darling Foundation, which he steered toward the creation of a Lewis and Clark trail zone that would also provide habitat for wildlife. Encouraged by Udall, representatives of the foundation, federal agencies, and the states through which the Lewis and Clark trail passed met in Portland, Oregon, in the fall of 1962 to discuss the Darling proposal.[3]

In 1963 the U.S. Congress approved a trail plan in principle, and the Bureau of Outdoor Recreation began to study development along a ten-mile corridor for inclusion in a proposed nationwide system of scenic trails. On August 7, 1964, legislation that would create a national commission to conduct hearings on the Lewis and Clark trail was introduced in the House of Representatives by John Kyl and Ben F. Jensen of Iowa; shortly thereafter, Iowa senator Jack R. Miller introduced a similar bill in the U.S. Senate. The bills moved through committee very quickly, and H.R. 12289 was soon passed by both houses of Congress. On October 6, 1964, President Lyndon Johnson signed Public Law 88-630 authorizing creation of a Lewis and Clark Trail Commission to promote public understanding of the expedition's historical significance and review proposals for developing "desirable long-term conservation objectives" and recreation opportunities along its length. The commission was also authorized to advise government agencies on selecting and marking a "suitable connecting network of roads" along the route.[4] Of the twenty-seven members, ten represented the states of Missouri, Kansas, Iowa, Nebraska, South Dakota, North Dakota, Montana, Idaho, Washington, and Oregon (in 1966 a member from Illinois was added). Four were congressmen and four were senators, five represented cabinet departments, and four were appointed by the Darling Foundation.[5] Sherry Fisher chaired the commission during its five-year existence. It met several times a year in various cities along the trail, including St. Louis, Bismarck, Billings, and Portland. Thus began an institutionalizing of the route the Corps of Discovery took between 1804 and 1806.

The Lewis and Clark Trail Commission's mandate drew on several streams of reform energy. It authorized a high-profile assault on water and air pollution and other forms of environmental degradation. It tied together the concept, if not the reality, of wilderness with symbols of national identity and heritage. It called for restitution of wildlife and natural conditions in conjunction with expansion of public recreation facilities. In pursuing these ideals, the commission enlisted the support of a number of states and municipalities in cooperation with agencies of the federal government. Along with current support for rescuing historical traces on the landscape, it could count on burgeoning enthusiasm about the expedition that had developed during the sesquicentennial celebrations in the Pacific Northwest.

The new Lewis and Clark Trail Commission would serve as a clearinghouse for ideas and a disseminator of information. It would listen to advice and offer recommendations for action. It would educate a populace generally ignorant of history, especially of Lewis and Clark, and promote tourism. It would work closely with seven agencies within the Department of the Interior to coordinate the national government's effort. Particularly significant was the Bureau of Outdoor Recreation. At its second meeting, held in St. Louis, the commission considered and accepted the report of a two-year study of historical preservation and recreational potential along the expedition route carried out by the Bureau of Outdoor Recreation. *The*

Lewis and Clark Trail—A Proposal for Development proposed, among other things, acquisition of lands along the Lewis and Clark route for historical interpretation sites and outdoor recreation. The Land and Water Conservation Fund Act of 1965 authorized the bureau to dispense matching grants to the various states and local governments along the trail for acquiring such parcels. The report also stressed "interpretations of segments of the Trail" and designation of "existing roads and highways" that followed the original route as closely as possible as portions of a Lewis and Clark Highway.[6]

While anxiety over the closing of the frontier may have stimulated interest in Lewis and Clark at the end of the nineteenth century, anxiety in the 1960s over the loss of parts of the historical landscape almost certainly did the same for stimulating national interest in a designated Lewis and Clark trail. The route's relative isolation following construction of the new interstate highway system probably contributed as well. The traffic flow of tourism in the plains states and the West moved too quickly to make much contact with historical sites associated with Lewis and Clark. Who would search out or even notice the markers and plaques denoting those sites? Donald B. Alexander, executive director of the National Conference on State Parks, complained in 1966 that the expedition had disappeared into the history books and that, except for "a few memorial stones and restored camp sites"—few of which could be seen from the new interstate highways—almost nothing of historical interest remained. More serious, at least for portions of the route, was the fact that the landscape itself had been altered to the point that no access to the original sites remained.[7]

The same year Alexander lamented the fact that superhighways were helping to consign historical remembrance to the ash heap, Roy E. Appleman wrote that "only in the high Bitterroot Range of Idaho and in the badlands of the White Rocks section of the Missouri in Montana can one today see this western wilderness for any considerable extent essentially as Lewis and Clark saw it." Appleman, a National Park Service historian, laments that sites had been obscured or wiped out by industrial activity and especially by dam construction on the Missouri, Snake, and Columbia rivers. Around 2,350 miles of Missouri River bottomland, on which the expedition camped,

Appleman complains, had disappeared beneath the waters of impoundments, accounting for more than 500 miles of shoreline in South Dakota alone.[8] Hydroelectric power dams had shorn the Great Falls of the Missouri and its companion waterfalls of much, and in some cases all, of their spectacular beauty. Camp Fortunate, where Lewis and Clark had conferred with the Shoshone and bargained for horses to cross the mountains and where Sacagawea had immeasurably improved their chances for success by recognizing her brother Cameahwait, was covered over by reservoir waters behind Clark Canyon Dam in 1963. On the Clearwater River at Kamiah, Idaho, a sawmill had obliterated the site of Long Camp, where the expedition had prepared to recross the Bitterroots in the spring of 1806.[9]

In the mid-1960s Ted Yates set out to produce a documentary film for NBC that would tie the landscapes through which Lewis and Clark traveled to descriptions from the expedition's journals. He found the task nearly "impossible." Yates bemoaned the "relentless civilizing" that had made the country Lewis and Clark saw vanish as a result of cultivation, dam building, and other forms of development. As for the Columbia River, Yates found it "impossible to photograph most of the way. Its technology, its wires and signs and roads and motels and picnic sites and highways and barges and locks and docks defied our best efforts to film the wild and awesome river that the explorers wrote about." Even without "road signs and high-tension wires," the Lolo Trail was difficult to photograph, he said, because of the pervasive evidence of clear-cut logging. Yates concluded that he and his crew had, with great difficulty, "reconstructed America to look the way many of us dream [that] it looks," yet they had also managed to add to the "delusion" and "sustain" the myth of American scenic beauty.[10]

The scenes from the journals had largely vanished. "We followed the Missouri River west nearly two thousand miles," Yates later wrote, "before we came upon remnants of the land they saw." The river itself had also changed. "It is corseted, dammed, and polluted, a kind of superbly engineered sewer. . . . Our film remained unexposed until we reached North Dakota," where sixty miles of free-flowing river could be found. Of the Great Falls of the Missouri, in western Montana, Yates noted that the film crew had to arrange "with the Montana Power Company to put some water over one of the falls

Fig 5.1 *Concrete monument marking the site of Camp Fortunate at Armstead, Montana, had to be moved to higher ground when Clark Canyon Reservoir filled in 1963. Photographer unidentified. Courtesy, Beaverhead County Museum, Dillon, Montana.*

---

for us." Numerous dams built by the Army Corps of Engineers had altered aspects of the route along the Snake and Columbia rivers as well. Two of the dams, The Dalles and Bonneville, erased a fifty-five mile stretch of cascades, falls, and rapids through which the Corps of Discovery had passed with great difficulty on both the outward and return trips. In general, it can be said that the mission carried out by the Corps of Discovery ushered in developments that resulted in such alterations to the landscape and the expedition's path of discovery. In any case, the conditions confronting Ted Yates were the same as those that confronted the National Lewis and Clark Commission in 1964, when it began to study and designate a national trail honoring the expedition. Inundated portions of the route represented a particular challenge for interpretation. For this reason, perhaps, public recreation appears to have been as important as history, at least in the case of the lower Missouri, where the emphasis was on developing water recreation sites—something both the Army Corps of Engineers and the Bureau of Reclamation had been pursuing for some time.[11]

Of course, not all changes have been caused by human settlement and industry. Even in Lewis and Clark's time, the Missouri River was in a constant state of flux. Flooding, siltation, and bank erosion created new channels, islands, and bends while abandoning old ones. Floodplain cottonwood groves and thickets of willows and other vegetation grew in some stretches of the river and dried up or were inundated in others, all of which has altered or eliminated many sites associated with the expedition. The most significant locations affected by river activity include the approximate site of Camp Wood, where the Corps of Discovery wintered in 1803–1804 before setting out on the expedition. The bed of the Missouri River has moved several miles to the south, that of the Mississippi has moved east, and the mouth of the Wood River in Illinois has moved northeast. In short, the geographical site today is believed to be on the Missouri side of the Mississippi and well north of the mouth of the Missouri River. The Council Bluffs site, where Lewis and Clark first conferred with Missouri Valley tribes, has moved west three miles from the river into Nebraska. The actual location of the winter camp of 1804–1805, Fort Mandan in North Dakota, has wandered into the body of the stream.[12] Within fifty years of his burial, erosion of the riverbank near Sioux City, Iowa, had threatened the original grave of Sergeant Charles Floyd, the only member of the expedition who perished. In 1857 Floyd's remains were moved 600 feet from the river and re-interred.[13]

Interest in tracing the route Lewis and Clark took by way of the Missouri River, as opposed to land, goes back at least seventy-five years. Few enthusiasts attempted to follow the trail upstream by water, although that had been a common—if hazardous—option by river steamer upstream to Fort Benton, Montana, before completion of the Northern Pacific. The Missouri River was changeable and dangerous, as the expedition journals note abundantly, and the currents were notoriously strong and treacherous at times.[14] In 1928 travel writer Lewis R. Freeman rode a light steel skiff *down* the Yellowstone and Missouri rivers and described his adventure along a portion of the Corps of Discovery's water route in *National Geographic Magazine*. Beginning at Livingston, Montana, Freeman braved whitewater "riffles," snags, and shallow bars as he bobbed down the Yellowstone, carefully noting likely locations and topographical features mentioned in Clark's journal. Freeman floated all the way to the confluence of the Missouri and Mississippi rivers, romantically conscious of the fact that the shorelines were redolent of history. "From the Grand [River] on down," he wrote, "every bend and every bluff was peopled with memories of the men who had blazed the way. Every hedge and point beyond reach of the claws of the river I knew had been looked upon and probably camped upon by earlier explorers."[15]

Upriver attempts to trace the Missouri portion of the route by boat or canoe have encountered much greater difficulty, although east to west has traditionally been the direction to follow the trail, by land or by water. Once the middle Missouri had turned into a series of long lakes, boating likely became a more practical alternative, although in many places the current was actually stronger than it had been during the nineteenth century. In 1968 an eight-person "Lewis and Clark Scientific Field Expedition" from Charles County Community College in La Plata, Maryland, set out in sixteen-foot canoes to follow the route and survey ecological conditions and recreational possibilities. The currents were so much stronger than those the explorers had encountered in 1804, said one member of the group, that "the original expedition couldn't have run upstream with [the Charles County expedition's] equipment." That same summer, seventy-two-year-old Ray Burkett, in a solo attempt to follow the trail upriver, found that he had to exchange the five-horsepower motor with which he had equipped his small boat in St. Louis for a ten-horsepower outboard to make any headway. Even then, he had to upgrade to an eighteen-horsepower outboard before reaching North Dakota.[16] In 1971 a contingent of twenty-nine Green Beret combat veterans from Fort Bragg, North Carolina, made its way up the Missouri, traveling by canoe from St. Louis to Three Forks, Montana, then overland to the Columbia River and down to the site of Fort Clatsop near Astoria, Oregon. Boy Scouts participated in numerous canoe expeditions along various segments of the river, particularly during the sesquicentennial commemorations in 1955. In 1972 the Great Lakes of South Dakota Association joined with Boy Scout groups in the area to establish a Lewis and Clark Historical Canoe Trail from Pickstown, South Dakota, to Sioux City, Iowa.[17]

Despite such attempts to follow the Lewis and Clark route by watercraft, the National Lewis and Clark Commission and its successor organizations faced formidable difficulties in establishing and interpreting a commemorative trail along the middle Missouri River, where the most severe alterations to the original route had taken place. Even before the commission came into being, dams and reservoirs created as part of the massive Pick-Sloan project had obliterated much of the route and displaced descendants of the tribes with which the Corps of Discovery had spent its first winter en route to the Pacific Coast.

This is not to imply that mid–twentieth-century dam builders had ravaged a virgin wilderness. Human attempts to alter the Missouri began long before 1941, when the U.S. Congress authorized the Bureau of Reclamation and the Corps of Engineers to construct the mainstem dams of the Pick-Sloan project. The project, however, had done little to counter the biggest problem in navigating the river—fluctuating water levels. The dugouts and keelboats of the fur trade, as well as the later paddlewheelers that seasonally steamed up the river as far as Fort Benton, faced virtually the same obstacles that had plagued members of the Corps of Discovery in 1804 and 1805. At times, the water on the upper river was too shallow to safely operate large craft. As Stanley Vestal has pointed out, "The trouble with going up the Missouri River in a boat is that you have to take the boat along."[18]

In addition to presenting navigability headaches, the Missouri periodically flooded farms and cities that had grown up in its floodplains. By the 1880s, U.S. Army engineers had begun to systematically remove trees and snags and to attempt to curtail the river's tendency to change course, usually to little avail. Locally financed flood-control levees and efforts by the Corps of Engineers to improve navigation by digging channels were also ineffective in the early twentieth century. Particularly devastating floods in 1943, however, stimulated the U.S. Congress to pass a flood-control act authorizing the Army Corps of Engineers to develop an overall plan for protection along the river's course. Meanwhile, the Bureau of Reclamation was drawing up its own plan for harnessing the Missouri and its tributaries. The Dust Bowl droughts of the 1930s, when populations in the Missouri Basin declined sharply, had added irrigation to the reasons for clearing and stabilizing the river. The many purposes of the massive Missouri River Basin Project, established in 1944, reflected the competing aims of these two agencies. The Corps of Engineers was concerned primarily with flood control, river navigation, and production of hydroelectric power. Colonel Lewis A. Pick, of the Omaha office, proposed a system of dams above Sioux City, Iowa, and levees or channelization on the lower river. The Bureau of Reclamation, for its part, favored development of irrigation, with power production a secondary consideration. The bureau was especially distressed that comprehensive reclamation development in the basin might be adversely affected by the corps' activities in improving river navigability. The bureau's plan, drawn up by William Glenn Sloan, called for a large number of smaller dams and reservoirs and numerous power plants.[19]

The agencies lobbied heavily for their respective proposals—the Pick Plan and the Sloan Plan. But when the U.S. Congress threatened to take responsibility for the Missouri River away from both agencies and set up an independent authority, the corps and the bureau met to find a way to cooperate. What Pick and Sloan eventually agreed on in October 1944 was something less than a compromise, however. Rather than half a loaf, each side settled for the entire plan. The resulting Missouri River Basin Project agreement basically included the main goals of both plans. Eventually, the project was renamed the Pick-Sloan project.[20]

Dam building on the Missouri did not begin with Pick-Sloan, however. The Corps of Engineers had already constructed the massive Fort Peck earth-fill dam in northeastern Montana between 1933 and 1937. The reservoir that filled in behind the dam covers the river's course for 180 miles upstream and is 16 miles wide at its widest point.[21] The first of the Pick-Sloan dams to be completed in the 1950s were Fort Randall and Gavins Point in South Dakota. Garrison Dam in North Dakota, which formed Lake Sakakawea, and Oahe Dam near Pierre, South Dakota, soon followed. The last major main-stem dam in the project was Big Bend, completed in 1963, which backed up Lake Sharpe above Chamberlain, South Dakota.[22] By the time it was completed, the system was presenting a thorny problem for those planning and promoting the commemorative trail. In the late 1960s, however, the National Lewis and Clark Commission shifted its focus to such problems as road access and descriptions of sites that no longer existed above water, thus ignoring an entire aspect of the expedition's historical heritage.

In terms of the lives of Indian peoples, the ecology of the river itself, and the route of Lewis and Clark regarded as an extended historical site, the impact of the Pick-Sloan project must be considered devastating rather than simply underachieving. The economic, social, and cultural costs to Indians who lived in the vicinity of the Missouri River widely overshadow the difficulties of restoring historical authenticity, yet the indirect relationship between the two suggests a dark irony. Inundation of lands behind the new dams had an immediate and lasting impact on descendants of the Indian peoples Lewis and Clark had encountered on the journey upriver in 1804 and with whom the expedition had wintered before setting out for the Pacific Coast in early 1805. As they filled, the Pick-Sloan reservoirs swiftly covered bottomlands used to grow food and shelter livestock by the Three Affiliated Tribes: the Hidatsa, Mandan, and Arikara in North Dakota. The tribes' Fort Berthold Reservation was rent asunder by Lake Sakakawea. Land also disappeared on five Sioux reservations in South Dakota: Standing Rock, Cheyenne River, Yankton, Crow Creek, and Lower Brulé. Lewis and Clark's edgy councils with the Teton (Lakota) Sioux took place just downstream from where the Oahe Dam is today, but the Cheyenne River and Standing Rock reservations would eventually border, and lose ground to, the great reservoir behind the dam.[23]

Altogether, the five dams took away "more than 550 square miles of tribal land and dislocated more than 900 Indian families." Compensation for lost land turned out to be paltry, substituted lands were of poor quality, and the relocation process was traumatic. In addition, the adverse effect on these peoples has not been confined to loss of land. Shore erosion, reduction of fish and game habitat, destruction of bottomland and river ecology, and an inability to utilize many benefits of the projects—for example, electrical power, irrigation, and recreational tourism—are just some of the economic disadvantages for Native Americans that came in the wake of the dam building. In general, Pick-Sloan has damaged attempts to reduce poverty on the reservations and disrupted or destroyed community and traditional culture, severing native peoples from much of the river that had nourished them long after they were sequestered on small reservations.[24] Vine Deloria Jr. has called Pick-Sloan "the single most destructive act ever perpetrated on any tribe by the United States." The same inundations that deprived the Indians of wooded bottomlands also impoverished the natural environment of the upper Missouri and obscured the historical relationship between the two.[25]

The Pick-Sloan and other dams have made seeing the route of Lewis and Clark even remotely the way the explorers saw it a much more strenuous act of imagination. Not only has a considerable portion of the Missouri River become lake, but vegetation, wildlife habitat, and landforms have been obliterated as well. Channelization has corseted the river and cut through its bends, preventing it from spreading out to form or extend zones of vegetation and habitat. Most striking, perhaps, is the loss of timber and shade along many stretches of riverbank.[26] Sites of Indian camps have disappeared, as have the more recent sites occupied by the Corps of Discovery. A survey and search for artifacts initiated in 1946 under the aegis of the Inter-Agency Archeological Salvage Program yielded much archaeological data on plains Indians. But historical points "looked upon and probably camped upon by earlier explorers," at which Lewis Freeman had marveled in his 1928 journey down the Missouri, will be looked upon no more.[27] Gone are most of the sites related to William Clark's description and commentary in the journal entries except those for about a week sometime between August 31 and October 19, 1804, including the Arikara villages upstream from Oahe Dam; from April 9 to April 22, 1805; and from May 10 to May 22, 1805.

These are just the portions of the outward-bound route affected by the Pick-Sloan and Fort Peck reservoirs. Numerous other sites described in the journals and occupied by the expedition are now inaccessible to tourists attempting to trace the route. Even before the reservoirs had filled, it became apparent that one type of accessibility had also disappeared. Roadways that had followed both banks of the Missouri were now under the waters of Lake Sakakawea, Lake Oahe, and other reservoirs in the Dakotas. For a time, there was no way to approach the Lewis and Clark trail by automobile along any of the Pick-Sloan impoundments. On the Columbia River in the Pacific

Northwest, Bonneville Dam, built in the mid-1930s, and The Dalles Dam, built in the mid-1950s, back up reservoirs that cover more than forty miles of the Lewis and Clark route. No longer visible are Celilo Falls, the cascades of The Dalles, or the Short and Long narrows that had bedeviled the expedition on its way both down and back up the river. More portions of the route were inundated by the John Day and McNary dams along the lower Columbia.[28]

The National Lewis and Clark Commission and the Bureau of Outdoor Recreation thus faced a daunting task in proposing ways to mark and interpret a historical route that was, in effect, a linearly extended historical site that now existed primarily in the imagination. The search for recreational opportunities, however, shored up the more tenuous historical aspects. In view of "Ding" Darling's original concerns, the congressional mandate to explore multiple uses is unsurprising, particularly with respect to the Missouri River portion of the route. The Corps of Engineers had already set out to provide water recreation sites on the lakes it had created, and individual states quickly saw an opportunity to copperplate their chances for attracting tourism by dotting the trail with recreational facilities. It is safe to say that nothing that equaled the scope of the National Historic Trail would have been possible without a strong emphasis on outdoor recreation and wildlife preservation.[29] Along much of the Missouri and Columbia rivers, over the preceding two decades the explorers' route had become exceedingly watery. Long segments of both rivers were now chains of reservoirs. The problem of luring tourists off the interstate highways and onto designated trail secondary highways where they would discover history was solved in part by the appeal of a "recreational ribbon" of day-use parks, campgrounds, and boating facilities. Designating and interpreting the proposed historic trail, however, was more complicated.[30]

For tourists, highways would serve as surrogates for the path of exploration, and officially marking the appropriate highways was one of the earliest issues that concerned the commission. For uniformity and continuity, a standard logo had to be agreed upon. In 1964 the Bureau of Outdoor Recreation announced a contest and a $500 prize for the best design, as judged by the J. N. "Ding" Darling Foundation. Although the prize was awarded, the winning insignia "depicting Sacagawea and her baby Baptiste" was not adopted, for reasons undisclosed. Instead, all designated roadways would bear signs depicting Lewis and Clark in silhouette, one holding a rifle and the other pointing, above the words "Lewis and Clark Trail."[31] Also to be worked out were means by which sites along the trail would be interpreted for travelers. South Dakota Historical Society director Will Robinson pointed out that the minimal symbol markers would tell travelers that they were on part of the Lewis and Clark trail but not "what they [the explorers] did here and where did they do it . . . the REAL MEAT of the program." Helping tourists *visualize* events associated with particular places, such as the meeting with the Teton Sioux at the mouth of the Bad River or the first encounter with the Nez Perce in Idaho, might, one federal official thought, "be the most important and perhaps the most difficult aspect of the entire Trail concept."[32]

The National Lewis and Clark Commission spent much time discussing the concept of a "continuous" Lewis and Clark trail highway. At its November 1968 meeting in Portland, Oregon, the commission called upon the U.S. secretary of transportation to seek congressional funds to expedite "the interstate planning and coordination" of such a highway.[33] A few months later, an article in the *Wall Street Journal* conveyed criticisms, such as those levied by Congressman John Kyl of Iowa, that the commission had tried to "expand into the roadbuilding business" with "ambitions [that] were getting it off the track." Sherry Fisher responded that a continuous road was needed because many parts of the trail were far from existing highways. "How in the hell," Fisher is quoted as asking, "is anybody going to enjoy these wilderness areas if you can't get people there so they can look [at them]?"[34]

It is true that the reservoirs had wiped out most road access along the river route, but there were no "wilderness areas" to be found along the middle or lower Missouri River. Still, following the Lewis and Clark route by automobile had become extremely difficult because of river dams, especially in the Dakotas and eastern Montana. A University of Wisconsin professor wrote to Fisher complaining about his frustration in four attempts to follow the expedition route along the Yellowstone and Missouri rivers. "It was all well and good," he wrote, "to mark the highways as you have done," but, for the most part, the highways designated did not come anywhere near the trail in the Dakotas.[35]

Actually, there never had been highways as such along the Missouri River in South Dakota, even before the dams were built. In the 1920s a proposal had surfaced to construct a "River Highway" from Sioux City, Iowa, to the North Dakota line. This route, a South Dakota Highway Commission editorial stated, "would give the tourists a different inspiration of South Dakota . . . a highway that would be both scenic and historic."[36] The proposal was never realized, however. A 1949 highway map of the state indicates, with few exceptions, dirt or gravel road access to the river. By the mid-1960s plans were being drawn up to construct a system of perimeter roads along the reservoirs in South and North Dakota to replace those that had been inundated. A 1965 engineering study report for the South Dakota Department of Highways proposed nearly 422 miles of paved perimeter roads that would provide recreation access. No mention was made of historical significance.[37]

Criticism, such as that reported in the *Wall Street Journal* in May 1969, that the Lewis and Clark Trail Commission was involving itself in road building probably stemmed from state attempts to squeeze the federal government for more construction funding on the excuse that the perimeter roads were integral to the creation of an official Lewis and Clark trail highway across the country.[38] Although it refused to succumb to such a scheme, the commission did resolve to designate new paved reservoir perimeter roads in North and South Dakota as part of the trail.[39] In 1969 the North Dakota Highway Department numbered the new highways 1804 on the east bank and 1806 on the west to commemorate the years in which the expedition passed up the Missouri (1804) and, on its return, back down (1806). Eventually, South Dakota adopted the same numbering system.[40]

By October 1966 the commission had designated the existing highways that would bear the official Lewis and Clark trail signs. It had also held four meetings. Following an organizational meeting in Washington, D.C., in January 1965, the members went to work on September 30 and October 1, 1965, in a meeting at the Old Court House in St. Louis, at which time the Bureau of Outdoor Recreation presented its plan and the commission accepted the highway marker symbol. Among other recommendations made at the meeting were that the Recreation Advisory Council study and appropriately implement the Bureau of Recreation plan, that consideration be given to acquiring the Pompey's Pillar historical site, and that the Lewis and Clark trail be surveyed for archaeological sites in danger of being "destroyed or marred." In addition, the commission recommended that "a fitting memorial to commemorate the achievement of Captain Clark in establishing mutual trust and goodwill [with and among the Missouri River Indian tribes] be erected at an appropriate location along the trail." Following the session, the group traveled by boat to the mouth of the Missouri River and visited a site near the 1803–1804 Wood River encampment, where the state of Illinois was planning to establish a commemorative state park. In mid-February 1966 the commission convened its third meeting in Portland, Oregon, reviewing proposals from various agencies and groups and touring Lewis and Clark sites near the mouth of the Columbia River, including Fort Clatsop in Oregon and Chinook Point, Washington. In early July 1966 commission members took a three-day float on the Yellowstone River and attended "the official dedication of Pompey's Pillar as a registered national historic landmark." Meeting in Billings, Montana, on July 11 and 12, the commission heard reports on progress in designating and marking official Lewis and Clark trail highways and prepared its first interim report to President Richard Nixon and the U.S. Congress.[41]

By the summer of 1966, all the states along the Lewis and Clark route had formed trail committees. Many had had active advisory groups before the creation of the national commission, but these organizations "were given new life by the Commission's actions." The members of these diverse committees included "housewives, bankers, representatives of State agencies, editors, and amateur historians." One of the most active states was Missouri. Governor Warren E. Hearnes appointed a thirteen-member Lewis and Clark Committee in December 1965. In addition, twenty-five Missouri counties responded to the governor's request that each county form its own three-member committee to help promote the trail efforts and "select sites of historic, archeologic, and recreation interest." The state committee held meetings at communities along the Lewis and Clark trail, including Jefferson City, Boonville, and Herman. A regional meeting in St. Joseph that included committee members from Nebraska, Iowa, and Kansas was held to discuss "mutual problems" and exchange ideas. The Missouri State Committee also published a newsletter. State agencies began to acquire lands along the river to develop small lakes and build campgrounds and "group camping facilities." The state legislature passed several laws intended to reduce water pollution in recreation areas.[42]

Kansas, Iowa, and North and South Dakota took similar measures. The Montana Trail Committee noted that the state had 1,650 miles of designated Lewis and Clark highways. Thirty-seven Lewis and Clark historical markers, which the Montana Highway Department had placed on the state's highways "for many years," were being relocated to nearby rest areas. Montana, its delegation reported, had asked the Department of the Interior to designate the part of the Missouri River between Fort Benton and the western end of Fort Peck Reservoir "for immediate Wild River status in pending legislation." The Montana committee also organized an advisory group of "interested and informed persons" who lived along the Lewis and Clark routes to, among other tasks, "help develop educational programs" and recommend specific historical sites. The Idaho legislature donated Spalding State Park and the Canoe Camp site near Orofino to the Nez Perce National Historical Park. In Washington state, interpretive displays were added at Sacajawea State Park south of Pasco, Beacon Rock State Park in the Columbia Gorge, and Fort Columbia State Park across the river from Astoria, Oregon. In addition to acquiring lands for state parks and constructing recreational facilities in the Columbia Gorge, Oregon reported marking the trail across Tillamook Head and the trek to the Salt Cairn from Fort Clatsop.[43]

In May 1968 the Jefferson National Expansion Memorial was dedicated. The stainless steel Gateway Arch, towering 630 feet over the St. Louis riverfront, had originally been authorized in the mid-1930s as a memorial to Thomas Jefferson and the Louisiana Purchase, as well as to the Lewis and Clark Expedition and other developments related to U.S. westward expansion. Historian Hal K. Rothman wrote that the monument "was designed to articulate the glory of the American past and to link it to the future of the nation," but unlike Williamsburg, whose "physical structures" had been restored, the memorial in St. Louis "rehabilitated ideas, giving them new vitality."[44] Both federal and city funds were appropriated for the project, and the National Park Service acquired a site. Architect Eero Saarinen's design was selected in 1949, but the gigantic arch was not built until the 1960s. Construction of the $15 million structure took place between February 1964 and October 1965. The arch easily spans the football field–sized Museum of Westward Expansion, which includes an "overview" of the Lewis and Clark Expedition.[45]

Montana, one of the states along the Lewis and Clark route invited to participate in the dedication of the arch, sent a "display" illustrating the role of the Lewis and Clark Expedition in that state and depicting the paths of the Missouri and Yellowstone rivers. The large Montana group attending the ceremony included several who had volunteered their efforts for years to preserve and interpret Lewis and Clark sites: Orvin B. Fjare, state advertising director and chair of the Montana Lewis and Clark Trail Committee; Harold Stearns, Harlowton publisher and vice chair of the committee; and E. E. "Boo" MacGilvra of Butte, a state committee member.[46] On the Fourth of July 1968, around 2,400 Boy Scouts and their leaders participated in commemorating both the Gateway Arch and the Lewis and Clark Expedition by setting up relays along the route to the Pacific Coast. They traveled by boat and canoe, backpacked, rode bicycles and horses, "floated in rubber rafts," and "piloted motor schooners" to retrace the path the Corps of Discovery had taken.[47]

In addition to publicizing the trail, coordinating the plans presented by various government and private groups, and preparing recommendations, the National Lewis and Clark Commission listened to proposals from organizations and individuals seeking financial support for their projects. Perhaps the most grandiose and interesting proposal for a monument was made in 1968 by sculptor Archie M. Graber, who had designed a "landsculpture . . . for the space age" that would use earth-moving equipment to alter the natural topography at the confluence of the Missouri and Yellowstone rivers and "create cameo-like statues of the explorers" visible from the air, with one head facing east and the other west. This super-heroic commemoration never became reality, but it demonstrates the degree of imaginative vision the commission's mandate inspired.[48]

Another request came from the Lewis and Clark Festival Association in Oregon. The association wanted to build a permanent outdoor amphitheatre in Clatsop County where summer performances dramatizing the expedition could be held. At the National Lewis and Clark Trail Commission meetings in November 1968, Festival Association director Jim Cameron made his pitch for the project, using a miniature model crafted by artist Bill Steidel of Cannon Beach. The theater, estimated to cost between $300,000 and $500,000, "would feature a revolving grandstand with a convertible cover and a man-made body of water to represent the Missouri and Columbia rivers."[49] The sponsoring Festival Association had been formed in 1965 for the purpose of conducting "an annual arts festival" in the Astoria-Seaside area, but the group's first activity—a forty-car caravan that traveled the route to the Salt Cairn—indicated that Lewis and Clark was actually their main consideration.[50] Within two years the Festival Association was seeking a "professional dramatist" to "get the show on the road"—the show being a summer dramatic production called *Oregon Dream* that would depict the part of the expedition that had taken place in the area. *Oregon Dream*, written in part by arts donor and activist Virginia Haseltine, was based on the expedition journals and touted as "highly accurate." It was hoped that the drama would be staged annually at Ecola State Park or elsewhere in Clatsop County. The group set out to raise $4,000 in donations to employ an executive director. Cameron, who had been director of the Portland Civic Theatre, agreed to take on the task. He also coordinated various community theater projects in the vicinity, including those at Clatsop Community College, where he became an instructor.[51]

Finding a permanent location for the performances proved difficult, however, since officials in charge of both Ecola State Park and the Fort Clatsop National Historic Site turned down the proposal. The *Oregon Dream* was not presented that summer. A December 1967 joint meeting of the Oregon Arts Commission, Oregon's Lewis and Clark Trail Advisory Committee, and the Festival Association was to provide the occasion for an evening of readings drawn from the journals, written by Haseltine and directed by Cameron. The presentation was to be multimedia, combining "numerous films, slides, maps, and tape recordings," as well as dramatic readings. Cameron, who had attended "a national convention on outdoor drama," told the association members that he had been strongly encouraged by writers and directors throughout the country, including Paul Green, who won the Pulitzer Prize for an outdoor pageant that had successfully dramatized the Lost Colony at Roanoke for thirty-four years. Green, according to Cameron, pointed out "that we have one of the best stories in the world to tell here . . . it's a natural."[52]

The Festival Association received a $3,000 grant from the National Endowment for the Arts that month. It pressed on with its plans to float a major summer production about the Lewis and Clark Expedition, trying to raise the remainder of the money it needed by presenting musicals and other popular theater offerings. Cameron expressed the hope that an outdoor drama would become a reality "within five years," comparing the possibility with the highly successful Ashland Shakespearean Festival. However, the organization was beginning to run out of operating funds. The 1968 summer season proved financially "bleak," but the outdoor theater proposal revived hope. Unfortunately, the National Lewis and Clark Commission, although impressed by the plan for an outdoor amphitheatre with a revolving stage, could not offer any funding. The idea withered on the vine. In December 1968 the Lewis and Clark Association Festival was forced to release its executive director and relinquish, for the time being at least, the dream of an annual historical extravaganza.[53]

By the time the commission issued its final report in October 1969, much had been done to interpret the trail and to draw public attention to it through various activities, including canoeing and hiking expeditions. Four new National Historic Landmarks had been designated along the trail: Weippe Prairie, north of the Clearwater River in Idaho, and the Portage Route, Camp Disappointment, and Pompey's Pillar in Montana. The commission reported that "the Missouri State Committee identified the probable locations of the Expedition's fifty-two campsites in Missouri." In addition, the Bureau of Land Management had mapped "12 miles of the most probable route of the Expedition in the Lemhi Pass area of Montana and Idaho, located eight of the expedition's campsites in the area, and selected nine additional historical sites on the Yellowstone River," while the Forest Service had installed sixty interpretive signs in national forests in Montana and Idaho and acquired several "key areas along the trail." In Montana, "Mr. and Mrs. Charles Urquhart, Sr., conveyed a Great Falls Portage site to the Boy Scouts of America." Local volunteer organizations initiated projects for establishing and developing additional sites. While relocating "an old Indian graveyard on the banks of the Snake River," archaeologists from Washington State University discovered one of the original Jefferson peace medals "given by Lewis and Clark to important Indian chiefs."[54]

By 1969 numerous memorials had "been dedicated along the Trail," and congressional legislation had changed the name of Garrison Reservoir to Lake Sakakawea. The J. N. "Ding" Darling Foundation paid for a bronze plaque commemorating Captain Clark's "fairness in dealings with the Indians," which "can be considered a measure of his character, since it took place in an era when such treatment was uncommon." The plaque text goes on to extol Clark's success in fostering "mutual trust and good will" with the native peoples, somewhat ironically concluding that "by so doing Clark and his small band of men advanced the western expansion of this nation and strengthened its claim to all of the land in the Missouri River and Columbia River systems."[55]

The creation of a national trails system gave both the National Lewis and Clark Commission and the Bureau of Outdoor Recreation new possibilities to consider.[56] In March 1966, Secretary of the Interior Stewart Udall proposed legislation creating a national system of trails "for hiking, horseback riding, bicycling, and motorbike riding." There would be three categories: scenic long-distance trails, "recreation trails in Federal and State parks and forests, and metropolitan area trails." The same legislation authorized a study of the Lewis and Clark route for inclusion as a national scenic trail. Other proposed scenic trails related to the Lewis and Clark trail included the Oregon, Mormon, Mississippi River, and Santa Fe trails. While these routes would be historically interpreted, generally followed, or paralleled by highways, the proposed Pacific Crest and Continental Divide trails would be primarily for hiking. A Bureau of Outdoor Recreation study that supported the legislation had originated "as a result of a directive in President [Lyndon] Johnson's Natural Beauty Message of February 8, 1965."[57] In 1966 the Bureau of Outdoor Recreation was also directed "to study the Missouri River between Fort Benton, Montana, and Yankton, South Dakota, to determine whether the entire stretch of the river or portions thereof should be managed as a National Recreation Area."[58]

The commission held eleven meetings and three public hearings during its five-year existence—gathering information, promoting public interest, coordinating efforts at all levels, issuing fifty-six resolutions and three reports, and approving an icon for signs to mark highways designated as part of the system.[59] Public and official consciousness had been raised about environmental issues, particularly with respect to clean water. But the process of creating a national historic trail had only begun. In the waning months of its authorized existence, the commission became the focus of controversy over whether it should be extended, since guidance and a high public profile were necessary to maintain momentum for the project. Members at a Portland meeting in early 1969 voted to recommend national legislation that would, in effect, make the commission permanent. Senators Jack Miller (R-Iowa) and Quentin Burdick (D–North Dakota) cosponsored a bill that would have extended the life of the commission to the end of 1974.[60]

Objections quickly followed from different quarters. The *Wall Street Journal* article that had lambasted the commission for promoting road building had also criticized it for blending "historical scholarship and promotional showboating" and "succumbing to crassly commercial tourist promotion."[61] *Life Magazine* called on *all* federal commissions to dissolve themselves, and even Representative John Kyl of Iowa, who had authored the bill creating the National Lewis and Clark Commission, opposed granting indefinite life to temporary commissions on principle.[62] Kyl's suggestion that the commission be replaced by a private organization was echoed by North Dakota commissioner John Greenslit, who also served as coordinator of the North Dakota State Outdoor Recreation Agency. He acknowledged that "a new organization is needed with state initiative," since Congress appeared unlikely to renew the commission.[63] Indeed, the U.S. Congress rejected a bill to extend the National Lewis and Clark Commission for five more years, and it was disbanded in October

1969. Within days, representatives of the eleven states that had participated in the commission's work began to seek ways to continue the project themselves, in cooperation with various citizen volunteer groups and federal agencies.[64]

The initiative now rested with local, state, and regional organizations. In every state that had been represented on the National Lewis and Clark Commission, groups—both public and private—began to implement the commission's recommendations. Even more important, perhaps, the volunteers and state organizations worked to maintain public interest in the Lewis and Clark trail. County committees had been established in Missouri and Iowa. In many of the other eleven states concerned, governors appointed state committees to pick up the slack, but an umbrella organization that would continue to coordinate efforts and keep the idea of a national historic trail in the public eye was clearly needed.[65]

One of the final recommendations the National Lewis and Clark Commission had made was that "one or more groups should be organized to further the broad program" it had originated. In 1970 a nonprofit organization, the Lewis and Clark Trail Heritage Foundation, Inc., was formed for that purpose.[66] Also, a mimeographed publication, *The Lewis and Clark Journal*, edited by G. Edward "Gus" Budde of the Lewis and Clark Trail Committee of Missouri, appeared quarterly during the early 1970s. The publication reported on meetings, legislative efforts, issues related to historical sites, trail development news, and projects supported by the Heritage Foundation. Budde, described in a newspaper article as "one of the last of the old-time publicity men," had "personally retraced" the trail from Wood River to Fort Clatsop eight times.[67] In the winter of 1974–1975 the first issue of *We Proceeded On*, the official publication of the Lewis and Clark Trail Heritage Foundation, noted that the Bureau of Outdoor Recreation was ready to submit legislation to the U.S. Congress to establish historic as well as scenic trails.[68] In the summer of 1976 the Valley County (Montana) Lewis and Clark Trail Society began to publish *A Squawl of Wind*, a periodical dedicated to articles and news about Lewis and Clark sites in northeastern Montana. Much of the writing was done by Bob Saindon of Glasgow, who later served as president of the Lewis and Clark Trail Heritage Foundation.[69]

These and similar activities were dependent on the enthusiasm of Lewis and Clark buffs and others who had long sought to institutionalize a national trail. It seems doubtful that a top-down campaign by the federal government could have maintained interest at such a high pitch through the late 1960s and early 1970s or acted as quickly to preserve threatened landmarks. For example, a group of concerned citizens, led by one-time president of the Montana Historical Society E. E. MacGilvra, sought to save Beaverhead Rock from partial demolition. The rock, located near Twin Bridges northeast of Dillon, was famous as a landmark Sacagawea recognized as the Corps of Discovery moved past the forks of the Jefferson River on August 8, 1805, thereby assuring the explorers that they were close to the ultimate source of the Missouri and to Sacagawea's people. In 1970 most of Beaverhead Rock was on private property and destined to be quarried for "rip-rap," rocks used to line riverbanks. A Butte newspaper claimed that Meriwether Lewis had carved his name on the rock face but that it had been obliterated sometime before 1970 by blasting at the site. Public "resentment" and a letter to the property owner from Senator Mike Mansfield of Montana led to a halt of the blasting, and eventually the site was nominated for protection as a National Historic Place.[70]

While much of the post-commission activity took place at the local and regional levels, the task of developing a plan for legislation to create a national trail fell to the Bureau of Outdoor Recreation within the Department of the Interior. During the early 1970s the bureau began to investigate a way to fit the Lewis and Clark route within the recently enacted National Trails System. The study, which would define "the associated scenic, historic, natural, cultural, and recreational qualities which establish the national significance of the route," focused primarily on the "main river courses . . . within a 10-mile corridor," adhering "as accurately as practicable to the main historic route." One of the criteria for National Scenic Trails was "national significance." The "scenic, historical, natural, or cultural qualities of the areas through which" the trails passed were to be superior to, presumably, run-of-the-mill trails: "National scenic trails should, with optimum development, be capable of promoting interest and drawing power that could extend to any section of the conterminous

United States." Trails "of major historic significance should adhere as accurately as possible to their main historic route or routes." National Scenic Trails were to be several hundred miles long and "primarily land based." Further, they were required to be continuous—that is, not intermittent—and to have access from other trails "at reasonable intervals" as well as allowing for "trips of shorter duration." By 1975 the Pacific Crest Trail and the Appalachian Trail had been so designated, and numerous candidates other than the Lewis and Clark route were being studied—including the Mormon, Santa Fe, Continental Divide, Natchez Trace, Oregon, and Alaska Gold Rush trails. But it was becoming apparent that large segments of the Lewis and Clark trail did not qualify as "land based national scenic trail." Little of the trail had potential for bicycling or hiking, for example, except in specific locales such as parks. However, a "historic" trail alternative soon came into being that would permit a different conception of what constituted a national trail.[71]

The adoption of a National Historic Trail and Travelway category provided for extended routes that were hundreds of miles long. Portions would be used for foot or non-motorized travel, travel along or on waterways, or motorized travel along marked public highways and roads. The trails' national historic significance would be sufficiently documented, and they would be marked by interpretive sites to "provide the user with the intangible elements of historic feeling and association." In a preliminary report (1975), the Bureau of Outdoor Recreation recommended that while the entire 3,700-mile Lewis and Clark route should be so designated, development was to be restricted to 135 miles of land and 2,010 miles of water within twenty-one "selected federally administered and complementing State and locally administered components." Considered a "travelway," authorized segments of the Lewis and Clark route could fit into the designation under less restrictive criteria.

As might be expected, the new routes authorized under this category by the U.S. Congress were to be "substantially of a historic nature" and to "possess exceptional values or qualities which illustrate or interpret the heritage of our Nation." They would be either "recreation/interpretive" trails on which "only travel by foot, horseback, bicycle, or other non-motorized means would be permitted," or they

Fig 5.2 *An expedition to Beaverhead Rock near Twin Bridges, Montana, probably in the 1920s. The rock, an important landmark on the Lewis and Clark trail, was saved from blasting in 1970. Photographer unidentified. Courtesy, Montana Historical Society Research Center, Helena.*

would comprise "selected public highways and roads approximating the historic alignment of a historic route and [be] marked to facilitate retracement of the route by motorized vehicle or bicycle." They could also be a combination of the two. Segments of historic trails and travelways had to "retain much of their historic character" and be largely free of "man-made developments of a disruptive or distracting nature" to be considered. However, segments that ran through agricultural or otherwise developed areas could qualify if they contributed, through "proper interpretation," to the trail user's "knowledge of the country through which the trail passes." Furthermore, although designated highways were expected to closely follow "the route's historic location," exceptions could be made "to maximize recreation opportunities." The implementation of both historic trails and historic travelways was required to preserve wildlife habitat, "fragile areas of vegetation," and archaeological sites, as well as historical sites. Most of the Lewis and Clark trail did not qualify "as a land based national scenic trail" since the expedition had traveled primarily by water, and it was doubtful that the public would make much use of any hiking trail that ran along the original route, even if only on the overland segment.

By the time the Bureau of Outdoor Recreation's final report was completed in April 1977, most of the states along the Lewis and Clark route had established related trail systems and completed the interpretive projects they had pledged to the National Lewis and Clark Commission in the 1960s. Much of the work had been done to locate and mark historical sites related to the expedition. Planned access roads and recreation areas had also been developed by the states, the Bureau of Reclamation, the U.S. Forest Service, and the Army Corps of Engineers. The Bureau of Outdoor Recreation noted that although about 50,000 travelers intersected the trail routes every day by automobile, mostly on interstate highways, only a "very small percentage of the total use of the Lewis and Clark Trail [was] expected to come from people attempting to trace the entire route . . . an arduous task which takes several weeks and would not appeal to most trail users."[73]

The Lewis and Clark National Historic Trail officially came into existence on November 10, 1978.[74] The result on the middle Missouri River turned out to be a necessary compromise in many ways: a travelway rather than a scenic trail in the usual sense, a recreation ribbon through the Dakotas in a segment of the trail where proposed recreation sites outnumber located historical sites by a ratio of nearly three to one. Yet from both the ecological and historical points of view, significant efforts have been made to preserve portions of the river in a way that resembles its state at the time the Corps of Discovery passed along it. The Big Muddy National Wildlife Refuge in Missouri, the Hamburg Bend Wildlife Management Area in Nebraska, and the DeSoto National Wildlife Refuge in Iowa, for example, have resulted from cooperation among the U.S. Fish and Wildlife Service, the Army Corps of Engineers, and other federal and state agencies. Tasks include restoring habitat and countering the negative effects of channelization by digging "chutes," or side channels, through some of the bends to form backwaters and wetlands, thereby allowing the river to "manage itself," to some extent. More than thirty similar projects are planned for the lower Missouri River. Many important historical locations have been spared inundation and remain available in free-flowing segments of the river above and below Bismarck, North Dakota, and downstream from Oahe and other dams. The 149-mile White Rocks section between Fort Benton and the head of Fort Peck Reservoir in Montana has been preserved as part of the National Wild Scenic River System, as have fifty-nine miles in South Dakota and Nebraska, downstream from Gavins Point Dam. Despite 100-foot-deep slack water from the Holter hydroelectric dam north of Helena, Montana, the Gates of the Mountains portion of the route looks much as it did when the expedition encountered it. The Three Forks of the Missouri, as well as the Jefferson River upstream, remain generally unspoiled.[75]

Guidebooks and published accounts of automobile journeys along the Lewis and Clark National Historic Trail began to appear even before the trail bill was signed and rapidly proliferated as the nation prepared for the expedition's bicentennial in 2003–2006, demonstrating the importance of motor routes for public appreciation of the new national trail and of autotourism for personal exploration of the West. In 1978, for example, Archie Satterfield, a member of the Washington State Lewis and Clark Trail Committee, published a short narrative on the expedition and an account of an automobile tour he and his family took from the Pacific Coast eastward along most of the Lewis and Clark route. Much of the book summarizes the history of the expedition, but in an appendix Satterfield describes the look of "the trail today," in the tradition of Wheeler and Gray, and includes a series of maps depicting segments of the route and a key to trail sites and recreational areas and facilities.[76]

On their journey east, the Satterfield family sought to explore the Lewis and Clark route (as well as provide grist for a book), but they did not pursue the quest as dedicated expedition buffs. As is the case with most vacationers who follow the trail, they were also looking for recreational opportunities and were selective in choosing which historical sites to visit. In his book, Satterfield offers a short, chatty narrative of his family's summer trip to Missouri, which included inspection of only some segments of the Lewis and Clark route. He wrote that he did not recommend following "the exact route," much of which he considered "uninteresting" (for example, the locations of Traveler's Rest, Canoe Camp, and Camp Disappointment on Cut Bank Creek). "There is no sense of discovery involved," he wrote, "while standing elbow-to-elbow with a crowd of people atop Pompey's Pillar." He was also unimpressed with Lolo Pass.[77]

While it is not clear what qualifications a site had to possess to impart "moments of illumination" or a "sense of discovery," the Satterfields went on to visit Giant Springs and the Great Falls of the Missouri, the Gates of the Mountains, and the general location of Camp Fortunate, vowing to hike up to Lemhi Pass on a future trip. From there they took in Yellowstone National Park before rejoining the trail at Livingston, Montana, and following the Yellowstone River down to Fort Union, near the location where the Yellowstone meets the Missouri: "We drove down the Missouri a few miles on a road so rough that we expected at almost any minute to find it dead-ending in some rancher's corral."[78] The next day they drove to a point near Washburn, North Dakota, to see the replica of Fort Mandan built in the late 1960s and early 1970s by the McLean County Historical Society. After traveling south through Pierre, South Dakota, and Sioux City, Iowa, where they stopped to visit the Sergeant Floyd monument, Satterfield and his family left the Lewis and Clark route. "Below Sioux City," Satterfield complained, "the Missouri River loses nearly all its remaining charm and becomes less and less a river. Instead, it is something of a liquid highway. So we gave up our diligent route tracing and drove directly south to visit my family."[79]

Much more thoughtful and introspective is the approach to tracing Lewis and Clark's path by road and highway taken by author and filmmaker Dayton Duncan. Duncan expressed the feelings of many in his 1987 account, *Out West: An American Journey*: "The route I plan to take—and the spirit in which it is followed—will be the same as theirs. Nearly everything else will be vastly different."[80]

CHAPTER SIX

Commemoration and Authenticity on the Trail

E

VEN BEFORE THE U.S. CONGRESS officially added the Lewis and Clark trail to the National Scenic Trail system, interest in the history of the expedition was heightened by the nation's bicentennial, celebrated in 1976. Within a few years of that event, the Lewis and Clark Trail Heritage Foundation began to establish local chapters. Eventually, individual chapters all along the trail began to host the organization's annual summer meetings, at which members attended lectures on various topics, watched costumed reenactments, visited nearby expedition sites, and socialized. In 1980, nearly two years after the creation of the National Historic Trail, Bert Hansen's pageant was revived at the Three Forks of the Missouri. To commemorate the 175th anniversary of the expedition's arrival at the headwaters, Nick Nixon of Bozeman, Montana, wrote and produced a revised version of the pageant, which was performed at Missouri

Headwaters State Park on July 26 and 27, 1980.[1] The performance by a cast of forty took place between the west side of Fort Rock and the river. The roles of "Sacajawea" and her brother Cameahwait were played by Oliviane Baier of Bozeman, a White Mountain Apache, and Rodger Spotted Eagle of Three Forks, a Blackfeet, while many other Native Americans appeared as villagers and Indian horseman. The same cast performed the pageant the following summer, aided by the Waa-No-Inee-Git Indian dancers.[2]

While Native Americans participated in the expedition's sesquicentennial, major differences in their attitudes toward it and future events have developed over the past fifty years. The Salish Indians who took part in Bert Hansen's 1955 pageants in Three Forks and Missoula, for example, added authenticity and color to what were essentially celebrations of the Lewis and Clark Expedition. The same might be said of members of the Nez Perce tribe who camped that summer by the Clearwater River at Lewiston, Idaho, and of lower Columbia River Indians who appeared at sesquicentennial ceremonies in Astoria, Oregon. Those who claimed to be direct descendants of "Sacajawea" appeared as featured guests in major sesquicentennial functions and pageants. By the end of the twentieth century, however, Native Americans who lived along the route had become divided in their opinions about the upcoming bicentennial and of Lewis and Clark in general. These opinions ran the gamut from bitter opposition, on one hand, to a desire to at least share in the expected profits and to use the event as a springboard for educating non-Indians about Indian history.

Even those who supported participation in the bicentennial argued that it should be a commemoration rather than a celebration. Their view, shared by bicentennial organizers, was that one commemorates an event or individuals to remember them in significant ways rather than necessarily to exalt them. There is often bitterness in recognizing the cost to Native American peoples of the expansion of white America that followed in the wake of the Corps of Discovery. The journals themselves offer cause for resentment: for example, the attitudes Clark expressed about the Teton band of Lakota that confronted the expedition in South Dakota or Lewis's account of the fracas near the Marias River that resulted in the deaths of two Piegan Blackfeet warriors. A traditional Blackfeet explanation of what happened insists that the "warriors" were actually twelve- and thirteen-year-old boys who had been invited to camp overnight with Lewis and his men but who were attacked when they tried to leave during the night. This account denies, however, that the Piegans tried to steal a rifle and a horse. Morever, many Blackfeet today appear to regard Lewis and Clark with either indifference or anger—as insignificant or villainous.[3]

This attitude is widely shared. At a 1992 conference at the University of Montana, held to discuss the expedition's impact, scholar Betty White—a member of the Salish tribe—criticized the explorers for the way they dehumanized the native peoples they encountered, treating them as objects in the same cold, "scientific" way they treated plant specimens. White also excoriated the expedition for its mission to spy in the far West in preparation for the ultimate conquest and destruction of the region's native inhabitants.[4] In 2004 a reenactment of the Corps of Discovery's meeting with Teton Sioux at Fort Pierre, South Dakota, met with protest from twenty Lakota tribal members, one of whom carried an upside-down American flag and another a sign accusing the explorers of "genocide." The group promised to carry on its protest at other commemorative reenactments upriver. Even tribal members who participated in the reenactment expressed agreement with the protesters.[5]

As was the case with the paid Lakota reenactors at Fort Pierre, commemoration of historical events does not necessarily entail approval of those events, but it can offer profitable advantages and an opportunity to reassess the past.[6] This was clearly evidenced in a resolution passed by the National Congress of American Indians in 2001 entitled "Preparation for, and the Safeguarding of, Native American Interests during the Lewis and Clark Bicentennial Commemoration." In addition to the demand that Indian peoples benefit economically from the festivities, the resolution, among other things, called for the opportunity to educate visitors about "culturally appropriate and legal conduct in, on and near Indian lands," to "restore vitality to fragile and irreplaceable natural resources," to "rejuvenate" native culture, and to "unite" native communities.[7]

In addition to Native Americans' points of view, an array of differing opinions regarding not only Lewis and Clark but commemorative heritage sites in general has arisen over the years since the Lewis and Clark National Historic Trail came into being. In the introduction to their collection of essays on "American sacred space," editors David Chidester and Edward T. Linenthal note that the movement to preserve and manage historical sites in an effort to promote "patriotic orthodoxy" and national unity has ignored diverse and competing views of history and of the sacredness of historical space.[8]

To some extent, this diversity of opinion reflects or parallels historians' competing interpretations. But it is also grounded in the multifarious claims of popular memory, the imaginative and symbolic engagements with the past that Pierre Nora has described as essential to different groups' identities. In John Bodnar's terms, it might be said that diverse views of the past emerge at both the "vernacular" and local levels. Both Nora and Bodnar see interaction between commemorative expressions of popular memory and those instigated and supported by government. For Nora, historical commemoration (in France) underwent a shift in the decades following World War II, from "the concentrated expression of a national history" to growing accommodation by the state to "a series of initiatives with no central organizing principle, each subject to the overlapping and intersecting influences of the media, the tourist trade, the entertainment industry, and advertising and marketing." However, Nora's explanation of this breakdown within French national history clearly does not apply to the United States because of much different circumstances. For example, Nora ascribes the change in France to the country's decline as a world power after the mid-twentieth century, but the United States has assumed increasingly greater global power and influence during that same period. Also, as this book has shown with respect to Lewis and Clark, the media, tourism, entertainment, and advertising have always shared the stage in historical commemoration.[9]

Regarding the "official," or governmental, role, Bodnar points out that institutional and cultural leadership in the United States has tended to adopt and channel "vernacular" expressions of public memory as means of serving the demands of unity, patriotism, and nationalism.[10] Yet preparations for the Lewis and Clark bicentennial seemed to indicate that a new spirit of cooperation had developed during the last few decades of the twentieth century between official and grassroots, or local, efforts. Furthermore, greater sensitivity to multicultural views has made commemoration in general more inclusive and less Anglo- or Eurocentric. The resulting input on issues involving historical commemoration seems to parallel Erika Doss's observation, in reference to public art, that controversy has been largely resolved by open debate, demonstrating "an outstanding example of how cultural democracy is being rediscovered and reconsidered."[11]

The meaning of the Lewis and Clark Expedition for most Americans has developed over time, especially in the last half century, adding the respect for scientific accomplishment inherent in the "literate elite" image to the glorification of national exploration and expansion characteristic of the "folk" image. The ways such common meanings are commemorated have changed as well. The Lewis and Clark National Historic Trail has become a vehicle for public education, although historian Mark Spence has pointed out that serious consideration of the legacies of the Lewis and Clark Expedition has been overwhelmed by a "tourism juggernaut." Commemorations, interpretation centers, and various promotions spurred by the bicentennial tended to portray the expedition primarily as a great adventure into the wilderness. Spence argues that the journals do not constitute a literary epic and that sentimentalizing or romanticizing the exploits of Clark, Lewis, and the other expedition members can only obscure an understanding of their purposes and of how our national attitudes toward nature are derived from the past.[12]

In general, relationships between the publicly perceived meaning of the Lewis and Clark trail and ways the significance of that trail is represented help shed light on ways the American public views its history, particularly with respect to questions of interpretation and authenticity. Interpretation, in this case, usually means establishing historical context and conveying portions of the narrative in as succinct and simple a manner as possible. It zeros in on *fact* and on the relation of fact to place. As Michael Kammen points out, the American public has come to suspect any other forms of historical interpretation and to believe that "trustworthy history consists of true facts . . . accurately organized and presented. No more and no less."[13]

Authenticity is the desired effect, one that appears to confer most of the educational value on which the appeal to tourism is based. In this sense, authenticity means genuine, realistic, and accurate. But in reality its meaning is rarely straightforward, even in terms of visitors' experience and perceptions of historic sites. Since the mid-1990s, considerable scholarly attention has been paid to questions regarding both historical interpretation of heritage tourist sites and historical authenticity. What counts as authentic or even simply genuine can change as cultural values and expectations change. Early–twentieth-century historical pageants appeared less genuine and real to audiences fifty years later. Bert Hansen's pageant scripts from the 1950s may seem stilted and artificial to audiences today. In addition, historical authenticity depends largely on interpretation, both visual and textual, and such interpretation tends to eliminate other possibilities of, and viewpoints on, history. Authenticity, for example, may embody richness and depth of meaning (closer to the way historians would define the word) or aesthetic considerations. An obvious problem for the creation and management of heritage sites is how to offer an interpretation that will at least appear authentic to the largest number of tourists. What appears to be authentic may not actually be so in the most objective sense. In other words, tension seems to exist between factual accuracy, on one hand, and interpretation processed to satisfy the present-day visitor to historical sites, on the other.[14]

Reproductions, which have the effect of bringing the past vividly into the present, represent one aspect of that tension. For example, such replicas as Fort Mandan on the Missouri River and Fort Clatsop near the mouth of the Columbia River—based on plans described in the Lewis and Clark journals—may have more authenticity for the modern tourist than would preserved ruins (if they existed). While carefully constructed replicas seem satisfying, any tampering, if apparent to the visitor, adversely affects a site's perceived authenticity. Yet certain kinds of unavoidable distortion remain transparent to the visitor.[15] Tourism scholar Peirce Lewis notes that the very existence of markers, viewing points, graphic and textual signs, and other interpretive aids contrives to "funnel our attention and to isolate the historical site from its present-day surroundings, roping off certain sites, as if everything else around them was *not* historical or worth paying attention to."[16] Thus, historical tourism often becomes a matter of hurrying from one sanctified and somewhat artificial site to the next, with little regard for what lies between. The modern highway system gives tourists the freedom to do just that.

Automobile tourism, especially the quest for historical sites and specific scenic attractions, has been a bonanza for small towns throughout the West. This is particularly true for those not located on railroad trunk lines or near popular tourist destinations. Communities quickly exploited whatever curiosities, landscapes, or historical claims to fame they possessed or could create in the public mind through promotion. In this quest they were aided by state and federal historical markers and monuments, as well as by commercial organizations that advertised vacation highway loops and routes that offered motorists the most efficient use of their travel time. Making contact with the historical past increasingly became a major motivation to explore the West by automobile after World War II. As historian John Jakle has noted, "Historical sites offered a sense of permanence in an ever-evolving world of new, highly standardized landscapes."[17]

As economic expansion wiped out material traces of that past and threatened the ties to national identity that historical consciousness provides, pressure grew to preserve physical manifestations of, and links to, the past. Members of the middle class who began to support environmental preservation in the 1960s tended to also support historical preservation. The fact that attitudes in western communities, large and small, began to change from those of "slash-and-burn renewal" to preservation of historic structures during this period can be seen as the result of both a new preservationist ethic and awareness of the commercial opportunities inherent in convincing tourists that an authentic historical past was available for their enjoyment and for the education of their children.[18] While most communities had to rely on their ties to individual historical events, those on or near the routes of the Corps of Discovery could exploit a broad continuity that connected them to other towns and to a unified theme; they did not have to establish completely different appeals or draw potential tourists away from other attractions. The Lewis and Clark trail potentially represented a linearly extended heritage site, in many ways the perfect raison d'être for a designated tourist route. Yet it faced problems of access and interpretation. By the mid-twentieth century, dams on the Missouri and Columbia rivers had inundated sites along a considerable portion of the trail. Although a few enthusiasts traveled those segments by water, in boats and canoes, the general public would not do so. To identify in the public mind secondary highway routes with this linearly extended site and provide adequate interpretation, initially, an effort was needed to institutionalize the expedition's route as a National Historic Trail.

While public representation of the Lewis and Clark Expedition and its relationship to a far-flung sequence of geographic sites focuses on fact and narrative over interpretation and analysis, the trail has some unusual characteristics and a unique authenticity. For one thing, the Lewis and Clark trail exists more as an imaginative construct than do most other heritage objects, such as buildings and historic districts. Administered today by the National Park Service, the trail constitutes little more than interpretation added to landscape; that interpretation, largely in the form of official signage, instantiates our understanding of the expedition's journals. The Lewis and Clark National Historic Trail can be considered a sort of historical replica that extends for thousands of miles—"replica" because virtually no trace remains of the expedition's journey, and much of the route today is covered by water. Except for William Clark's etching of his name and the date on Pompey's Pillar during his party's return along the Yellowstone River, no known trace of the route has survived. Relics left behind (as opposed to those purposely sent east) are also few: they include only some Jeffersonian peace medals and a branding iron bearing Lewis's initials.

Since virtually no traces of the Corps of Discovery remain upon the landscape, replicas of structures, salt cairns, and dugout canoes must fill the gap. Reconstructing the Lewis and Clark trail essentially demands such an approach. The fact that signs and other interpretive figurations subtly alter the historical landscape and condition our perception of it, as Euro-American settlement and industrial and agricultural development more obviously have, is beside the point if the entire trail is viewed as a sort of imaginative replica. Linkages between the journals and the trail as a linearly extended heritage site, on the one hand, and between the trail and the landscapes through which it runs, on the other, may inspire in the visitor an imaginative vision that overcomes the impress of progress and civilization. At best, the trail and the transformed landscape may blend in the viewer's mind to reestablish continuity between past and present. It is much more likely, however, that tourists will try to see what is *not* there—unfettered waterfalls on the upper Missouri and lower Columbia rivers or the Bitterroot forest as Lewis and Clark saw it, for example—and not see what actually *is* there: extensive clear-cuts, high-power transmission lines, hundreds of miles of reservoirs, paper mills, cabins, towns, and so forth.

For more than twenty years, efforts continued to carry out the general recommendations of the National Lewis and Clark Commission, and it is safe to say that the bicentennial commemoration—particularly as manifested in the Lewis and Clark National Historic Trail—both reflected and molded public attitudes toward this historical enterprise. Today, the National Park Service has overall responsibility for the trail, but development and management of individual sites have largely been carried out by other agencies and organizations. By the end of the twentieth century there were four major interpretive centers along the route: the Jefferson National Expansion Memorial and the Gateway Arch in St. Louis, the Fort Clatsop National Monument and Interpretive Center near Astoria, Oregon, the North Dakota Fort Mandan Interpretive Center at Washburn, and a newer Lewis and Clark Interpretive Center in Great Falls, Montana. Located along the Missouri River, just upstream from the Rainbow Falls overlook, the Great Falls center opened with a week-long celebration in July 1998. As the bicentennial approached, existing facilities—such as Cape Disappointment (Fort Canby State Park) at the mouth of the Columbia River in Washington state, the Nez Perce National Historic Park in Spalding (donated by the state of Idaho), and the Lolo Pass Interpretive Center on the Montana-Idaho state line (renovated in 2002)—were joined by numerous other commemoration locations, including the Sacajawea Interpretive Cultural and Education Center in Salmon, Idaho; the Travelers' Rest State Park and National Historic Landmark near Lolo, Montana; Pompey's Pillar National Monument on the Yellowstone River northeast of Billings, Montana; and the Wood River/Camp Dubois State Park in Illinois.[19]

The route taken by the Corps of Discovery and its institution-alization as the Lewis and Clark National Historic Trail represent the fusing of two twentieth-century phenomena: the rise of auto tourism as a form of personal exploration, or "frontiering," and the movement to establish an authentic historical heritage as a basis for both education and commercial opportunity. For modern auto tour-ists, the designated highway—with its distinctive periodic logo signs depicting the explorers pointing the way—merges with, and become equivalent to, the trail itself. After all, except for the occasional canoe trip or chartered boat ride, it is virtually the only way to experience the route. Passing through eleven states between Illinois and Oregon, this is not primarily a hiking trail. Further, unlike the Santa Fe Trail, none of it has been romanticized as a major tourist destination. With the exceptions of Interstate 84 through the Columbia Gorge in Oregon and Interstate 90 along the Yellowstone River in Montana, most of the highways along or adjacent to the route of exploration are secondary, two-lane roads. To follow the trail is to abandon the interstate superhighway and explore "blue" highways and even the occasional unpaved road, such as the one that crosses the Continental Divide at Lemhi Pass or the more treacherous Lolo Motorway, Forest Road 500 in Idaho.

Although it faces challenges of interpretation similar to those of other heritage projects, the Lewis and Clark trail has enjoyed unique advantages, not the least of which is the way viewers con-tinually reinforce its historical authenticity through reenactments. Like recreational tourism, this form of heritage tourism invites par-ticipation rather than simple observation. But in terms of historical consciousness, the trail has also bound together communities in the northern mountain states and the Pacific Northwest with those in the Midwest and the high plains, a web of interrelationships that was only strengthened by the 200th anniversary commemoration of the Lewis and Clark Expedition.

Notes

INTRODUCTION

1. Helen B. West, "Lewis and Clark Expedition: Our National Epic," *Montana: The Magazine of Western History* 16, no. 3 (July 1966): 3–5.

2. Pierre Nora, "General Introduction," in *Realms of Memory: Rethinking the French Past,* vol. 1, ed. Pierre Nora, trans. Arthur Goldhammer (New York: Columbia University Press, 1996), 18.

3. Pierre Nora, "The Era of Commemoration," in ibid., vol. 3 (1998), 636.

4. John Bodnar, *Remaking America: Public Memory, Commemoration, and Patriotism in the Twentieth Century* (Princeton, N.J.: Princeton University Press, 1992), 13.

5. Ibid., 15.

6. Wilbur Zelinsky, *Nation into State: The Shifting Symbolic Foundations of American Nationalism* (Chapel Hill: University of North Carolina Press, 1988), 80.

NOTES

7. John Mullan, handwritten draft of speech at Fort Owen, Montana, December 24, 1861, 31 and 38, SC 547, Montana Historical Society archives, Helena (hereafter referred to as MSHS).

8. Paul Allen, ed., *History of the Expedition under the Command of Captains Lewis and Clark to the Sources of the Missouri, Thence across the Rocky Mountains and down the River Columbia to the Pacific Ocean. Performed during the Years 1804–5–6* (Philadelphia: Bradford and Inskeep, 1814) (This is usually referred to as the Biddle edition; Nicholas Biddle began the editing, but Allen completed it); Elliott Coues, ed., *History of the Expedition under the Command of Lewis and Clark*, a new edition in four volumes (New York: Francis P. Harper, 1893).

9. Paul Russell Cutright, *A History of the Lewis and Clark Journals* (Norman: University of Oklahoma Press, 1976), 77, 80–81, 88 (original emphasis).

10. Reuben Gold Thwaites, ed., *Original Journals of the Lewis and Clark Expedition, 1804–1806*, 8 vols. (New York: Dodd, Mead, 1904–1905).

11. Cutright, *History of the Lewis and Clark Journals*, 227 (original emphasis); Olin D. Wheeler, *The Trail of Lewis and Clark 1804–1904*, 2 vols. (New York: G. P. Putnam's Sons, 1926).

12. Donald Jackson, "The Public Image of Lewis and Clark," *Pacific Northwest Quarterly* 57, no. 1 (Jan. 1966): 1–2.

13. Milo M. Quaife, ed., *The Journals of Captain Meriwether Lewis and Sergeant John Ordway* (Madison: State Historical Society of Wisconsin, 1916); Ernest Staples Osgood, ed., *Field Notes of Captain William Clark, 1803–1805* (New Haven: Yale University Press, 1964); Donald Jackson, ed., *Letters of the Lewis and Clark Expedition with Related Documents, 1783–1854* (Champaign: University of Illinois Press, 1962); Bernard DeVoto, ed., *The Journals of Lewis and Clark* (New York: Houghton Mifflin, 1953).

14. John L. Allen, " 'Of This Enterprize': The American Images of the Lewis and Clark Expedition," in *Voyages of Discovery: Essays on the Lewis and Clark Expedition*, ed. James P. Ronda (Helena: Montana Historical Press, 1998), 268–269 (second quote), 270 (first quote).

15. Ibid., 261–263, 276.

16. Zelinsky, *Nation into State*, 29.

17. Michael Frisch, "American History and the Structures of Collective Memory: A Modest Exercise in Empirical Iconography," *Journal of American History* 75, no. 4 (March 1989): 1132, 1140.

18. Jackson, "Public Image of Lewis and Clark," 4.

19. Allen, "Of This Enterprize," 276.

20. E. W. Carpenter, "A Glimpse of Montana," *Overland Monthly and Out West Magazine* 2, no. 4 (April 1867): 379–380.

21. C. M. Scammon, "In and Around Astoria," *Overland Monthly and Out West Magazine* 3, no. 6 (December 1869): 495–499.

22. Josiah Copley, "The Rocky Mountains," *Debow's Review* 4, no. 6 (June 1843): 521; William Bradford, "Discovery, Characteristics, and Resources," *Debow's Review* 20, no. 5 (May 1856): 549; J.D.B. Debow, "Climate of the United States," *Debow's Review* 23, no. 5 (November 1857): 507.

CHAPTER 1: MONUMENTS

1. Carl Abbott, *The Great Extravaganza: Portland and the Lewis and Clark Exposition* (Portland: Oregon Historical Society, 1981), photo facing p. 1, 12–14.

2. Ibid., 3.

3. Burton Benedict et al., *The Anthropology of World's Fairs: San Francisco's Panama Pacific International Exposition of 1915* (Berkeley: Scolar Press and the Lowie Museum of Anthropology, 1983), 6–7.

4. Robert W. Rydell, *All the World's a Fair: Visions of Empire at American International Expositions, 1876–1916* (Chicago: University of Chicago Press, 1984), 18–19.

5. Warren L. Susman, *Culture as History: The Transformation of American Society in the Twentieth Century* (New York: Pantheon Books), 1984. For an example of the phrase "our national epic," see Helen B. West, "Lewis and Clark Expedition: Our National Epic," *Montana: The Magazine of Western History* 16, no. 3 (July 1966): 4–5, although the phrase was used as early as the 1905 exposition in Portland.

6. *Lewis and Clark Journal: Official Publication of the Lewis and Clark Fair* (February 1904): 4.

7. Ann Rogers, "We Met Them at the Fair: Lewis and Clark Commemorated at the 1904 Louisiana Purchase Exposition," part 1, *We Proceeded On* 21, no. 3 (August 1995): 21–22; part 2, 21, no. 4 (November 1995): 21.

8. Karal Ann Marling, *George Washington Slept Here: Colonial Revivals and American Culture, 1876–1986* (Cambridge: Harvard University Press, 1988), 156.

9. H. W. Scott, "Historical Significance of the Lewis and Clark Expedition," *Lewis and Clark Journal: Official Publication of the Lewis and Clark Fair* 1, no. 1 (January 1904): 6.

10. Abbott, *Great Extravaganza*, 3, 16.

11. Scott, "Historical Significance," 7.

12. Ella E. Clark and Margot Edmonds, *Sacagawea of the Lewis and Clark Expedition* (Berkeley: University of California Press, 1979), appendix D: Sacagawea Memorials.

13. Donna Kessler, *The Making of Sacagawea: A Euro-American Legend* (Tuscaloosa: University of Alabama Press, 1996), 55.

14. Esther Burnett Horne and Sally McBeth, *Essie's Story: The Life of a Shoshone Teacher* (Lincoln: University of Nebraska Press, 1998), 144–148.

15. Ibid.

16. Laura McCall, "Sacagawea, a Historical Enigma," in *Ordinary Women, Extraordinary Lives: Women in American History*, ed. Kriste Lindenmeyer (Wilmington, Del.: SR Books, 2000), 39.

17. Ibid., 40.

18. Historian Grace Hebard championed the Wind River tradition in *Sacajawea: A Guide and Interpreter of the Lewis and Clark Expedition* (Glendale, Calif.: A. H. Clark, 1933).

19. Horne and McBeth, *Essie's Story*, 148–150. The authors point out (p. 150) that mixed feelings toward Sacagawea developed on the Wind River Reservation, with many viewing her as a cause of Indian woes because she helped Lewis and Clark.

20. Ibid., 150–151.

21. McCall, "Sacagawea, a Historical Enigma," 48.

22. Kessler, *Making of Sacagawea*, 66–67; Eva Emery Dye, *The Conquest: The True Story of Lewis and Clark* (Chicago: A. C. McClurg, 1902).

23. *Lewis and Clark Journal: Official Publication* (February 1904): 26.

24. Ronald W. Taber, "Sacagawea and the Suffragettes: An Interpretation of a Myth," *Pacific Northwest Quarterly* 58, no. 1 (January 1967): 7–11.

25. Kessler, *Making of Sacagawea*, 90.

26. Bert Huffman, [untitled poem], *Lewis and Clark Journal* (January–March 1904): 8–9.

27. Laura Tolman Scott, paper presented to the Montana Federation of Women's Clubs, Lewistown, Montana (June 1914), VF 2606, Washington State University Special Collections, Pullman. In North Dakota the preferred spelling is the Hidatsa "Sakakawea"; most historians use Sacagawea.

28. Stone marker quotes in "Historical Sites Preserved and Markers Erected by the Montana Society, Daughters of the American Revolution and Its' [sic] Chapters," VF, MSHS.

29. Eva Emery Dye, *The Conquest: The True Story of Lewis and Clark* (New York: Grosset & Dunlap, 1914).

30. Scott, paper to the Montana Federation of Women's Clubs.

31. Marker description and Clark quoted in Carroll van West, "Montana's Monuments: History in the Making," *Montana: The Magazine of Western History* 40, no. 4 (Fall 1990): 17.

32. Zillah Harris's lullaby in unattributed news story, "What Became of Sacajawea?" dated April 9, 1916, Astoria (Oregon) Heritage Museum VF, C-boxes.

33. "Historical Sites Preserved and Markers Erected by the Montana Society, DAR . . . 1899–1917," VF Lewis and Clark Expedition—Statuary, Markers, Monuments, etc. MSHS.

34. Brass plate inscription from Harris, "What Became of Sacajawea?"

35. Mobridge monument in *The Wi-Iyohi* (monthly bulletin of the South Dakota Historical Society) 8, no. 5 (August 1, 1954): 9.

36. Astoria (Oregon) *Evening Budget*, February 10, 1922.

37. Michael Kammen, *Mystic Chords of Memory: The Transformation of Tradition in American Culture* (New York: Alfred A. Knopf, 1991), 505.

38. More spectacular than the grave markers for Clark and Lewis is that of Sergeant Charles Floyd near Sioux City, Iowa. The 100-foot sandstone obelisk dedicated to Floyd, the only member of the Corps of Discovery who died during the expedition, was dedicated in 1901. In 1960 it became the first registered National Historic Landmark, a category created in part as a compromise between Iowa's congressional delegation and the National Park Service, which refused to accept a gravesite as an official historic site. Barry MacKintosh, *The Historic Sites Survey and the National Historic Landmarks Program, a History* (Washington, D.C.: Historical Division, National Park Service, Department of the Interior, 1985), 41–46.

39. *The Unveiling of the Lewis-Clark Statue at Midway Park in the City of Charlottesville, Virginia* (Charlottesville, Va.: City of Charlottesville, 1919), frontispiece.

40. Astoria *Evening Budget*, July 22, 1926; John E. Goodenberger, "Column Tells Astoria's Story," *Daily Astorian 125th Anniversary Issue*, September 25, 1998. Time and weather, in fact, would not be kind to the decorative historical frieze that covers the Astoria Column. According to the 125th anniversary issue, Pusterla returned ten years later to restore his deteriorating artwork. Subsequent efforts would also be required to protect the frieze, most recently the application of a water repellent in 1995, which, it is hoped, "will preserve the column for another 50 years or more" (Goodenberger, "Column Tells Astoria's Story").

41. Astoria (Oregon) *Daily Astorian Centennial Edition*, July 22, 1976.

42. Astoria (Oregon) *Evening Budget*, July 22, 1976.

43. Description of 1925 and 1926 Columbia River historical expeditions from Michael Kammen, *In the Past Lane: Historical Perspectives on American Culture* (New York: Oxford University Press, 1997), 134–138.

44. Astoria (Oregon) *Evening Budget*, July 21, 1926.

45. Seaside (Oregon) Chamber of Commerce press release, April 29, 1968, LC VF, Astor Library, Astoria, Oregon.

46. Jane Steel, "Misspelling on End of Trail Sign at Beach Draws Attention," *Daily Astorian*, March 16, 1967.

47. The history of the early attempts to fund the statues discussed in this paragraph is from Dr. H. J. Wunderlich (Lewis and Clark Bicentennial Celebration Committee) to Montana Governor Stan Stephens, February 9, 1991, VF Lewis and Clark Expedition X Statuary, Markers, Monuments, etc. MSHS.

48. H.B. 167, 15th Session, Montana Legislative Assembly, 1917, *House Journal*, 167, 305, 637.

49. "History of the Henry Lion Bronze, etc.," VF MHS, Lewis and Clark Memorial Committee, MSHS.

50. "The Three Forks of the Missouri River: Logical Site of a National Memorial to Captains Lewis and Clark" (Three Forks, Montana: Chamber of Commerce, 1928), 3, 13, 16, Leggat-Donahoe Collection, Montana State University Special Collections, Bozeman.

51. Papers of the 1929 Lewis and Clark Memorial Commission: Minutes of May 1, May 26, and September 10 meetings, and undated copy of the final report to the Montana Legislature, RS-164, folders 1–4, MSHS.

52. *River Press* (Fort Benton, Montana), June 9, 1976.

53. Ibid.; *Billings* (Montana) *Gazette*, May 21, 1976. Although Russell's statue design was never used, the artist did paint a 12-foot by 25-foot mural for the State House of Representatives chambers in the Montana capitol in Helena depicting the explorer's encounter with Flathead (Salish) Indians in Ross's Hole in September 1805.

54. Rogers, "We Met Them at the Fair," part 1, 23.

55. Stephen Ambrose, *Undaunted Courage: Meriwether Lewis, Thomas Jefferson, and the Opening of the American West* (New York: Simon & Schuster/Touchstone, 1996), 457–458.

56. Howard Betts, *In Search of York: The Slave Who Went to the Pacific with Lewis and Clark*, rev. ed. (Boulder: University Press of Colorado and Lewis and Clark Trail Heritage Foundation, 2000).

CHAPTER 2: TRACING THE ROUTE

1. I have generally avoided repeating "the present-day site of" and similar phrases when referring to towns or other modern locations now at or near places referred to in the journals. I believe the reader will recognize that few such referents existed in 1804–1806. Further, I have not altered spellings in direct quotations from the journals. The description of the expedition's routes that follows is based primarily on Gary Moulton ed., *The Journals of the Lewis and Clark Expedition*, volumes 2–8 (Lincoln: University of Nebraska Press 1987–1993). Only direct quotes from entries and the editor's notes are

cited. Unless otherwise indicated, all citations of the journals are from the Moulton edition and, for convenience, are indicated by volume and page in brackets in the text (e.g., [VI, 87] for volume six, page 87, or [VIII, 166n12] for volume 8, p. 166, note 12).

2. Jefferson's instructions are in Frank Bergon, ed., *The Journals of Lewis and Clark* (New York: Penguin Books, 1989), xxiv–xxvi.

3. Paul Russell Cutright, *Lewis and Clark: Pioneering Naturalists* (Lincoln: University of Nebraska Press/Bison Books, 1989), 48.

4. Daniel B. Botkin, *Passage of Discovery: American Rivers Guide to the Missouri River of Lewis and Clark* (New York: Berkly/Perigee, 1999), 36, 38.

5. Cutright, *Lewis and Clark,* 50.

6. Ibid., 63.

7. James P. Ronda, *Lewis and Clark among the Indians* (Lincoln: University of Nebraska Press, 1984), 21.

8. Cutright, *Lewis and Clark,* 79.

9. On Sioux expansion, see Richard White, "The Winning of the West: The Expansion of the Western Sioux in the Eighteenth and Nineteenth Centuries," *Journal of American History* 65 (September 1978): 319–343; for Sioux territory in 1856, see Edwin Thompson Denig, *Five Indian Tribes of the Upper Missouri,* ed. John C. Ewers (Norman: University of Oklahoma Press, 1961), 64–65. See also Anthony McGinnis, *Counting Coup and Cutting Horses: Intertribal Warfare on the Northern Plains, 1738–1889* (Evergreen, Colo.: Cordillera, 1990) and Theodore Binnema, *Common and Contested Ground: A Human and Environmental History of the Northwestern Plains* (Norman: University of Oklahoma Press, 2001) for relations among Missouri River and Northern Plains tribes at the time of the Lewis and Clark Expedition.

10. Ronda, *Lewis and Clark among the Indians,* 28; Jefferson quote on p. 30.

11. Ibid.

12. Interpretation of the encounter with the Brulé band is from ibid. 31–41.

13. Ibid., 42–44.

14. Ibid., 44–45.

15. Cutright, *Lewis and Clark,* 134.

16. Ibid., 137–138.

17. Ronda, *Lewis and Clark among the Indians,* 158–159.

18. Ibid., 167–169; D. W. Meinig, *The Great Columbia Plain: A Historical Geography, 1805–1910* (Seattle: University of Washington Press, 1968), map of plateau tribes on 22–23.

19. Ronda, *Lewis and Clark among the Indians,* 170.

20. Clark also waited anxiously for a group of four men led by Sergeant Nathaniel Pryor, who had been sent ahead down the Yellowstone to obtain

horses at the Mandan Villages. Pryor and his men lost the few horses they had and were forced to float down the river on bull boats behind the main party.

21. Pierre Cruzatte apparently mistook his captain for game while they were hunting on August 11. The following day they met up with Clark.

CHAPTER 3: THE NEW EXPLORERS

1. David Dary, *The Oregon Trail: An American Saga* (New York: Oxford University Press, 2004), 310–326. Meeker's journeys are also discussed in David M. Wrobel, *Promised Lands: Promotion, Memory, and the Creation of the American West* (Lawrence: University of Kansas Press, 2002), 109–113. Meeker described his twentieth-century wagon journeys in several similar accounts, including (in collaboration with Howard R. Driggs) *The Busy Life of Eighty-Five Years: Ventures and Adventures* (Seattle: pub. by the author, 1916) and *The Ox Team, or the Old Oregon Trail, 1852–1906* (Mt. Vernon, Ind.: repr. Windmill Publications, 1992). Meeker never stopped boosting the Oregon Trail. In addition to making another wagon trip west, he traced the overland route by automobile in 1916 and flew over it as a passenger in an open-cockpit U.S. Army plane in 1923. Meeker was one of the founders of an organization that became the Oregon Trail Memorial Association in 1926, a group that forged close ties with the National Highways Association—appropriately, since Meeker's ultimate aim was to establish an Oregon Trail memorial highway.

2. Olin D. Wheeler, *The Trail of Lewis and Clark, 1804–1904*, 2 vols. (New York: G. P. Putnam's Sons, 1926), vol. I, xi–xiii, 52.

3. Ibid., xiii.

4. Ibid.

5. Mullan, handwritten original of speech at Fort Owen, Montana, December 24, 1861, SC 547, MSHS archives, 26–27, 31, 38.

6. Ted Van Arsdol, "Pioneer of Travel Routes: The Story of C. C. Van Arsdol," *Latah Legacy* (Latah County Historical Society, Moscow, Idaho) 15 (Spring 1986): 10, 15; quote (in article) is from the *Yakima* (Washington) *Republic*, January 26, 1900, 15.

7. Wheeler, *Trail of Lewis and Clark*, vol. II, 84.

8. Ibid., 85.

9. Ibid., 81–82.

10. John Leiberg quote, report to the director of the USGS, in ibid., 84–85.

11. Ibid., 85–86.

12. Ibid., 89.

13. Ibid., 87–89.

14. Ibid., 89.

15. Ibid., 85, 87; Kirby Lambert, "Through the Artist's Eye: The Painting and Photography of R. E. DeCamp," *Montana: The Magazine of Western History* 49, no. 2 (Summer 1999): 47–48. As in Chapter 2, I am citing material from the Moulton edition of the journals in square brackets within the text.

16. Wheeler, *Trail of Lewis and Clark*, vol. II, 85.

17. Ibid., 86.

18. Ibid., 98–100.

19. Ibid., 158.

20. Ibid., 164, 206.

21. Ingvard Eide, *American Odyssey: The Journey of Lewis and Clark* (New York: Rand McNally, 1969); Albert Salisbury and Jane Salisbury, *Two Captains West: An Historical Tour of the Lewis and Clark Trail* (Seattle: Superior Publishing, 1950); Ralph Space, *The Lolo Trail: A History of Events Connected with the Lolo Trail since Lewis and Clark* (Lewiston, Idaho: Printcraft Printing, 1970); John J. Peebles, "Rugged Waters: Trails and Campsites of Lewis and Clark in the Salmon River Country," *Idaho Yesterdays* 8, no. 2 (Summer 1964): 2–17, and Peebles, "On the Lolo Trail: Route and Campsites of Lewis and Clark," *Idaho Yesterdays* 9, no. 4 (Winter 1965–1966): 2–15.

22. Weippe [Idaho] Hilltop Heritage Society, Inc., "Lewis and Clark on the Weippe Hilltop" (grant proposal, 2001); *Clearwater Tribune* (Orofino, Idaho), June 26, 1932. I am also indebted to Robben Johnston, archaeologist for the Clearwater National Forest, and Bernice Pullman of the Clearwater Historical Museum (Orofino) for some of the information about Sewell and Harlan.

23. Space, *Lolo Trail*, 41–43 (third quote), 58 (first two quotes).

24. Ibid., 52–53.

25. Peebles, "On the Lolo Trail," 15.

26. Ibid., 14–15.

27. Peebles, "Rugged Waters," 5 (map legend).

28. Anne Farrar Hyde, *An American Vision: Far Western Landscape and American Culture, 1820–1920* (New York: New York University Press, 1990), 117.

29. Earl Pomeroy, *In Search of the Golden West: The Tourist in Western America* (New York: Alfred A. Knopf, 1957), 135.

30. Wheeler, *Trail of Lewis and Clark*, vol. I, 53.

31. Curt McConnell, *Coast to Coast by Automobile: The Pioneering Trips, 1899–1908* (Palo Alto: Stanford University Press, 2000), 59–62.

32. Ibid., 225.

33. Ibid., 307.

34. Ibid., 305.

35. John A. Jakle, *The Tourist: Travel in Twentieth Century North America* (Lincoln: University of Nebraska Press, 1985), 103.

36. Taussig's book, privately printed in San Francisco in 1910, cited in Michael Vinson, *Motoring Tourists and the Scenic West, 1903–1948* (Dallas: Southern Methodist University De Golyer Library, 1989), 37.

37. James J. Flink, *Car Culture* (Cambridge: MIT Press, 1975), 53.

38. Drake Hokanson, "'To Cross America, Early Motorists Took a Long Detour,'" *Smithsonian* 16, no. 5 (August 1985): 59.

39. Joe McCarthy, "The Lincoln Highway: The First Transcontinental Paved Road," *American Heritage* 25, no. 4 (June 1974): 32–34.

40. Hokanson, "To Cross America," 59.

41. *Lewiston (Idaho) Morning Tribune,* November 3, 1916.

42. Vinson, *Motoring Tourists,* 21.

43. Marilyn Wyss, *Roads to Romance: The Origins and Development of the Road and Trail System in Montana* (Helena: Montana Department of Transportation, 1992), 24, 28.

44. Virginia Rishel, *Wheels to Adventure: Bill Rishel's Western Routes* (Salt Lake City: Howe Bros., 1985), 37–38.

45. See Oral Bullard, *Lancaster's Road: The Historic Columbia River Scenic Highway* (Beaverton, Ore.: TMS Book Service, 1982); Ronald J. Fahl, "S. C. Lancaster and the Columbia River Highway Engineer as Conservationist," *Oregon Historical Quarterly* 74 (June 1973): 101–144.

46. Robert G. Athearn, *The Mythic West in Twentieth Century America* (Lawrence: University Press of Kansas, 1986), 153; see also Warren James Belasco, *Americans on the Road: From Autocamp to Motel, 1910–1945* (Cambridge: MIT Press, 1979), 37.

47. Hal K. Rothman, *Devil's Bargains: Tourism in the Twentieth Century American West* (Lawrence: University Press of Kansas, 1998), 153.

48. Athearn, *Mythic West,* 147.

49. The term "interstate highway system" was commonly used to refer to the federally funded highways built in the 1920s, as well as the later system of four-lane highways.

50. Federal Writers Project (WPA), *South Dakota: A Guide to the State,* 2nd ed., rev. M. Lisle Reese (New York: Hastings House, 1952), 187–188, 197, 239.

51. John R. Borchert, *America's Northern Heartland: An Economic and Historical Geography of the Upper Midwest* (Minneapolis: University of Minnesota Press, 1987), 74–76.

52. State Map of Montana, 1938.

53. Theodore E. Lang, "Bringing Montana out of the Mud," *Montana: The Magazine of Western History* 44, no. 4 (Autumn 1994): 35.

54. Lewis and Clark Memorial Association (Lewiston, Idaho), Report of First Annual Meeting (October 30, 1929), RS 164, folder 4, MSHS archives, first three unnumbered pages (quotes are from pp. 2–3).

55. Ibid., 3–7.

56. Ibid., 11–12.

57. *Lewiston* (Idaho) *Morning Tribune*, September 3, 1933.

58. Lewis and Clark Memorial Association, Report, 3–7.

59. Neal Parsell, *Major Fenn's Country* (Seattle: Pacific Northwest National Parks and Forests Association, n.d.), 21.

60. Space, *Lolo Trail*, 53.

61. Louis F. Hartig, *Lochsa, the Story of a Ranger District and Its People in Clearwater National Forest*, ed. Shirley Moore (Seattle: Pacific Northwest National Parks and Forests Association, 1981), 172.

62. Lolita Brown, *Pioneer Profile: A Bicentennial Salute to Kamiah and the Upper Clearwater Region* (Kamiah, Idaho: Clearwater Valley Publishing, 1976), 126.

63. Space, *Lolo Trail*, 53.

64. Ralph Gray, "Following the Trail of Lewis and Clark," *National Geographic Magazine* (June 1953): 707, 709.

65. Ibid., 714 (second quote), 731 (first quote).

66. Ibid., 738.

67. Ibid., 748.

68. Ibid., 746, 748.

69. Gerald S. Snyder, *In the Footsteps of Lewis and Clark* (National Geographic Society, 1970), 41, 116, 139.

70. The account that follows is from Wallace G. Lewis, "Building the Lewis-Clark Highway," *Idaho Yesterdays* 43, no. 3 (Fall 1999): 13–23.

71. George W. Woolery, "A New Northwest Passage," *Westways* 56, no. 5 (May 1964): 29.

CHAPTER 4: THE 1955 SESQUICENTENNIAL

1. "Review of *The Far Horizons*," *Time Magazine*, June 6, 1955, 110.

2. *The New York Times*, May 21, 1955, 11.

3. Ibid., May 8, 1955; Northwest Lewis and Clark Sesquicentennial Committee Minutes, December 18, 1954, and undated committee report, 5–6, Lewis and Clark Trail Papers, Box 3, South Dakota State Historical Society archives (hereafter referred to as LC/SDSHS), Pierre.

4. Lancaster Pollard (superintendent of the Oregon Historical Society), "Lewis and Clark at Seaside," report for Seaside, Oregon, Chamber of Commerce, n.d., VF 906, Washington State University Special Collections, Pullman.

5. *Evening Budget* (Astoria, Oregon), August 17, 1955. Lydia Large's claim depended on the Wyoming theory that "Sacajawea" had lived to be an old woman and was buried on the reservation near Fort Washakie in that state. According to the certificate quoted in the news story, that lineage named Lydia's father, Fred Large, as the "son of Maggie Basil Large Coy . . . daughter of Basil . . . son of the Otter woman, who was the sister of Sacajawea."

6. Ibid., August 10, 1953, for a description of the Fort Clatsop vicinity.

7. Ibid., July 10 and 16, 1948, and January 25, 1955; *Oregonian* (Portland), May 31, 1955.

8. *Evening Budget*, July 12, 1955 (photo caption); Dedication program, Fort Clatsop National Memorial and Visitor Facilities, August 25, 1963, Astoria Heritage Museum/Clatsop County Historical Society; Richard Neuberger, Senate speech, July 12, 1955 (Washington, D.C.: Government Printing Office, 1955), VF 906, Washington State University Special Collections, Pullman. This replica of Fort Clatsop burned in 2005 and was reconstructed the following year during the Lewis and Clark Bicentennial.

9. James Stevens, Robert MacFarlane, and Kenn E. Johnston, *Lewis and Clark: Our National Epic of Exploration* (Tacoma: Northern Pacific Railway Co. and Washington State Historical Society, 1955).

10. Chapin D. Foster, letter to Ferris Weddle, May 19, 1955, LC/SDSHS.

11. Jules Loh, "Westward to the Sea," Associated Press story in *Lewiston* (Idaho) *Morning Tribune*, September 19, 1971, Lewis and Clark VF, Asotin County Historical Society, Clarkston, Wash., no pages.

12. Letters, clippings, and state monument description in the Clark M. Maudlin Scrapbook, Three Forks, Montana, Public Library; Lyle K. Williams, *Historically Speaking: Tales of the Men and Women Who Explored and Settled the Missouri River Headwaters* (Three Forks, Mont.: pub. by author, n.d.), 54–56.

13. Maudlin Scrapbook.

14. David Glassberg, *American Historical Pageantry: The Uses of Tradition in the Early Twentieth Century* (Chapel Hill: University of North Carolina Press, 1990), 4, 148, 151, 231, 249.

15. MacKaye cited in Naima Prevots, *American Pageantry: A Movement for Art and Democracy* (Ann Arbor, Mich.: UMI Research Press, 1990), 1–2, 3 (second and third quotes), 72 (first quote).

16. Ibid., appendix A, 13, 15, 22–23.

17. Ibid., 121, quoting Frederick Henry Koch, *The Dakota Playmakers*, reprinted as a booklet from the *Quarterly Journal of the University of North*

Dakota 9, no. 1 (October 1918): 15–16. The spelling can actually be found, attributed to the Bureau of Ethnology, in *The Lewis and Clark Journal: Official Publication*, 1904, LC/SDSHS.

18. *Dillon* (Montana) *Daily Tribune*, September 3, 1915.

19. Dick Riggs (president of the Nez Perce County Historical Society), commentary accompanying a photograph of the Lewis-Clark Hotel for the society's 2004 calendar. Lewis and Clark VF, Nez Perce County Historical Society, Lewiston, Idaho.

20. Catherine Cocks, "The Chamber of Commerce's Carnival: City Festivals and Urban Tourism in the U.S., 1890–1915," in *Being Elsewhere: Tourism, Consumer Culture, and Identity in Modern Europe and North America*, ed. Shelley Baranowsky and Ellen Furlough (Ann Arbor: University of Michigan Press, 2001), 98.

21. David Lowenthal, in *The Past Is a Foreign Country* (New York: Cambridge University Press, 1985), 295, refers to "a growing cult of authenticity" and "fanatical" attention to research that still characterizes many historical reenactors.

22. Albert Erickson, letter to Clark Maudlin, September 22, 1949, Clark Maudlin Scrapbook.

23. Bert Hansen, "Sociodrama in a Speech Communication Program," *Quarterly Journal of Speech* 33, no. 2 (April 1947): 163, 165.

24. Carla Homstad, "Two Roads Diverged: A Look Back at the Montana Study," *Montana: The Magazine of Western History* 53, no. 3 (Autumn 2003): 18.

25. Bert Hansen, "Tale of the Bitterroot: Sociodrama in a Small-Community Therapy Program," repr. as a booklet from *Sociatry* 1, no. 1 (March 1947): 163–165.

26. Ibid., 93–94; Homstad, "Two Roads Diverged," 24.

27. Hansen, "Tale of the Bitterroot," 94.

28. Homstad, "Two Roads Diverged," 25.

29. Hansen, "Tale of the Bitterroot," 95.

30. Homstad, "Two Roads Diverged," 25.

31. Bert Hansen and Virginia Buttleman, *Corridor of an Empire*, Bert Hansen Papers, MSHS archives.

32. Ibid., Episode I, 1.

33. Ibid., Episode II, 1–4.

34. Ibid., Episode III, 7.

35. Ibid., Episode IV, 11.

36. *Montana Standard* (Butte-Anaconda), July 24, 1955.

37. *Dillon* (Montana) *Daily Tribune*, July 28 and August 1, 1955.

38. Dillon/Camp Fortunate pageant program, July 31, 1955, Beaverhead County Historical Society, Dillon, Mont.

39. *Your Land Forever* pageant program, K. Ross Toole Archives, Mansfield Library, University of Montana, Missoula.

40. *The Salmon River Saga* by Vio Mae Powell pageant program, August 20–21, 1955, VF 2609, Washington State University Special Collections, Pullman.

41. *Salt Lake Tribune*, August 29, 1955.

42. Lewiston (Idaho) *Morning Tribune*, July 9 and October 10, 1955.

43. *Clearwater Progress* (Kamiah, Idaho), October 7, 1955.

44. *Montana Standard* (Butte), June 17, 1955.

45. "Washington State Committee's Speech Outline for the Sesquicentennial" (undated) and "Suggested Programs for Clubs and Organizations" (prep. Ruth M. Babcock; undated), both in VF 906, Washington State University Special Collections, Pullman.

46. *Great Falls* (Montana) *Tribune*, February 18, 1945.

47. The Magnuson measure was S.R. 88, 85th Congress, 1st Session (May 8, 1957); Department of the Interior, Bureau of Outdoor Recreation, *The Lewis and Clark Trail: A Proposed National Historic Trail* (Washington, D.C., 1975), 6.

48. Will Robinson to Chapin D. Foster, July 24, 1957, in LC/SDSHS.

CHAPTER 5: THE NATIONAL COMMISSION

1. Walter Nugent, *Into the West: The Story of Its People* (New York: Alfred A. Knopf, 1999), 344.

2. Daniel B. Botkin, in *Passage of Discovery* (New York: Berkly/Perigee, 1999), 58–59, points out that agricultural pesticides such as DDT and Dieldrin may have contributed to major fish kills in the lower Missouri during the 1960s.

3. David L. Lendt, *Ding: The Life of Jay Norwood Darling* (Ames: Iowa State University Press, 1979), 50, 70, 85, 154 (quote), 166.

4. *U.S. Statutes at Large* 88 (1964), 630, and 89 (1966), 475.

5. Lewis and Clark Trail Commission, *Interim Report to Congress and the President*, 1966, 6–7, SC 1961, MSHS.

6. Ibid.

7. Donald B. Alexander, "Tracking down a Heritage," *Parks and Recreation* 1 (March 1966): 224.

8. Roy E. Appleman, "Lewis and Clark: The Route 160 Years After," *Pacific Northwest Quarterly* 57, no. 1 (January 1966): 10–12.

9. Ted Yates, "Since Lewis and Clark," *American West* 2, no. 4 (Fall 1965): 24–25, 30.

10. Ibid., 23–26.

11. Ibid., 28.

12. Roy E. Appleman, *Lewis and Clark: Historic Places Associated with Their Transcontinental Exploration, 1804–06* (Washington, D.C.: U.S. National Park Service, 1975), 261–262.

13. Wheeler, *Trail of Lewis and Clark,* vol. I, 88–89.

14. Ibid., xi–xiii, 51–53.

15. Lewis R. Freeman, "Trailing History down the Big Muddy," *National Geographic Magazine* 54 (July 1928): 73, 77, 117 (quote).

16. *Bismarck* (North Dakota) *Tribune,* July 8, 1968.

17. *Lewis and Clark Journal* (newsletter) 2, no. 3 (1971), and 3, no. 4 (1972), LC/SDSHS.

18. Stanley Vestal, *The Missouri* (New York: Farrar & Rinehart, 1945), 11.

19. John E. Thorson, *River of Promise, River of Peril: The Politics of Managing the Missouri River* (Lawrence: University Press of Kansas, ca. 1994), 64–67.

20. Ibid.

21. Vestal, *The Missouri,* 282.

22. Thorson, *River of Promise,* 15.

23. Michael L. Lawson, *Dammed Indians: The Pick-Sloan Plan and the Missouri River Sioux, 1944–1980* (Norman: University of Oklahoma Press, 1982), 27, 45.

24. Ibid., 27 (quote), 181–193.

25. Vine Deloria Jr., preface to ibid., xiv.

26. Botkin, *Passage of Discovery,* 38–39.

27. Appleman, *Historic Places,* 258–259.

28. Ibid., 260–261.

29. Lendt, *Ding,* 154.

30. *U.S. Statutes at Large* 88 (October 6, 1964), 630.

31. *Great Falls* (Montana) *Tribune,* May 26, 1964.

32. Will Robinson, letter to Curtis B. Mateer, July 19, 1967, and Keith G. Hay (Fish and Wildlife Service, U.S. Department of the Interior), memo, September 23, 1966, both in LC/SDSHS.

33. Lewis and Clark Trail Commission, Resolution of Portland Meeting (November 1968), LC/SDSHS.

34. Arlen Large, "Onward! Lewis and Clark Trail Commission Can't Bring Itself to Quit," *Wall Street Journal,* May 7, 1969.

35. Lawrence W. Lichty, letter to Sherry Fisher, July 2, 1968, LC/SDSHS.

36. Editorial in *South Dakota Hiway Magazine* 2, no. 9 (September 1927): 11.

37. South Dakota Department of Highways, *Missouri River Perimeter Road System: Upper Big Bend and Oahe Reservoirs, Pierre to Northern Boundary of*

South Dakota (Mobridge, S.D.: Nance Engineering Study, 1965), 3, 9, SDSHS archives, Pierre.

38. Large, "Onward."

39. North Dakota Lewis and Clark Trail Committee meeting minutes, March 14, 1975, Neff Papers, North Dakota State Historical Society archives, Bismarck.

40. North Dakota, *State Outdoor Recreation Agency Digest* 4, no. 5 (May 15, 1969): map.

41. Lewis and Clark Trail Commission, *Interim Report*, 9, 14–17.

42. Ibid., 9–10, 14–15.

43. Ibid., 16–17. Montana had already designated that segment of the Missouri River, as well as the stretch of the Yellowstone River from Yellowstone National Park to Pompey's Pillar, as "state recreation waterways."

44. Rothman, *Devil's Bargains*, 155–156.

45. National Park Service Web site, www.np.gov/jeff/arch (accessed November 25, 2002).

46. Associated Press stories in the Missoula, Montana, *Missoulian*, *Great Falls* (Montana) *Tribune*, and *Montana* (Butte/Anaconda) *Standard*, May 16, 1968.

47. Boy Scouts of America, "Report on the Lewis and Clark Trail Project," 1968, LC/SDSHS.

48. Archie Satterfield, "Park with Land Sculptures Proposed," *Seattle Times*, January 28, 1968.

49. Astoria, Oregon, *Daily Astorian*, November 20, 1968.

50. Ibid., September 27, 1965.

51. Ibid., January 20, February 8, April 21, October 23, and November 9 and 17, 1967.

52. Ibid., October 23 (potential sites; second and third quotes) and November 9 (anticipated performances of the Lewis and Clark story) and 17 (first quote), 1967.

53. Ibid., December 4, 1967 (grant; 1968 summer production plans), March 29 (first quote), June 9 (second quote), and December 19, 1968 (release of the executive director).

54. Lewis and Clark Trail Commission, *Final Report*, October 1969, 3, 5–6, Lewis and Clark Trail Commission Records, MSHS, SC 1961.

55. Ibid., 7.

56. The National Trails System Act became Public Law 90-543 on October 2, 1968 (16 U.S. Code 1241).

57. Department of the Interior, Bureau of Outdoor Recreation, *The Lewis and Clark National Historic Trail*, 3.

58. Lewis and Clark Trail Commission, *Interim Report*, 19.

59. Lewis and Clark Trail Commission, *Final Report*, 1, 3.

60. *Omaha Register*, May 7, 1969.

61. Large, "Onward."

62. Letter to *Life Magazine* editor George P. Hunt, February 14, 1969; Clark Mollenkopf story in *Des Moines* (Iowa) *Register*, May 1, 1969; and Sherry Fisher, letter to Dayton Canaday, February 7, 1969, all in LC/SDSHS. (Fisher was responding to a squib in *Life* on February 7, 1969, entitled "A Hero among Bureaucrats" and retorted that the commission relied on very little public funding; the funding it did receive was used for travel.)

63. John Greenslit, letter to Christopher D. Koss, August 11, 1969, LC/SDSHS.

64. *St. Louis Post-Dispatch*, October 12, 1969.

65. Lewis and Clark Trail Heritage Foundation, "South Dakota Report," presented at meeting in Helena, Montana, August 9, 1972, and Dayton Canaday, letter to Lester F. Faber (Bureau of Outdoor Recreation), March 29, 1974, both in LC/SDSHS.

66. Lewis and Clark Trail Commission, *Final Report*, 22–23.

67. *St. Louis Post-Dispatch*, February 9, 1968.

68. Editorial comment, *We Proceeded On* 1, no. 1 (Winter 1974–75): 9.

69. Bob Saindon wrote a thirty-two-page newspaper supplement entitled "Lewis and Clark in Northeast Montana" that accompanied the July 19, 1974, issue of the *Glasgow Courier*.

70. *Montana Standard* (Butte/Anaconda), February 6, 1970.

71. Department of the Interior, Bureau of Outdoor Recreation, *The Lewis and Clark Trail: A Potential Addition to the National Trails System*, 1974, PAM 3263, MSHS, and *The Lewis and Clark Trail: A Proposed National Historic Trail*, 1975, 1, appendix B, 3, PAM 3262, MSHS.

72. Department of the Interior, Bureau of Outdoor Recreation, *Proposed National Historic Trail*, 7 (first quote); appendix B, 2–3 (fifteenth quote), 73 (second through sixth quotes), 74 (seventh through fourteenth quotes).

73. Department of the Interior, Bureau of Outdoor Recreation, *Final Report to Congress*, 45–46, House Document 277, vol. 13211-1 (Washington, D.C.: Government Printing Office, 1978).

74. *U.S. Statutes at Large* 95 (1978), 625.

75. Botkin, *Passage of Discovery*, 33–34, 64–65, 76, 104.

76. Archie Satterfield, *The Lewis and Clark Trail* (Harrisburg, Penn.: Stackpole Books, 1978).

77. Ibid., 162.

78. Ibid., 170, 174–175, 177 (quote).

79. Ibid., 181–182, 185–186 (quote).

80. Dayton Duncan, *Out West: An American Journey* (New York: Viking, 1987) x, 4–5. More recent guides include Julie Fanselow, *The Traveler's Guide to the Lewis & Clark Trail* (Helena, Mont.: Falcon, 1994); Barbara Fifer and Vicky Soderberg, *Along the Trail with Lewis and Clark* (Great Falls: Montana Magazine, 1998).

CHAPTER 6: COMMEMORATION
AND AUTHENTICITY ON THE TRAIL

1. *Three Forks* (Montana) *Herald*, May 19, 1980; Bozeman, Montana, *Daily Chronicle*, July 18, 1980, and July 27, 1981.

2. Gallatin County Historical Society newsletter, April 16, 1980, Lewis and Clark VF, Gallatin Historical Society and Pioneer Museum, Bozeman Mont.; Lewis and Clark Three Forks 1980 and 1981 pageant programs, Three Forks Public Library, Three Forks, Mont.

3. Angie Wagner, "Seekers Who Destroyed," AP story in the *Denver Post*, May 5, 2003.

4. John Stromnes, "Explorers Depicted as Sent Oppressors," Missoula, Montana, *Missoulian*, September 13, 1992.

5. Jim Hughes, "Lewis and Clark Re-enactors Stir Indian Debate," *The Denver Post*, September 26, 2004.

6. Margot Roosevelt, "Tribal Culture Clash," *Time Magazine* (July 8, 2002): 66–68.

7. National Congress of American Indians, Resolution #SPO-01-112, adopted at its 58th Annual Session, 2001; "Along the Lewis and Clark Trail," American Native Press Archives, www.anpa.ualr.edu/f_lewis_clark.htm (accessed November 17, 2002).

8. David Chidester and Edward T. Linenthal, eds., *American Sacred Space* (Bloomington: Indiana University Press, 1995), 27, 29.

9. Nora, "Era of Commemoration," 626 (first quote), 615 (second quote).

10. Bodnar, *Remaking America*, 247.

11. Erika Doss, *Spirit Poles and Flying Pigs: Public Art and Cultural Democracy in American Communities* (Washington, D.C.: Smithsonian Institution Press, 1995), 248.

12. Mark Spence, "The Unnatural History of the Lewis and Clark Bicentennial," *Montana: The Magazine of Western History* 53, no. 2 (Summer 2003): 57–58.

13. Kammen, *In the Past Lane*, 219.

14. On issues of authenticity and interpretation, see also, for example, Dean MacCannell, *The Tourist: A New Theory of the Leisure Class* (New York:

Schocken, 1976); David Glassberg, *Sense of History: The Place of the Past in American Life* (Amherst: University of Massachusetts Press, 2001); Barbara Kirshenblatt-Gimblett, *Destination Culture: Tourism, Museums, and Heritage* (Berkeley: University of California Press, 1998); Peirce Lewis, "Taking down the Velvet Rope: Cultural Geography and the Human Landscape," in *Past Meets Present: Essays about Historic Interpretation and Public Audiences*, ed. Jo Blatti (Washington, D.C.: Smithsonian Institution Press, 1987); Lowenthal, *The Past Is a Foreign Country*; Zelinsky, *Nation into State*. Since the late 1980s, the number of articles that discuss site authenticity has grown steadily in journals specializing in tourism studies and public history.

15. For issues of presentism and selective public memory, see Sven Birkerts, *Readings* (St. Paul, Minn.: Greywolf, 1999), 26–27; Daniel J. Boorstin, *The Image, or What Happened to the American Dream?* (New York: Atheneum, 1962), 108; Kammen, *In the Past Lane*, 219. On the historical immediacy of reproductions, see Lowenthal, *The Past Is a Foreign Country*, 265, 326–327.

16. Lewis, "Taking down the Velvet Rope," 25 (original emhasis).

17. Jakle, *The Tourist*, 286–287, 289.

18. Nugent, *Into the West*, 344.

19. National Council of the Lewis and Clark Bicentennial brochure, 2003 (St. Louis, author's copy).

Bibliography

BOOKS AND ARTICLES

Abbott, Carl. *The Great Extravaganza: Portland and the Lewis and Clark Exposition.* Portland: Oregon Historical Society, 1981.

Alexander, Donald B. "Tracking down a Heritage." *Parks and Recreation* 1 (March 1966): 221–226.

Allen, John L. "'Of This Enterprize': The American Images of the Lewis and Clark Expedition." In *Voyages of Discovery: Essays on the Lewis and Clark Expedition,* ed. James P. Ronda. Helena: Montana Historical Press, 1998.

Allen, Paul, ed. *History of the Expedition under the Command of Captains Lewis and Clark to the Sources of the Missouri, Thence across the Rocky Mountains and down the River Columbia to the Pacific Ocean. Performed during the Years 1804–5–6.* Philadelphia: Bradford and Inskeep, 1814.

Ambrose, Stephen. *Undaunted Courage: Meriwether Lewis, Thomas Jefferson, and the Opening of the American West.* New York: Simon and Schuster/ Touchstone, 1996.

Appleman, Roy E. *Lewis and Clark: Historic Places Associated with Their Transcontinental Exploration (1804–06)*. Washington, D.C.: U.S. National Park Service, 1975.

———. "Lewis and Clark: The Route 160 Years After." *Pacific Northwest Quarterly 57*, no. 1 (January 1966): 8–12.

Athearn, Robert G. *The Mythic West in Twentieth Century America*. Lawrence: University Press of Kansas, 1986.

Belasco, Warren James. *Americans on the Road: From Autocamp to Motel, 1910–1945*. Cambridge: MIT Press, 1979.

Benedict, Burton, et al. *The Anthropology of World's Fairs: San Francisco's Panama Pacific International Exposition of 1915*. Berkeley: Scolar Press and the Lowie Museum of Anthropology, 1983.

Bergon, Frank, ed. *The Journals of Lewis and Clark*. New York: Penguin Books, 1989.

Betts, Howard. *In Search of York: The Slave Who Went to the Pacific with Lewis and Clark*, rev. ed. Boulder: University Press of Colorado and Lewis and Clark Trail Heritage Foundation, 2000.

Binnema, Theodore. *Common and Contested Ground: A Human and Environmental History of the Northwestern Plains*. Norman: University of Oklahoma Press, 2001.

Birkerts, Sven. *Readings*. St. Paul, Minn.: Greywolf, 1999.

Bodnar, John. *Remaking America: Public Memory, Commemoration, and Patriotism in the Twentieth Century*. Princeton, N.J.: Princeton University Press, 1992.

Boorstin, Daniel J. *The Image, or What Happened to the American Dream?* New York: Atheneum, 1962.

Borchert, John R. *America's Northern Heartland: An Economic and Historical Geography of the Upper Midwest*. Minneapolis: University of Minnesota Press, 1987.

Botkin, Daniel B. *Passage of Discovery: American Rivers Guide to the Missouri River of Lewis and Clark*. New York: Berkly/Perigee, 1999.

Bradford, William. "Discovery, Characteristics, and Resources." *Debow's Review 20*, no. 5 (May 1856): 540–571.

Brown, Lolita. *Pioneer Profile: A Bicentennial Salute to Kamiah and the Upper Clearwater Region*. Kamiah, Idaho: Clearwater Valley Publishing, 1976.

Bullard, Oral. *Lancaster's Road: The Historic Columbia River Scenic Highway*. Beaverton, Ore.: TMS Book Service, 1982.

Carpenter, E. W. "A Glimpse of Montana." *Overland Monthly and Out West Magazine 2*, no. 4 (April 1867): 378–386

Chidester, David, and Edward T. Linenthal, eds. *American Sacred Space*. Bloomington: Indiana University Press, 1995.

Clark, Ella E., and Margot Edmonds. *Sacagawea of the Lewis and Clark Expedition*. Berkeley: University of California Press, 1979.

Cocks, Catherine. "The Chamber of Commerce's Carnival: City Festivals and Urban Tourism in the U.S., 1890–1915." In *Being Elsewhere: Tourism, Consumer Culture, and Identity in Modern Europe and North America*, ed. Shelley Baranowsky and Ellen Furlough. Ann Arbor: University of Michigan Press, 2001.

Copley, Josiah. "The Rocky Mountains." *Debow's Review* 4, no. 6 (June 1843): 520–536.

Coues, Elliott, ed. *History of the Expedition under the Command of Lewis and Clark*, a new edition in four volumes. New York: Francis P. Harper, 1893.

Cutright, Paul Russell. *A History of the Lewis and Clark Journals*. Norman: University of Oklahoma Press, 1976.

———. *Lewis and Clark: Pioneering Naturalists*. Lincoln: University of Nebraska Press/Bison Books, 1989.

Dary, David. *The Oregon Trail: An American Saga*. New York: Oxford University Press, 2004.

Debow, J.D.B. "Climate of the United States." *Debow's Review* 23, no. 5 (November 1857): 506–521.

Deloria, Vine, Jr. Preface. In Michael L. Lawson, *Dammed Indians: The Pick-Sloan Plan and the Missouri River Sioux, 1944–1980*. Norman: University of Oklahoma Press, 1982.

Denig, Edwin Thompson. *Five Indian Tribes of the Upper Missouri*. Ed. John C. Ewers. Norman: University of Oklahoma Press, 1961.

DeVoto, Bernard, ed. *The Journals of Lewis and Clark*. New York: Houghton Mifflin, 1953.

Doss, Erika. *Spirit Poles and Flying Pigs: Public Art and Cultural Democracy in American Communities*. Washington, D.C.: Smithsonian Institution Press, 1995.

Duncan, Dayton. *Out West: An American Journey*. New York: Viking, 1987.

Dye, Eva Emery. *The Conquest: The True Story of Lewis and Clark*. Chicago: A. C. McClurg, 1902; repr. New York: Grosset & Dunlap, 1914.

Editorial comment. *We Proceeded On* 1, no. 1 (Winter 1974–1975): 1.

Eide, Ingvard. *American Odyssey: The Journey of Lewis and Clark*. New York: Rand McNally, 1969.

Fahl, Ronald J. "S. C. Lancaster and the Columbia River Highway Engineer as Conservationist." *Oregon Historical Quarterly* 74 (June 1973): 101–144.

Fanselow, Julie. *The Traveler's Guide to the Lewis & Clark Trail*. Helena, Mont.: Falcon, 1994.

Federal Writers Project (WPA). *South Dakota: A Guide to the State*, 2nd ed. Rev. M. Lisle Reese. New York: Hastings House, 1952.

Fifer, Barbara, and Vicky Soderberg. *Along the Trail with Lewis and Clark*. Great Falls: Montana Magazine, 1998.

Flink, James J. *Car Culture*. Cambridge: MIT Press, 1975.

Freeman, Lewis R. "Trailing History down the Big Muddy." *National Geographic Magazine* 54 (July 1928): 73–120.

Frisch, Michael. "American History and the Structures of Collective Memory: A Modest Exercise in Empirical Iconography." *Journal of American History* 75, no. 4 (March 1989): 1130–1155.

Glassberg, David. *American Historical Pageantry: The Uses of Tradition in the Early Twentieth Century*. Chapel Hill: University of North Carolina Press, 1990.

———. *Sense of History: The Place of the Past in American Life*. Amherst: University of Massachusetts Press, 2001.

Gray, Ralph. "Following the Trail of Lewis and Clark." *National Geographic Magazine* (June 1953): 707–750.

Hansen, Bert. "Tale of the Bitterroot: Sociodrama in a Small-Community Therapy Program." *Quarterly Journal of Speech* 33, no. 2 (April 1947): 162–166.

Hartig, Louis F. *Lochsa, the Story of a Ranger District and Its People in Clearwater National Forest*. Ed. Shirley Moore. Seattle: Pacific Northwest National Parks and Forests Association, 1981.

Hokanson, Drake. "To Cross America, Early Motorists Took a Long Detour." *Smithsonian* 16, no. 5 (August 1985): 58–65.

Homstad, Carla. "Two Roads Diverged: A Look Back at the Montana Study." *Montana: The Magazine of Western History* 53, no. 3 (Autumn 2003): 16–29.

Horne, Esther Burnett, and Sally McBeth. *Essie's Story: The Life of a Shoshone Teacher*. Lincoln: University of Nebraska Press, 1998.

Huffman, Bert. [untitled poem]. *Lewis and Clark Journal* (January-March 1904): 8–9.

Hughes, Jim. "Lewis and Clark Re-enactors Stir Indian Debate." *The Denver Post*, September 26, 2004.

Hyde, Anne Farrar. *An American Vision: Far Western Landscape and American Culture, 1820–1920*. New York: New York University Press, 1990.

Jackson, Donald. "The Public Image of Lewis and Clark." *Pacific Northwest Quarterly* 57, no. 1 (January 1966): 1–7.

Jakle, John A. *The Tourist: Travel in Twentieth Century North America*. Lincoln: University of Nebraska Press, 1985.

Jackson, Donald, ed. *Letters of the Lewis and Clark Expedition with Related Documents, 1783–1854*. Champaign: University of Illinois Press, 1962.

Kammen, Michael. *In the Past Lane: Historical Perspectives on American Culture.* New York: Oxford University Press, 1997.

———. *Mystic Chords of Memory: The Transformation of Tradition in American Culture.* New York: Alfred A. Knopf, 1991.

Kessler, Donna. *The Making of Sacagawea: A Euro-American Legend.* Tuscaloosa: University of Alabama Press, 1996.

Kirshenblatt-Gimblett, Barbara. *Destination Culture: Tourism, Museums, and Heritage.* Berkeley: University of California Press, 1998.

Lambert, Kirby. "Through the Artist's Eye: The Painting and Photography of R. E. DeCamp." *Montana: The Magazine of Western History* 49, no. 2 (Summer 1999): 38–49.

Lang, Theodore E. "Bringing Montana out of the Mud." *Montana: The Magazine of Western History* 44, no. 4 (Autumn 1994): 28–39.

Large, Arlen. "Onward! Lewis and Clark Trail Commission Can't Bring Itself to Quit." *Wall Street Journal*, May 7, 1969.

Lawson, Michael L. *Dammed Indians: The Pick-Sloan Plan and the Missouri River Sioux, 1944–1980.* Norman: University of Oklahoma Press, 1982.

Lendt, David L. *Ding: The Life of Jay Norwood Darling.* Ames: Iowa State University Press, 1979.

Lewis, Peirce. "Taking down the Velvet Rope: Cultural Geography and the Human Landscape." In *Past Meets Present: Essays about Historic Interpretation and Public Audiences,* ed. Jo Blatti. Washington, D.C.: Smithsonian Institution Press, 1987.

Lewis, Wallace G. "Building the Lewis-Clark Highway." *Idaho Yesterdays* 43, no. 3 (Fall 1999): 13–23.

Lowenthal, David. *The Past Is a Foreign Country.* New York: Cambridge University Press, 1985.

MacCannell, Dean. *The Tourist: A New Theory of the Leisure Class.* New York: Schocken, 1976.

MacKintosh, Barry. *The Historic Sites Survey and the National Historic Landmarks Program, a History.* Washington, D.C.: Historical Division, National Park Service, Department of the Interior, 1985.

Marling, Karal Ann. *George Washington Slept Here: Colonial Revivals and American Culture, 1876–1986.* Cambridge: Harvard University Press, 1988.

McCall, Laura. "Sacagawea, a Historical Enigma." In *Ordinary Women, Extraordinary Lives: Women in American History,* ed. Kriste Lindenmeyer. Wilmington, Del.: SR Books, 2000.

McCarthy, Joe. "The Lincoln Highway: The First Transcontinental Paved Road." *American Heritage* 25, no. 4 (June 1974): 32–37.

McConnell, Curt. *Coast to Coast by Automobile: The Pioneering Trips, 1899–1908.* Palo Alto: Stanford University Press, 2000.

McGinnis, Anthony. *Counting Coup and Cutting Horses: Intertribal Warfare on the Northern Plains, 1738–1889*. Evergreen, Colo.: Cordillera, 1990.

Meeker, Ezra. *The Ox Team, or the Old Oregon Trail, 1852–1906*. Mt. Vernon, Ind.: Windmill, 1992.

Meeker, Ezra, in collaboration with Howard R. Driggs. *The Busy Life of Eighty-Five Years: Ventures and Adventures*. Seattle: pub. by the author, 1916.

Meinig, D. W. *The Great Columbia Plain: A Historical Geography, 1805–1910*. Seattle: University of Washington Press, 1968.

Moulton, Gary, ed. *The Journals of the Lewis and Clark Expedition*, vols. 2–8. Lincoln: University of Nebraska Press, 1987–1993.

Nora, Pierre. "General Introduction." In *Realms of Memory: Rethinking the French Past*, vol. 1 (of three). Ed. Pierre Nora; trans. Arthur Goldhammer. New York: Columbia University Press, 1996.

———. "The Era of Commemoration." In *Realms of Memory: Rethinking the French Past*, vol. 3. Ed. Pierre Nora; trans. Arthur Goldhammer. New York: Columbia University Press, 1998.

Nugent, Walter. *Into the West: The Story of Its People*. New York: Alfred A. Knopf, 1999.

Osgood, Ernest Staples, ed. *Field Notes of Captain William Clark, 1803–1805*. New Haven: Yale University Press, 1964.

Parsell, Neal. *Major Fenn's Country*. Seattle: Pacific Northwest National Parks and Forests Association, n.d.

Peebles, John J. "On the Lolo Trail: Route and Campsites of Lewis and Clark." *Idaho Yesterdays* 9, no. 4 (Winter 1965–1966): 2–15.

———. "Rugged Waters: Trails and Campsites of Lewis and Clark in the Salmon River Country." *Idaho Yesterdays* 8, no. 2 (Summer 1964): 2–17.

Pomeroy, Earl. *In Search of the Golden West: The Tourist in Western America*. New York: Alfred A. Knopf, 1957.

Prevots, Naima. *American Pageantry: A Movement for Art and Democracy*. Ann Arbor: UMI Research Press, 1990.

Quaife, Milo M., ed. *The Journals of Captain Meriwether Lewis and Sergeant John Ordway*. Madison: State Historical Society of Wisconsin, 1916.

"Review of *The Far Horizons*." *Time Magazine* (June 6, 1955): 11.

Rishel, Virginia. *Wheels to Adventure: Bill Rishel's Western Routes*. Salt Lake City: Howe Bros., 1985.

Rogers, Ann "We Met Them at the Fair: Lewis and Clark Commemorated at the 1904 Louisiana Purchase Exposition." Part 1: *We Proceeded On* 21, no. 3 (August 1995): 20–24, and Part 2: *We Proceeded On* 21, no. 4 (November 1995): 20–22.

Ronda, James P. *Lewis and Clark among the Indians*. Lincoln: University of Nebraska Press, 1984.

Roosevelt, Margot. "Tribal Culture Clash." *Time Magazine* (July 8, 2002): 66–68.

Rothman, Hal K. *Devil's Bargains: Tourism in the Twentieth Century American West*. Lawrence: University Press of Kansas, 1998.

Rydell, Robert W. *All the World's a Fair: Visions of Empire at American International Expositions, 1876–1916*. Chicago: University of Chicago Press, 1984.

Saindon, Bob. "Lewis and Clark in Northeast Montana." *Glasgow* (Mont.) *Courier*, July 19, 1974.

Salisbury, Albert, and Jane Salisbury. *Two Captains West: An Historical Tour of the Lewis and Clark Trail*. Seattle: Superior Publishing, 1950.

Satterfield, Archie. *The Lewis and Clark Trail*. Harrisburg, Pa.: Stackpole Books, 1978.

———. "Park with Land Sculptures Proposed." *Seattle Times*, January 28, 1968.

Scammon, C. M. "In and around Astoria." *Overland Monthly and Out West Magazine* 3, no. 6 (December 1869): 495–499.

Scott, H. W. "Historical Significance of the Lewis and Clark Expedition." *Lewis and Clark Journal: Official Publication of the Lewis and Clark Fair* 1, no. 1 (January 1904): 5–7.

Snyder, Gerald S. *In the Footsteps of Lewis and Clark*. National Geographic Society, 1970.

South Dakota Hiway Magazine (editorial) 2, no. 9 (September 1927): 11.

Space, Ralph. *The Lolo Trail: A History of Events Connected with the Lolo Trail since Lewis and Clark*. Lewiston, Idaho: Printcraft, 1970.

Spence, Mark. "The Unnatural History of the Lewis and Clark Bicentennial." *Montana: The Magazine of Western History* 53, no. 2 (Summer 2003): 56–63.

Steel, Jane. "Misspelling on End of Trail Sign at Beach Draws Attention." *Daily Astorian* (Astoria, Ore.), March 16, 1967.

Stevens, James, Robert MacFarlane, and Kenn E. Johnston. *Lewis and Clark: Our National Epic of Exploration*. Tacoma: Northern Pacific Railway Co. and Washington State Historical Society, 1955.

Stromnes, John. "Explorers Depicted as Sent Oppressors. Missoula, Montana, *Missoulian*, September 13, 1992.

Susman, Warren I. *Culture as History: The Transformation of American Society in the Twentieth Century*. New York: Pantheon Books, 1984.

Taber, Ronald W. "Sacagawea and the Suffragettes: An Interpretation of a Myth." *Pacific Northwest Quarterly* 58, no. 1 (January 1967): 7–13.

Thorson, John E. *River of Promise, River of Peril: The Politics of Managing the Missouri River*. Lawrence: University Press of Kansas, ca. 1994.

Thwaites, Reuben Gold, ed. *Original Journals of the Lewis and Clark Expedition, 1804–1806,* 8 vols. New York: Dodd, Mead, 1904–1905.

The Unveiling of the Lewis-Clark Statue at Midway Park in the City of Charlottesville, Virginia. Charlottesville: City of Charlottesville, 1919.

Van Arsdol, Ted. "Pioneer of Travel Routes: The Story of C. C. Van Arsdol." *Latah Legacy* (Latah County Historical Society, Moscow, Idaho) 15 (Spring 1986): 9–18.

van West, Carroll. "Montana's Monuments: History in the Making." *Montana: The Magazine of Western History* 40, no. 4 (Fall 1990): 12–25.

Vestal, Stanley. *The Missouri.* New York: Farrar & Rineholt, 1945.

Vinson, Michael. *Motoring Tourists and the Scenic West, 1903–1948* (bibliography). Dallas: Southern Methodist University/De Golyer Library, 1989.

Wagner, Angie. "Seekers Who Destroyed." AP story in the *Denver Post,* May 5, 2003.

West, Helen B. "Lewis and Clark Expedition: Our National Epic." *Montana: The Magazine of Western History* 16, no. 3 (July 1966): 3–5.

Wheeler, Olin D. *The Trail of Lewis and Clark, 1804–1904,* 2 vols. Introduction by Frederick S. Dellenbaugh. New York: G. P. Putnam's Sons, 1926.

White, Richard. "The Winning of the West: The Expansion of the Western Sioux in the Eighteenth and Nineteenth Centuries." *Journal of American History* 65 (September 1978): 319–343.

Williams, Lyle K. *Historically Speaking: Tales of the Men and Women Who Explored and Settled the Missouri River Headwaters.* Three Forks, Mont.: pub. by author, n.d.

Woolery, George W. "A New Northwest Passage." *Westways* 56, no. 5 (May 1964): 26–29.

Wrobel, David M. *Promised Lands: Promotion, Memory, and the Creation of the American West.* Lawrence: University Press of Kansas, 2002.

Wyss, Marilyn. *Roads to Romance: The Origins and Development of the Road and Trail System in Montana.* Helena: Montana Department of Transportation, 1992.

Yates, Ted. "Since Lewis and Clark." *American West* 2, no. 4 (Fall 1965): 23–30.

Zelinsky, Wilbur. *Nation into State: The Shifting Symbolic Foundations of American Nationalism.* Chapel Hill: University of North Carolina Press, 1988.

ARCHIVE SOURCES AND GOVERNMENT DOCUMENTS

"Along the Lewis and Clark Trail." American Native Press Archives, www.anpa.ualr.edu/f_lewis_clark.htm (accessed November 17, 2002).

Boy Scouts of America. "Report on the Lewis and Clark Trail Project," 1968. LC/SDSHS.

Canaday, Dayton. Letter to Lester F. Faber, March 29, 1974. LC/SDSHS.

Clark M. Maudlin Scrapbook. Three Forks Public Library, Three Forks, Mont.

Dedication program, Fort Clatsop National Memorial and Visitor Facilities, August 25, 1963. Astoria Museum/Clatsop County Historical Society, Astoria, Ore.

Department of the Interior, Bureau of Outdoor Recreation. *Final Report to Congress* [on Lewis and Clark National Historic Trail], 1977. House Document 277, vol. 13211-1. Washington, D.C.: Government Printing Office, 1978.

———. *The Lewis and Clark Trail: A Potential Addition to the National Trails System,* 1974. PAM 3263, MSHS.

———. *The Lewis and Clark Trail: A Proposed National Historic Trail,* 1975 report. PAM 3262, MSHS.

Dillon/Camp Fortunate pageant program, July 31, 1955. Beaverhead County Historical Society, Dillon, Mont.

Erickson, Albert. Letter to Clark Maudlin, September 22, 1949. Clark Maudlin Scrapbook, Three Forks Public Library, Three Forks, Mont.

Fisher, Sherry. Letters to Dayton Canaday, February 7, 1969, and to *Life Magazine* editor George P. Hunt, February 14, 1969. LC/SDSHS.

Foster, Chapin D. Letter to Ferris Weddle, May 19, 1955. LC/SDSHS.

Gallatin County Historical Society newsletter, April 16, 1980. Lewis and Clark VF, Gallatin Historical Society and Pioneer Museum, Bozeman, Mont.

Greenslit, John. Letter to Christopher D. Koss, August 11, 1969. LC/SDSHS.

Harris, Zillah. "Lullaby," in unattributed news story, "What Became of Sacajawea?" Dated April 9, 1916. Astoria Heritage Museum VF C boxes, Astoria, Ore.

Hansen, Bert. "Sociodrama in a Speech Communication Program." Repr. from *Western Speech* 33, no. 2 (April 1947). Bert Hansen Papers, MSHS.

Hansen, Bert, and Virginia Buttleman. *Corridor of Empire* (pageant script). Bert Hansen Papers, MSHS.

Hay, Keith G. Memo, September 23, 1966. LC/SDSHS.

"Historical Sites Preserved and Markers Erected by the Montana Society DAR . . . 1899–1917." Lewis and Clark Expedition—Statuary Markers, Monuments, etc., VF, MSHS.

"History of the Henry Lyons Bronze, etc." VF MHS, Lewis and Clark Memorial Committee, MSHS.

The Lewis and Clark Journal (newsletter) 2, no. 3 (1971), and 3, no. 4 (1972). LC/SDSHS.

Lewis and Clark Journal: Official Publication of the Lewis and Clark Fair 1, no. 1 (January 1904).

Lewis and Clark Memorial Association (Lewiston, Idaho). Report of First Annual Meeting, October 30, 1929. RS 164, folder 4, MSHS.

Lewis and Clark Memorial Commission (Montana). Minutes of May 1, May 26, and September 10, 1929, and meetings and undated copy of final report to Montana Legislature. RS 164, folders 1–4, MSHS.

Lewis and Clark Three Forks 1980 pageant program. Three Forks Public Library, Three Forks, Mont.

Lewis and Clark Trail Commission. *Final Report,* October 1969. Lewis and Clark Trail Commission Records, SC 1961, MSHS.

———. *Interim Report to Congress and the President,* 1966. Lewis and Clark Trail Commission Records, SC 1961, MSHS.

———. Resolution of Portland Meeting, November 1968. LC/SDSHS.

Lewis and Clark Trail Heritage Foundation. "South Dakota Report," presented at meeting in Helena, Montana, August 9, 1972. LC/SDSHS.

Lichty, Lawrence. Letter to Sherry Fisher, July 2, 1968. LC/SDSHS.

Loh, Jules. "Westward to the Sea." Associated Press story in *Lewiston* (Idaho) *Morning Tribune,* September 19, 1971. Lewis and Clark VF, Asotin County Historical Society, Clarkston, Washington, no pages.

Mullan, John. Handwritten draft of speech at Fort Owen, Montana, December 24, 1861. SC 547, MSHS.

National Congress of American Indians. Resolution #SPO-01-112, adopted at its 58th Annual Session, 2001.

National Council of the Lewis and Clark Bicentennial brochure, 2003. St. Louis, author's possession.

Neuberger, Richard. U.S. Senate speech, July 12, 1955. Washington, D.C.: Government Printing Office, 1955. VF 906, Washington State University Special Collections, Pullman.

North Dakota. *State Outdoor Recreation Agency Digest* 4, no. 5 (May 15, 1969): map.

North Dakota Lewis and Clark Trail Council meeting minutes, March 14, 1975. Neff Papers, North Dakota State Historical Society, Bismarck.

Northwest Lewis and Clark Sesquicentennial Committee minutes, December 18, 1954, and undated committee report. LC/SDSHS.

Pollard, Lancaster (superintendent of the Oregon Historical Society). "Lewis and Clark at Seaside." Report for Seaside, Oregon, Chamber of Commerce, n.d. VF 906, Washington State University Special Collections, Pullman.

Riggs, Dick. Commentary accompanying a photograph of the Lewis-Clark Hotel for the Nez Perce County Historical Society 2004 calendar. Lewis and Clark VF, Nez Perce County Historical Society, Lewiston, Idaho.

Robinson, Will. Letters to Chapin D. Foster, July 24, 1957, and Curtis B. Mateer, July 19, 1967. LC/SDSHS.

The Salmon River Saga program for Vio Mae Powell pageant, Salmon, Idaho. August 20–21, 1955. VF 2609, Washington State University Special Collections, Pullman.

Scott, Laura Tolman. Paper presented to the Montana Federation of Women's Clubs, Lewistown, Mont., June 1914. VF 2606, Washington State University Special Collections, Pullman.

South Dakota Department of Highways. Missouri River Perimeter Road System: Upper Big Bend and Oahe Reservoirs, Pierre to Northern Boundary of South Dakota. Mobridge, S.D.: Nance Engineering Study, 1965. South Dakota State Historical Society, Pierre.

"The Three Forks of the Missouri River: Logical Site of a National Memorial to Captains Lewis and Clark." Chamber of Commerce, Three Forks, Montana, 1928. Leggat-Donahoe Collection, Montana State University Special Collections, Bozeman.

U.S. Statutes at Large 88 (1964), 630; 89 (1966), 475; 95 (1978), 625.

"Washington State Committee's Speech Outline for the Sesquicentennial" (undated) and "Suggested Programs for Clubs and Organizations" (prep. Ruth M. Babcock; undated). VF 906, Washington State University Special Collections, Pullman.

Weippe (Idaho) Hilltop Heritage Society, Inc. "Lewis and Clark on the Weippe Hilltop" (grant proposal, 2001).

Your Land Forever, program for Bert Hansen pageant, Missoula, Mont. K. Ross Toole Archives, Mansfield Library, University of Montana, Missoula.

NEWSPAPERS

Billings Gazette (Billings, Mont.), May 21, 1976.

Bismarck Tribune (Bismarck, N.D.), July 8, 1968.

Clearwater Progress (Kamiah, Idaho), October 7, 1955.

Clearwater Tribune (Orofino, Idaho), June 26, 1932.

Daily Astorian (Astoria, Ore.), March 16, 1907; September 27, 1965; January 20, February 8, April 21, October 23, November 9 and 17, and December 4, 1967; March 29, June 9, November 20, and December 19, 1968; July 22, 1976 (U.S. Centennial issue); September 25, 1988 (Astoria 125th anniversary issue).

Daily Chronicle (Bozeman, Mont.), July 18, 1980; July 27, 1981.

Denver Post, May 5, 2003; September 26, 2004.

Des Moines Register (Des Moines, Iowa), May 1, 1969.

Dillon Daily Tribune (Dillon, Mont.), September 3, 1915; July 28 and August 1, 1955.

Evening Budget (Astoria, Ore.), February 10, 1922; July 21 and 22, 1926; July 10 and 16, 1948; August 10, 1953; January 25, July 12, and August 17, 1955; July 22, 1976.

Glasgow Courier (Glasgow, Mont.), July 19, 1974.

Great Falls Tribune (Great Falls, Mont.), February 18, 1945; May 26, 1964; May 16, 1968.

Lewiston Morning Tribune (Lewiston, Idaho), November 3, 1916; September 3, 1933; July 9 and October 10, 1955; September 19, 1971; February 14, 1999.

Missoulian (Missoula, Mont.), May 16, 1968; September 13, 1992.

Montana Standard (Butte/Anaconda, Mont.), June 17 and July 24, 1955; May 16, 1968; February 6, 1970.

The New York Times, May 8 and 21, 1955.

Omaha Register (Omaha, Neb.), May 7, 1969.

Oregonian (Portland, Ore.), May 31, 1955.

River Press (Fort Benton, Mont.), June 9, 1976.

Salt Lake Tribune, August 29, 1955.

Seattle Times, January 28, 1968.

St. Louis Post-Dispatch, February 9, 1968; October 12, 1969.

Three Forks Herald (Three Forks, Mont.), May 19, 1980.

Wall Street Journal, May 7, 1969.

LOCATIONS OF HISTORICAL PHOTOGRAPHS

Beaverhead County Library and Museum, Dillon, Mont.
Montana State Historical Society, Helena.

Index

Armstead, Montana: Camp Fortunate, 102, 134; monument site, 36, 134; 1915 pageant, 25–27, 27; Sacajawea plaque, 25, 115; sesquicentennial pageant, 122

Army Corps of Engineers (U.S.): dams on Snake and Columbia rivers, 134; Fort Peck Dam, 138; Pick-Sloan project, 137–138; recreation site development, 141, 155

Arrow Rock State Park (Missouri), 44

Ashland Shakespearean Festival, 148

Assiniboin (Native American tribe), 50, 53

Astor, John Jacob, 8, 29, 30

Astoria (book). *See* Irving, Washington

Astoria Column (Oregon), 31, 32; dedication, 29–33; preservative applied, 173(n40)

Astoria Evening Budget, 110

Astoria (Oregon), 29; American Legion Auxiliary, 110; Astoria Column and dedication, 30, 31–33, 31, 32; near 1805–1806 winter camp, 68; and Fort Columbia State Park (Washington), 147; near Fort Clatsop National Monument and replica, 111, 167; Green Beret canoe trip to, 136; Jaycees, 110; Lions Club, 110; Scammon trip to, 12; view of Columbia River from Astoria hill, 69

Astoria trading post. *See* Fort Astoria

Atchison (Kansas), 65

Athearn, Robert, 96

Augusta (Montana), 74

Automobiles, 89–93; clubs, 95; technology, 95–96

Auto tourism, xi–xii; accessing trail, 77; automobile manufacturing and improvements, 91–93; *Blue Book* guides, 92; Bureau of Outdoor Recreation and, 131–132, 143–144; commercial promotion, 108, 165; cross-country, 7, 91–95; exploration by motorcar, xii, 89, 96–97, 165; and federally funded highway system, 5, 90, 94; following

Lewis and Clark trail, 100–103, 142; guidebooks and travel accounts, 156; highway conditions and improvements, 95–97; highway route associations and names, 93–95; highways as tourist destinations, 90, 95–96; historical markers, xi–xii, 87–88, 98, 125, 149 165; historical tourism, 164–165; Lewis and Clark bicentennial, 160–163; Lewis and Clark Memorial Association and proposed memorial highway route, 98–99; Lewis and Clark National Trail Commission, 131–132, 143–144; to Lewis and Clark 1905 Portland exposition, 92; Lincoln Highway, 93–94; Meeker and, 77–78; and national trail system, 149–150; and railroad travel, 90; "tin can" tourists, 95; trail highway signs and logo contest, 141–142, 144–145, 168; U.S. Forest Service, 87–88, 149; visualizing history, 142; Wheeler expedition and promotional materials of route, 78–86. *See also* Bureau of Outdoor Recreation; *interstate highways by name*

Bad River. *See* Teton River

Baier, Oliviane, 160

Baker, George Pierce, 114–115

Baker's Bay, 12, 18

Bankhead Highway, 94

Bankside Theatre (University of North Dakota), 115

Baptiste. *See* Pompey

Basil, son of Otter Woman, 180(n5)

Beacon Rock (Washington state), 68

Beacon Rock State Park, 145

Bear Paw battleground, 33

Bear Paw Mountains, 54

Beaverhead Mountains, 63

Beaverhead River: Armstead 1915 pageant, 115; on expedition route, 60–62; sesquicentennial pageant, 121, 123, 154; Traveler's Rest, 71, 88

Beaverhead Rock, 21, 61, 102; protected, 152, 154

Montana (state), 33, 62, 80, 83, 123, 152; Armstead 1915 pageant, 115; attempts to establish heroic-size statues of Lewis and Clark, 34–38, 39; Bear Paw battleground, 33; Big Hole Valley, 62; Bitterroot Mountains, 80; buffalo country, 80; Camp Fortunate, 62; capitol murals, 83; Clark's party crosses Continental Divide going east, 62; commemoration of Lewis and Clark, 5–6; DAR, 25, 27, 115; eastern, 45, 49, 138, 142, 151; expedition route, 52–54, 88, 168; Fort Peck Dam and Reservoir, 53, 138; and Gateway Arch dedication, 146; Gibbons Pass, 62; Gray (Ralph) auto trip along trail, 101–103; Great Falls Interpretive Center, 167; Great Falls of the Missouri River, 12, 55–58, 56, 61, 74, 97, 133, 157; Hansen pageants, 117–123, 159–160; Helena parade for Lewis and Clark centennial, 20; high plains vegetation, 45; highways, 54, 96–97; Lemhi Pass, 148; Lewis and Clark centennial, 38, 39; Lewis and Clark highways designated, 145; Lewis and Clark National Trail Commission, 131; Lewis and Clark sesquicentennial, 38, 108, 112, 126; Lolo Creek, 81; Lolo Pass Interpretive Center, 167; Lost Trail Pass, 62; north-central, 54; Marias River, 30; and Missouri River, 52–54, 184(n43); Montana Trail Committee, 145; National Historic Landmark, 148; Northern Pacific Railway, 78; parkland donation to at the Three Forks, 113; portage site donated to, 149; Sacagawea "unsung heroine" of, 25; Saindon articles on Lewis and Clark sites, 151; shift in means for commemoration, 5–6; southwestern valleys, 61; state centennial, 38–39; State Highway 200, 54; state line with Idaho, 123; state line with North Dakota, 96; state recreation waterways, 184(n43); and U.S. bicentennial, 38; version of Sacagawea's death, 22; western, 88, 133; and Yellowstone River, 52–53, 62, 168; Yellowstone Trail Association, 94

Montana State Highway Commission, 116

Montana Study (the), 117–118

Monuments and statuary, xi; Armstead, 27; Astoria Column, 29–30, 31, 32; Camp Fortunate, 34; Clark statue and bronze bust for grave marker, 18; Floyd memorial, 101; and folk images, 37–38; Fort Benton, 37–38, 39; Fort Clatsop National Monument legislation, 111; Great Falls, 34, 36, 38; Historical Society of the Rocky Mountains, 8; Keck statue (Virginia), 28–29; Lewis and Clark column in Washington Park, Portland, 23, 28; Lewis and Clark grave markers, 27; Lewis and Clark Memorial Association, 37, 98; Lewis statue at Louisiana Purchase Exposition, 18; Montana's early attempts at Lewis and Clark statue 34–37; public interest in, 26–28, 38; Sacagawea first depicted with Lewis and Clark, 28; Sacajawea statue (Bird Woman) in Washington Park, Portland, 24, 25, 26; Sacagawea statues, number of, 19; St. Louis, 146; Seaside (Oregon), 26, 33, 35, 36; sesquicentennial, 5, 38; shift in mode of commemoration, 4, 40–41; site competition among Montana cities, 34–38; state and federal historical markers, 165; women's suffrage movement, 23–27. See also Memorials

Moreau River, 44, 50
Moreno, Jacob, 117
Mormon Trail, 149, 153
Morrison, Samuel Elliot, 30
Mosquitoes, 58
Mount Adams (Washington), 69
Mount Hood (Oregon), 69